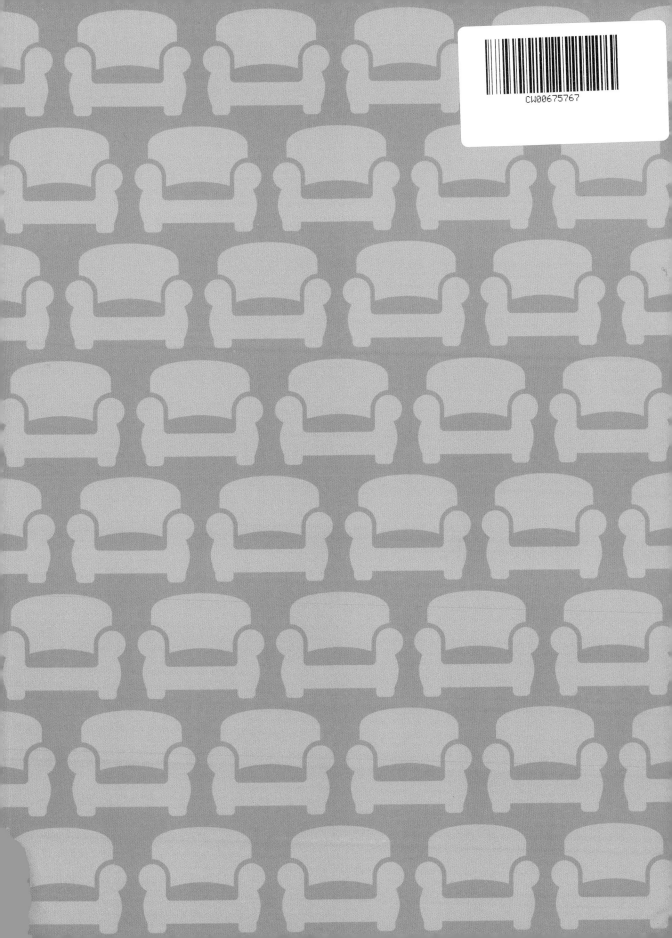

# Are You Going to do That Little Jump?

A life in TV, sitcom, film and theatre
The Adventure Continues

by Robert Gillespie

 jane Nightwork
PRODUCTIONS

Published in Great Britain by
Jane Nightwork Productions

A catalogue version of this book is available
from the British Library.

ISBN 978-1-9997993-1-1

Typeset in 11.5/16.5pt Minion Pro
by The Cutting Edge, Teddington Lock
Printed and bound by Harrier Print

In Rattigan's *Harlequinade* an actor, rehearsing a scene,
is hogging the stage. At last, it's his wife's turn to speak her lines.
She hasn't got far, when he executes a little movement to
attract attention to himself. She stops and asks him,
"Are you going to do that little jump?"

It's called 'upstaging'. There are many forms of it and can lead
to sharp words, even violence; sometimes to serious injury.

# Contents

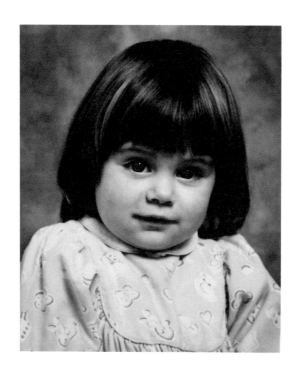

To my dear darling daughter Lucy,
…and all those readers who, with curiosity,
amusement and affection, have
followed my story in Part One of
*Are You Going to do That Little Jump?*,
here is the much-anticipated sequel.

**The story so far** (see Part One): I was born in France, escaped with my family to England from the advancing German army by the skin of my teeth (learnt English!), went to RADA, then to the Old Vic (the company was led by Richard Burton and Claire Bloom). I worked at Stratford East with Joan Littlewood, with Spike Milligan at the Mermaid, was present at the start of the great modernising movement at the Royal Court Theatre begun by George Devine, featured in a daring life of Jesus—live on TV, and walked down Bond Street as a troubled transvestite. I was in a hundred commercials, ending up on Table Mountain with Pauline Yates.

I hope, I believe, that reading Part Two will provide a complete and satisfying experience. This pleasure might be enhanced—let's say bestow the cherry on a super-rich cake—if you were to become familiar with the contents of Part One: it's still available, and I'll be referring to it, from time to time.

**This book, Part Two – The Adventure Continues,** is about how it happened that, for a time, I was stopped in the street several times a day, by the general public—about sitcom, of course. But the book is also about the highs and lows of provincial theatre—rep—from Ian McKellen's *Henry V* to Agatha Christie's potboiling *Murder at the Vicarage*. It tells why I began directing, and how television won, over theatre; about Ned Sherrin and writing for *That Was The Week That Was;* about sitting with a Polish-Aussie spy, trying to scribble a West End hit based on his adventures; about filming with Graham Stark, with Barry Humphries, and almost filming with Albert Finney in Nice. It's about my unexpected—but very pleasurable—return to classical drama with the RSC. Above all, it's how I was inducted into the specialised, disciplined and testing world of Situation Comedy—climaxing with my own series *Keep It in the Family*. Finally, it's about keeping on and on—lately, in *Lost in London* with Woody Harrelson, and in Mike Leigh's movie *Peterloo.*

If it's the sitcom you want, go to page 146. But if you fancy the whole journey, the build-up, and some provocative, some stimulating reflections with moments of sheer homage in honour of our curious and addictive trade, just read on from here.

# The last of the dinosaurs

On actor-managers (400 BC–1960 AD)

**So, as I was saying...** Picture an imposing figure, male, often loud, impatient, with a ready answer to a variety of problems: about the quality of performance, the setting, the behaviour of the audience, the sex life of his cast, the local digs, the railway service, and the demeanour of the town and corporation. A tribal chieftain, yes: an actor-manager!

Who's heard of Donald Wolfit? Well... he may linger on in more minds than you might suppose through Ronald Harwood's play *The Dresser* (1980), which evokes the essence of the man remarkably well. I saw Wolfit act many times: as Malvolio, Macbeth, King Lear (twice), Touchstone, Shylock and in Montherlant's *Malatesta*. He was a salutary example of the fast-disappearing actor-manager. He took the King's Theatre Hammersmith for some years—it's been demolished now—and I went time and again.

Indirectly, watching him, I learnt a lot about directing. He was a burly man, but light on his feet. He was never bad in anything—and sublime as Lear: a dream of mine was to have inserted Wolfit's Lear into Peter Brook's famous production; Paul Scofield played the old king and gave a beautifully modulated reading, but if Wolfit had played in that production the audience could have died happy—having seen perfection.

Wolfit was funny. He orchestrated Touchstone's tour-de-force about surviving challenges to duel... 'I did dislike the cut of a certain courtier's beard...' with huge panache. But his performances were solos—with cue-giving minions around him on stage. Time after time, I would see a semi-circle of actors only partially allowed to encroach on the lighted area, and tamely giving Donald his cues as he pranced energetically to and fro in the middle of the stage. Wolfit was good enough to invent, through his responses, what the rest of the cast should have been enacting for him. The other performers were given so little chance to shine that it was hard to tell how good any of them were. I believe Harold Pinter was in his company for a while, and it's entertaining to imagine this world-famous playwright-to-be tiptoeing deferentially round the edges of this theatrical titan.

Actor-managers ran everything themselves: couldn't delegate. Wolfit was the ultimate solo operator: every choice, every decision—no matter whom he consulted

*Robert Atkins, Anew McMaster, Donald Wolfit*

—was finally his alone; and it wasn't always the best one. And as with all dictators, in the end that flaw diminished what he achieved…

Wolfit had a wife, Rosalind Iden, and her hubby too often injudiciously put her centre stage—more or less. A nice woman, so it goes, and a great support to Donald. There are stories of Wolfit and Rosalind conducting business meetings with their staff from their bed. And he was famous for timing his descent to the rehearsal stage to the last thirty seconds.

Because Wolfit was a great actor, admirers tried to tempt him to lead a competent company: by some feat of alchemical persuasion, and presumably on the strength of his own stupendous reputation, Tyrone Guthrie set up a season starring Donald Wolfit at the Old Vic. It began with his performance as Lord Ogleby in *The Clandestine Marriage*. So good, I had to see it again at the King's Theatre.

The play begins with the washed out, dissipated Ogleby putting himself together at his dressing table in the morning, starting from an ageing human wreck, sagging everywhere, skin the colour of death, gradually, with the help of paints and powders and potions and creams and corsets and cummerbunds—and fine clothes—slowly reconstructing the shattered edifice and, at last, turning himself once more into a sparkling, fashionable, appealing gallant about town. It's not possible to convey how brilliant this routine was; it took ages—and Donald got a round for it, as he put the finishing touch to his toilette with a fine flourish. Unforgettable.

More magnificent still was his *Tamburlaine the Great*. It was one of the most splendiferous stage shows I will ever see. Directed by Tyrone Guthrie himself, it had a stunningly gifted cast—not a wrong note from anyone. Imagine the great tyrant entering the stage riding on his barbarous cart drawn by captive kings. I can still picture the death of a traitor, hauled up high, pierced with crossbow bolts, shot from the stage far below—the martyrdom of St. Sebastian brought to mind by a great director.

Donald was rehearsing the next production—when he found a quarrel and walked. Why? He'd (I understood) done the same thing at Stratford-on-Avon. Could he not bear to share the showers of praise and approval for these productions with the rest of the company? Everyone, the biz, was so pleased to see his immense talent framed in the high quality of production it deserved; but did he feel diminished to hear fellow actors complimented? What goes on in the head of someone like that?

*Donald Wolfit, Tyrone Guthrie, and 'the Dream' at Regent's Park*

I myself remember being asked whether, when directing, I didn't feel envious of my cast for the wonderful parts I wasn't (in that instance) playing; it's what my interlocutor felt, he told me, when he directed! I've never understood how it is to be there. It's such a delight to watch good actors succeeding.

To those of you who may have heard or read of Wolfit's antics at the curtain call: it's all true. After Lear, or any major role, he would part the curtains, reaching up with one hand for support and, hanging on to the great fall of red cloth, apparently drained by the exertions of his performance, would gravely bow to us in several directions. Then the tabs would open to reveal the rest of the cast, and the exhausted, unsteady bowing would continue, centre stage. But then, I am assured, as soon as the curtains closed and the company was dashing for the exits, he would clap hands to gather his chicks together, not a hint of tiredness or weariness of any kind, yelling for the tabs to open again, eager to pick up the last vestiges of any audience applause on offer.

Wolfit was in movies such as *Room At The Top* and bloody good in them too. I presume he couldn't come it grand on the movie set.

He might have matched the status Laurence Olivier achieved as a rounded, history making, first-rate theatre worker. Instead, that intrusive self-destructive streak eventually turned him into a bit of a—joke. I am fascinated by how people with tremendous qualities and abilities undermine themselves.

I woke up one morning in the 1960s and read that another actor-manager, Anew McMaster, was still alive and touring Ireland. This was like hearing that, if you were quick, there was a woolly mammoth you could visit, still padding about on a small Russian island. McMaster was running fit-ups, so I heard. Was it possible? Fit-ups are—were, rather—groups of actors, led by an actor-manager who constantly toured half a dozen plays with a set of flats and props to stage them, and they'd arrive at any village or town however small, adapting to each hall they came to—sometimes they played in tents, I came across actors who'd done that. They arrived with a limited repertoire—a bill of fare, like a menu—which they offered to perform. They would act a different play every evening. If the manager favoured a new text he would allocate parts, you'd learn your lines and after a day's rehearsal, you'd open the same night. Many companies listed the same popular texts. So that if you had, say, your Hamlet indisposed—or briefly unavailable for any other reason—you could contact another group and ask their Hamlet to step in; with almost no rehearsal. A very flexible system.

Older actors would give you glimpses of those times; it was a link with the 19th century and beyond, when there were few entertainments or distractions, apart from adultery. I wondered if McMaster was still using a caravan of carts, a Winnebago, or just taking the train, from hall to hall. I was poised to go and find him, he was still on the road, heading for Cork; and then his death was announced, and I missed him. However, his son, Chris, was still alive.

When I met Chris he was working for Southern Television, but he'd once played the Fool to his dad's Lear: he was touched by my interest in his father, and told me about the kind of thing that happened in these fit-ups on the road—many of the great, seminal theatre stories came from that period. Chris told me the story of the actor, playing Lysander in *The Dream,* who used a default speech from *Hamlet* whenever he dried in a Shakespeare. Which he did one night in the opening scene: couldn't remember a word of what came next and seamlessly began to say 'I am thy father's spirit, doomed for a certain term to walk the night, and for the day confined to fast in fires, till the foul crimes done in my days of nature are burned and purged away…' Then he remembered Lysander's lines and went on with… 'Apart from that, I am as well derived as he…'

Robert Atkins was another actor-manager, a last echo of an older school of acting, a living dinosaur. He was a large man, with a large, booming voice and a large booming persona, and he actor-managed the Open Air Theatre in Regent's Park. Atkins enchanted everyone, when it wasn't raining, with an electrically lit *Midsummer Night's Dream* played among real bushes, on real turf. Once, when a character did not appear, he wandered into the shrubbery to look, found the actress squatting by a shrub relieving herself, and is supposed to have said, 'If you're contemplating your entrance—you've missed it!' I saw his Bottom. Not bad.

For many years, if you walked into any company of actors and opened the fingers of your right hand, wide, and rotated your wrist one way and then the other, and said, in a cavernous voice, 'Let me explain something, old son…' you would get a laugh: Atkins' hallmark. It was like a Masonic sign: it proved you were part of a brother- or sisterhood. Stories aren't the same now, in the theatre. Now we flit in and out of studios, or are in limited runs, and we aren't together long enough for a common culture to stick.

# It'll do you good or it'll kill you

Repertory theatre (1950s to '60s)

**The term 'repertory' is misleading.** Once, it referred to the kind of fit-ups I've mentioned; but when I came to it, rep had declined to brief runs of plays one after the other—never repeated—always in a permanent venue.

I tried to do as little repertory theatre as possible, and I'm not sorry.

While still at grammar school, and shakily beginning to think I might not take the standard academic route to some sort of 'steady and safe' job, I flirted with the idea of becoming an actor—daring, unsafe, uncommon. I had a precedent. In my class at school, and a fellow actor in school plays, was Graham Armitage. He had joined a very large amateur dramatic group—The Altrincham Garrick Society. With a mixture of excitement and dread, I followed him. Crucially, the Altrincham Garrick set a very high standard and was rich and committed enough to employ a professional director, Edward Horton. Through Edward we discovered The Stage newspaper. I heard that one way in to the acting trade was via repertory: The Stage ran weekly advertisements for theatre jobs and my mother ordered the paper—she was keen on the arts!—and together we scoured through the many weekly and fortnightly reps offering places as assistant stage manager/play-as-cast—there were two or three hundred of them, then. But you mostly had to pay them—the management —so many pounds per three or six month season, to get the job. We were not well off and my father was shaken at this idea: pay to be employed!? Outlandish. My mother, always supportive of anything with an artistic aura, and hating 'business', was on my side. I wrote some letters and got a few answers (though see letter, Page 11, for a different view) but, to everyone's relief, the chance to go to RADA came up.

We were then living in Sale, south of Manchester, and at that distance RADA shone like a beacon. I was utterly convinced that it must be a Temple of Art. Sadly, in my time, it wasn't, and I write all about that in Part One. RADA didn't seem to think I'd amount to much in the theatre by the time I left so I somewhat shook the staff when I told them that I'd got myself an audition at the Old Vic, and been offered a year's work—which turned into two. My account of Michael Hordern's

*'Inspector' Roy Kinnear — managing not to laugh (Dial M for Murder)*

magnificent Malvolio, the conundrum of Burton's Hamlet, and the absurdity of the mob's responses in *Coriolanus,* I also cover in Part One.

But two years with the Old Vic, and bumming at Theatre Workshop with Joan Littlewood, and odd runs of TV, still leaves large gaps. I signed on—which I loathed—at Hammersmith Labour Exchange. However… there were funny little Theatre Agents' offices in Charing Cross Road where you could drop in daily and see if any work had come in: there was a famous wheeling-and-dealing sort of middle-man with one eye who levered me into my first ever night of feature filming; and some odd connection like that led to my introduction to weekly rep at Worthing.

There was a curiously gracious, stately feel about this seaside town, and the theatre was well-known to be run by what we now call 'gays'; who were also very stately, immensely civilised and courteous. Kenneth Ewing, a charming man, agreed to audition me for a brand new play (very unusual) *Hand In Glove,* which featured a large role for an 'idiot boy': this term was shorthand for a local person not fully equipped to cope with the complexities of life—its usage was country-wide, then. Novelists of every quality would write about 'village idiots'.

I got the part. The amazing Pat Routledge was in the cast. 'Idiot boys', by the way, are about the easiest thing to play, and if you have a yearning for an Oscar or some other award see if you can get yourself cast as an 'idiot boy': I guarantee success. I was, of course, a wow but I had the script for a fortnight, so I could learn the text accurately and also give the interpretation some thought. And my evenings were free so I took the opportunity to see the rest of the cast in their current show. An eye-opener… Crude characterisation, obvious paraphrasing and a sense of forced energy floating on chronic fatigue, with never enough time to do your work or live properly; that's what came over to me.

My actress friend Anne Robson (we were in the same company at the Old Vic) once worked in nearby Bexhill and, just out of drama school, was rehearsing with the company. In a break she cautiously approached the actor with whom she'd just played a scene. 'May I mention that the line you spoke—that wasn't my cue.' His reply: 'No cues given. None expected.' Was this quality of work worth paying to see?

I promised myself I would try to avoid working in rep as far as I could. Not always possible, though, and most often I went back to Ipswich rep. Very sadly, it had fallen into the hands of Geoffrey Edwards; a tall, sad, languid, bored 'Edwardian' character; straight out of a thirties novel. Of course there was a story, and I heard the full version later: apparently Geoffrey had been an approved actor on the Binkie Beaumont circuit and was understudying Cyril Cusack in the West End—in Shaw's *The Doctor's Dilemma*, I recall. One night Cyril arrived at the stage door so drunk he could barely stand. The stage management pumped black coffee into him—enough to enable him to make his first entrance. But as the caffeine wore off, the audience watched Cyril appear to get drunker and drunker (though he wasn't seen to touch a solitary drop on stage) and then he fell apart at the interval. Geoffrey was sent on for the rest of the show. He didn't know a line: he was always an idle sod. He had to go on with the book. Binkie fired him and banned him from the West End for ever.

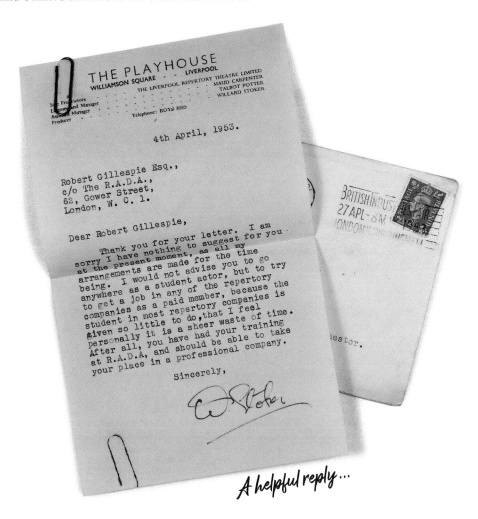

*A helpful reply...*

That was the artistic director Ipswich was blessed with. Very disappointed people rarely show much energy: Geoffrey recruited an under-strength company, and even though we had a mere two weeks to rehearse each full-length play he would dismiss rehearsals at 4p.m.—sheer loss of interest. Ipswich had a tolerable leading lady, Julia McCarthy, who shone when well-directed, otherwise relied on stock performance tricks; and Gawn Grainger was in the company, later to flourish.

Julia's was one of the oddest careers. She would work for a couple of seasons and then would be employed in an office for seven years, still calling herself an actress. Yet she was vindicated: all at once she'd be featuring at the Young Vic for a while—till her sharp mind—and tongue—would tempt her to come in on the wrong side of an argument with the management, and they'd edge her out. There'd be another gap, and then she'd land a big commercial television series; a really strange career. She became something of a friend, and died too young, of cancer.

One of the best things we did at Ipswich was a Soviet play called *Distant Point* (director Edward Burnham) in which Julia played an entirely believable local peasant woman—no cheap tricks—and where I met Walter Hall, later founder of the Basement Theatre, Soho, and a friend ever since. I, of course, played Matvei Malko, a middle-aged Soviet Army Lt. General, hair greyed up and all. Yvonne Coulette played my wife (see pic page 225).

Standard fare at Ipswich, however, was ex-West End potboiler successes supposed to attract the local folk so far from London. A few actors made a real effort to learn the texts as written by the author and even give accurate cues—but most didn't. We all learned to fudge and approximate. We were permanently exhausted: eating after a show and learning the next play's lines till two in the morning. For some, there were love affairs to fit in; jolly tiring.

I had hoped never to be in an Agatha Christie play: I've ended up in two. I was at Ipswich when Geoffrey announced *Murder at the Vicarage.* Till then, even in rep, I'd managed to learn my character's lines organically, never by rote but by digging into, exploring the rounded life of the bloke till the words sank in—I'd worked like this from RADA, from the Altrincham Garrick Society, from school. I was playing the Inspector in the Christie, and my opening line as I came on was 'Murder at the vicarage, eh?' There was no connection with anything living—or even interestingly dead—in this rotten text and for the first time in my life I sat up in my room going down the page with a ruler, mechanically absorbing the lines. Horrible. If I wanted to give a student an example of poor character dialogue and hideous English, I'd start with Agatha Christie. All she achieves that hooks her audience is plot. In America it has been possible to major at college in Agatha Christie; homage goes in waves. Because most Americans equate earning power with quality, they have to believe Christie is a fine writer. In fact she has outsold, so I'm told, every other writer that has so far lived. Only the Bible has an edge on her.

I go with Grayson Perry on this: democracy has bad taste. However I have, very recently, been told that there exists a 'feminist' work of hers which reveals some insights, some roundedness, some depth of character and narrative. I must look.

I will never forget a matinée of *Murder at the Vicarage* with fifteen in the audience, Julia mugging away as Miss Marple, some poor hexed youth of twenty chuntering on as a seventy-year-old colonel. I desperately wanted to step forward at the curtain call and say to the audience that theatre need not be as bad as this and please to give it another chance.

Playing Bamforth in *The Long and the Short and the Tall* at Ipswich was something of a high moment. Robert Chetwyn directed. Ian Cullen *(Z Cars)* played our radio operator. Many years later Ian, out of work, had starting hawking pension plans. He got in touch with me. I was astonished that a man of his young age could be so anxious, far-sighted, insecure as even to be thinking about pensions. He told me that he'd started saving in his first plan when he was fifteen, and twenty years later had cashed in his first income stream. He'd started a new plan every year since then. I was startled and full of wonder. Now of course I grasp the general idea but it seemed truly alien to me, then.

A memorable enough interlude at Ipswich was *Henry V,* Ian McKellen as the King. I sensed—difference. It wasn't the reading, the interpretation; it was about not being able to take your eyes off him. As if he carried a valuable secret, something to explore, to think about, that he never quite fully revealed, but was infinitely fascinating; spellbinding. Alan Bates (in my class at RADA) also had it. I scratch my head about this quality from time to time; indefinable.

I was at the new Belgrade Theatre, Coventry for a few shows. Amazing: they'd

Ipswich, Distant Point

built flats into the building for the actors! You couldn't be late for rehearsals—however hard you tried. Ian was there too, but not cast to cast spells! One of the most delightful people I've met in the theatre was the leading man, Bernard Kilby. He played Sir Thomas More in Bolt's *A Man For All Seasons* and I was The Common Man. Here follows a matter still hotly debated by thespians: in Act II of the play, a message from 'a higher place' is delivered on stage by releasing a paper from the flies. It's meant to plunk on stage in mid-scene for The Common Man (me) to retrieve—and read out… We are divided, us mummers, as to whether the rule is 'always learn a letter or telegram or page from a book', or 'don't be a tight-arsed prick and just read the bloody thing'.

Well, here's the bit of text that dropped down from the flies:

' "With reference to the old adage: Thomas Cromwell was found guilty of High Treason and executed on 28 July, 1540. Norfolk was found guilty of High Treason and should have been executed on 27 January, 1547, but on the night of 26 January, the King died of syphilis and wasn't able to sign the warrant. Thomas Cranmer—Archbishop of Canterbury", *(jerking thumb)* that's the other one "—was burned alive on 21 March, 1556." *(He is about to conclude but sees a postscript)* Oh. "Richard Rich became a Knight and Solicitor General, a Baron and Lord Chancellor, and died in his bed." So did I. And so, I hope, will all of you. *(He goes to MORE and rouses him)* Wake up, Sir Thomas.'

Who in their right mind would want to, try to, learn that? But the flies were high up, the stage manager hadn't studied the latent aerodynamics of letters and, one night, the thing flew into the front stalls. Oh for the kind Old Vic audience member inclined to hand back bits of stage rubbish… Not available. And, yes, you're ahead of me, I made a sow's breakfast of trying to remember the damned thing. Bernard was jelly, shaking to pieces with barely suppressed laughter; I thought he'd burst.

I played Aston in *The Caretaker,* Bernard was Davies, and Derek Newark, Mick. Aston's famous speech takes fourteen minutes—I timed it one night (before Pinter, Bernard Shaw held the record for a single speech, I think). We played Willis Hall's *Celebration,* and I was the photographer in *When We Are Married.* And then I was in my second Christie: *Black Coffee.* Bernard played Hercule Poirot with such inventive cheek that it was a pleasure to be on stage with him. Physically, vocally, he was daring and fresh, but never cheap. The constant invention kept him sane I suppose—but it killed him. Bridget Turner, a regular company member, told me what happened: soon after I left, Bernard was Poirot again, and to liven up the evening gave himself a leap over a sofa. Spectacular, very showy, but then one night he fell awkwardly, limped through the rest of the play and retired to his bed. 'It was nothing, nothing…' he said. A doctor was called in the middle of the night—Bernard was worsening—but no one turned up till the morning. The physician, quoted afterwards by Gillian Raine, Bernard's girl friend, said he 'knew better than to respond to emergency calls from actors in the middle of the night'. Bernard was rushed to hospital with internal injuries, lingered, and died. Another Agatha Christie victim. He would have played Fred Midway in David Turner's brilliant, satirical *Semi-Detached:* perhaps made his theatrical mark? Instead, Leonard Rossiter took over the Christie, and created Fred Midway, gobbling up and spitting out the lines as only he knew how. Leonard was very funny, likeable, and responded to people instantaneously—as if he'd known them for all his life. Coventry is where we first met, were on good terms ever after and crossed tracks in television later. Gillian Raine, another delightful person and a good actress, was hit hard, but all the signs are that Leonard more or less seamlessly took her over as well (10 years later they married).

The other rep-style venue I played was the Glasgow Citizens' Theatre. It had a high—and intermittently deserved—reputation. The theatre was a vast, almost clapped out Victorian building sited in the Gorbals, a picturesque slum full of knife fights and alcoholism, embedded in architecturally thrilling, but decaying, communal dwellings which soon—instead of being renovated—began to be destroyed, while I could see the new high-rise slums being built before my eyes in the west of the city.

Peter Duguid, a considerable talent with a distinguished career, hired me to play Captain Queeg in *The Caine Mutiny Court Martial*. I was twenty-four playing forty-five. If I'd got the reviews I attracted for this performance within a twenty-mile radius of the centre of London, I'd have shortened my clamber up the show-biz greasy pole by ten years. I was immediately offered local radio and TV—chances like this don't come often—but I'd agreed to stay on for *Twelfth Night*. There was no give, no compromise, on either side. I was playing Antonio in the Shakespeare—small-ish part—but the theatre management wouldn't give me the few hours' breaks to let me do even the radio. Because I had to refuse the immediate offer, Scottish radio and TV sulked and treated me, afterwards, as if I hadn't existed. Today, there'd be a conversation.

When a rep put on Shakespeare it was always hoped to boost the box office with schoolchildren. Little sign of that in the evenings, but whole matinées were sold to kids. It gave us a whiff of what might have happened at a rough performance at Shakespeare's Globe itself. Roy Kinnear was Sir Toby Belch, but the local Scots—Annette Crosbie as Viola, and Fulton Mackay (later in *Porridge*) as Sebastian—knew what we were in for: these kids, from the moment they were rammed and cajoled and shoved into their seats, kept up an undulating, low roar of private chatter; in the dimmed light, liberated from the classroom, what an opportunity to socialise! Many experienced theatregoers among them had bought tubs of ice cream, and immediately they'd scoffed the contents, they put them to their real use… These tubs were made of stiffened cardboard, and when torn up and folded in a particular way they made very good, very hard pellets. All the regulars had brought elastic bands with them, and as we came on stage we were hit in the face and hands—and everywhere else—with these carefully catapulted, painful missiles.

Miffing, the whole experience. It felt wrong to act a part in *Twelfth Night* with a hand held in front of your face. As we came off stage we complained, but the management wearily said they'd tried everything and it did no good: nothing changed. An announcement was made at the interval and the school staff asked to assert themselves, impose some discipline. Complete waste of breath. There were essentially two dramas going on: a vast, liberated talk-fest in the auditorium and an odd, private run-through of a Shakespeare play on stage, with a few futile attempts to raise our voices and project above the hubbub. Nothing missed the kids however so, whenever lovers showed the slightest hint of physical intimacy, that funny, sad wail of part shock, part embarrassment welled up from the crowd of children, shot through with wild giggles and a few colourful remarks from the older boys. I can't describe how un-amusing and tiresome that is for a group of professional actors. A little bit of me wanted to offer a class or two in modern sex-education and relationship counselling. Strangely freakish to watch actors play a comic scene in front of a crowd hugely more entertained by their own inventiveness.

The highlight of one matinée for me without any question was when, as I parted from Sebastian, having arranged to meet him later, I loped towards the right proscenium arch to leave the stage; my sword swung upward at my waist, its point pierced a

large stage flat and brought me to a screeching halt. There was a huge laugh, a round
of applause; that's what they'd really come for: screw-ups.

The third play I'd been hired for at the Glasgow Cits was *Dial M for Murder* and I actually played someone's (dodgy) lover. Roy Kinnear was the Inspector. The entire play
revolves around where someone had put a key (was it under the stair carpet?) and how
many keys there were. Roy and I had a scene together in which he had a long speech
about the various possibilities in the life and placement of one or two crucial keys. He
could never learn it accurately, and ominous signs of breaking-up showed at rehearsal.
Peter Duguid was a stern, puritanical, Geordie fellow, so he stamped on any fooling.
We got through the first performance, but after that I would watch as Roy's shoulders
began to shake as he ploughed into the 'key' speech. He tried to control his giggling and
sometimes he got a fair way into the speech before he stopped, shaking silently.

Giggles are infectious on stage, of course. It got worse and worse. We tried going
through the sequence before the performance, promising ourselves we'd take it all
terribly seriously—no good. It wasn't so bad for me, because Roy was really flying
solo: I could recover while he rambled on. One famous night he tied himself in such
knots with this stuff that he ground to a complete standstill—every wobbly bit of
him shaking like an unset jelly; he started again 'Was the key in your possession, the
key that…' and then he muttered, 'Who the fuck
cares anyway?' It was a big theatre—once more,
I don't think anyone picked it up.

Some time later, I was asked to go up
to Glasgow again to be in Brendan Behan's
*The Quare Fellow*—to find that Gerard
Dynevor was playing one of the prisoners.
I knew him from Theatre Workshop, but here
arose a perfect instance of my complete inability to judge whether anything Gerard
said was true or not. Before rehearsal actors

*Caine Mutiny Court Martial,*
*Fulton Mackay, RG*

would drop in to the Italian-run café alongside the theatre (of course, there'd been a knife fight outside the night before and so there was a lot of turmoil, talk, and clearing up). The boss's daughter was a very attractive dark-haired girl, about eighteen—I think her name was Maria—she served behind the counter. Gerard and I sat opposite each other at a table. 'Watch this,' he said. He tried to attract Maria's attention: 'She won't look at me.' He got up and went to the counter and waited as Maria flitted about, and then nailed her with an order. Smiling his crooked smile, he returned to our table. 'She won't look at me. I had her last night, and now she won't look at me.' To this day, I've no idea if he was telling the truth, or if this was just his way of dramatising his life. Maria certainly looked uncomfortable, but...

Another time, in the course of a proper political conversation, Gerard told us that the cells in Hammersmith police station were regularly used to beat up detainees suspected of serious crimes; that there was an arrangement with the firemen at the Fire Station next door to turn on their hoses so as to drown out the sounds of the shouting and the screaming and the beating. I didn't believe him; it seemed to come out of that sense of persecution common at Theatre Workshop and the harassed Left: just as Joan Littlewood would tell us that Shepherd's Bush was populated with burglars—and so represented a wonderful reservoir of working class protest against the establishment. I've owned a house in Hammersmith—just down the road from the Bush—since 1962. In the first years of my living there, a cock used to crow in the early morning from somewhere along Irving Road. I don't remember much in the way of burglars or working class protest: what I do remember about the Bush is the last of the totters, the rag and bone men and the street organ grinders and the door-to-door scissor and knife sharpeners; and after many years of observation I would say that in fact most thieves are capitalists.

However, not so long ago I read a press article that confirmed the beating-and-hoses story. They can't do it now, because the Fire Station has moved a few blocks down Shepherd's Bush Road. So Gerard—was he right about everything, then? Will anyone ever know?

The insult that was rep prompted me to write to the Arts Council. Audience numbers were falling, subsidies threatened, theatres closing and I wanted to tell the committee men that the product wasn't worth anybody's money. I got their standard answer of the day: 'any provincial theatre could depend on three per cent of its local population to attend their theatre. If the catchment population was too small, naturally attendances suffered'. This was the grossest piece of self-deception I've witnessed in an uncertain profession. First of all, the 'reliable' percentage was one and a half. And no one would address the enormous variability of the output of the provincial theatre companies. Birmingham rep, with its four-week rehearsal period, remained pretty well in a league of its own. Two or three other companies managed to find a way of rehearsing for three weeks—and achieve a tolerable standard. Television was providing smooth, professional looking entertainment, available without leaving your house. Why endure the mugging and fluffing—and hysterical giggling—of your local thespians as they battered their way through rapidly dating middlebrow plays in creaking, under-funded halls? Weekly rep was junk. Fortnightly rep largely dross. And because 'the establishment' refused to acknowledge this reality, provincial theatre eventually collapsed.

Just as well perhaps, because it gave fringe theatre virtually a blank canvas to write its new history on, and it drove actors to train and polish their craft so as to compete in an increasingly harsh show-biz world. Culminating, eventually, in the extraordinarily high standard of performance of recent years.

*Does a beard get you more work?*

# Meanwhile... Family

**In August 1954** my parents moved south. They found a bungalow in Ewell, near Epsom in Surrey. My mother had got hooked on never climbing stairs again—so modern, so convenient—though it probably shortened her life. Papa's life improved as he'd now been promoted to a management job at the Massey Ferguson Head Office in London, and they even sent him to Spain for a year and a half; he said 'yes, sure, he'd love to go', and added another language to his repertoire. As his company globalised he travelled everywhere, with glee.

They'd moved not long after my time at the Old Vic. Living in London had become so expensive that I made a decision to move back in with the family; I'd had to quit the YMCA—their policy was only to house transients, so I'd been 'frightfully lucky' to stay there for over a year. I wanted to see if I could scrape together enough cash to be part of a property owning democracy.

My mother began to glow: she blossomed, as she kept open house for her favourite people—actors; my friends. By now she could speak intelligible English, though her Hungarian accent, and idiosyncratic usage, never improved. It was a good time. Feasts were constantly in the calendar, gratefully scoffed by starving actors—

*Dear old friend! Fount of endless cups of illicit tea... at the YMCA and beyond*

Roy Kinnear came, Norman Rossington, Ken Cope, Bernard Bresslaw—tens of them. Joyce Snape, a young amateur star from the Altrincham Garrick, turned up once and I could tell she was shocked by the indecorous behaviour of 'real' actors; she was almost speechless as I saw her off to the station, making up her mind on the spot not to join the profession—too loud, too loose, too… threatening.

Soon after the war my father went back to Lille, to 'our' house. He knocked on the door and asked if anyone knew what had happened to our stuff. Germans had occupied the place, he was told. Our things? Well… who knows where they went? My mother never quite forgave him for not trying harder to put our belongings into safekeeping; he'd just turned the key and we fled (for more on our wartime adventures, see Part One).

I went back too, in the 1960s; drove there with a girl-friend; and here it was, the house I was born in, on Place Madeleine. I didn't knock.

Many, many years later, with Lucy (very small) and Anna, I was in Saint Jean de Luz again—our point of departure from France in 1940. We had a slap up meal at a free SardineFest on trestle tables out in the open at the same quayside. No sign of my mother's furs—you'll all be astonished to hear.

Some family, and actor friends

# Wrong!
# Chimpanzees
# can't do this

Writing

6 Religion
Why? Robert Gillespie & Charles Lewson

A Consumer Guide to Religions

The Week 'Your Consumer Guide' presents its report of Religions.
In seeing which was the best buy we first asked ourselves 'What should
a good religion do?' And we decided that, ideally, it should offer a
way of life, with strong reliable  support under all circumstances,
culminating in happiness.

  Of the dozens of products on the market we investigated the following
six: Judaism, the Roman Catholic Church, the Protestant Church, Islam
Buddhism and Communism.

# The Petrov Affair (mid 1950s)

**There was a time when I whiled away hours with a spy,** who was also a doctor, a violinist, and a conductor: Michael Bialoguski. *The Petrov Story*, a ghosted book about his counter-espionage coup, had just hit the headlines. I'd been introduced to him by Rosemary Hill, at that time the 'older woman' in my life (not that old), who had got interested in him and his life story—and passed him on to me because I understood the stage: I was to make a smash West End hit for him, out of his adventures.

Bialoguski (it means 'white goose') had escaped from the messy horror of WWII by going east, through to Vladivostock and then Australia, and was eventually responsible for the defection—in Australia—of soviet Colonel Petrov of the MGB.

Michael was Polish, right wing, and had become alarmed at how casual the Aussies were about the vast amount of subversive Marxist literature that was being pushed through their doors. He took a fistful to 'the authorities'; they laughed. So he offered to do his own sleuthing.

In Oz, he quickly discovered that Petrov, hidden as some Embassy second secretary, was a full MGB colonel. He cosied up to Petrov—Michael was a fluent Russian speaker—and got him to parties, which the Russian loved. 'Petrov', Michael explained 'had a brick outhouse of a wife, so found the local glamour irresistible'. Michael liked the Russians, in spite of their atrocities in his native Poland; he said they were sexy—and very open about it. They had countless jokey proverbs; the one that stays with me is 'You can't fuck them all—but you must try.' 'Sometimes I gave the girl flowers', said Michael 'and sometimes I gave her a fuck.' It was the 1950s, and it was the first time I'd ever heard a man describe doing such a thing with amused condescension. Different culture, specifically Polish? New. Then. To me. Michael was charming, attractive; but he described how hard it had been to persuade some girls to indulge Petrov: 'Christ, no, not with him Michael, I came for the beano…'

*Dr. Michael Bialoguski, 52, an Epsom general practitioner, rehearsing yesterday with the New Philharmonia Orchestra for the concert he is to conduct at the Albert Hall tonight. He is paying nearly £3,000 for hire of the orchestra and hall in an attempt to become established as a conductor.*

*Many strings to Bialoguski's bow*

# SPY DOCTOR'S CONCERT REHEARSAL COST £450

### By SEAN DAY-LEWIS, Arts Reporter

**D**R. MICHAEL BIALOGUSKI, one-time Australian double agent and now an Epsom general practitioner, had his first three hours with the New Philharmonia Orchestra at the Albert Hall yesterday. It cost him £450, and he said at the end: "I have learned much."

The 52-year-old Polish-born doctor has hired the orchestra and the hall for tonight's concert to make what he admits is "an all on one throw" attempt to establish himself in Britain as a serious conductor.

His bill afterwards is now expected to be close on £3,000—including such items as £450 for yesterday's extra rehearsal, £350 for the hire of the hall, £250 for publicity and £80 for programmes. He could break even if all 6,000 tickets were sold, but so far only 1,200 have been bought.

After his work in espionage, leading to the defection to Australia of the Soviet spy Colonel Vladimir Petrov, he was able to write a book about his experiences and make some money. It will all be gone after tonight.

★

He appeared yesterday modestly with a brown cardigan, a Beechamesque beard and a baton half the length of those favoured by his artistic backer, Sir Adrian Boult. There was no questioning the quiet authority

*'Nice legs', thought Colonel Petrov*

The day that Petrov was arrested at a party and then turned to Michael for help, only to realise that all the time he'd been led and tempted and conned by his friend into the trap, was a huge international Cold War score against the Soviet colossus—and that day was also one of his saddest, Michael told me, wiping a corner of one eye.

Rosemary was working at the BBC. The first thing Michael had asked when he met her was 'Who is the MI6 man at the BBC?' Bafflement. Michael assured her, and myself, that every large institution had a spook planted in some innocuous post to watch, sniff around, chat up, and report back.

Following a remark I made one day about high-ups at the BBC he asked me what was the English attitude to promotion. I told him it was welcomed; everyone looked forward to it. 'Ahhh. Because in Russia, they have commiseration parties' he said, 'when a colleague is promoted. In Russia, you aim to be number two or number three. The top man carries the can for everything and is in line for imprisonment, when the slightest thing goes wrong, or to be shot.' 'Exactly the opposite here,' I said. 'The higher you go the greater your immunity. The habit here is to blame your incompetent juniors, and if necessary fire them. Shooting is rare.' 'Ahhh, that is more hopeful,' said Michael. 'A theatre boss here might take our play.'

Michael, above everything, wanted to make money and be famous. He hired the Albert Hall and the New Philharmonia Orchestra, and conducted a popular programme, hoping to launch a musical career. It cost him three thousand pounds; borrowed. I went along. Not bad. Sadly, a good few of the orchestra didn't bother to turn up. He played violin gigs, sometimes. He loathed the NHS, and set up in private practice—expecting the local Surrey-folk to form queues for his services: they didn't. His French au pair, Danielle, was very indiscrete: 'Michael's little son could do no wrong; Michael adored him and allowed him everything—defecating against the sitting room wall was forgiven, to his wife's fury'. We were busy writing one morning when Nonnie, his bouncy Australian wife, strode into the room and announced 'I've just seen rhinos copulating on television. They take about an hour. I think you could learn something from them, Michael.'

The West End triumph we giggled and scribbled to slam together was utter crap (and never finished), but enormous fun. Michael diagnosed his own cancer and went, very philosophically, to an early grave.

# BBC TV's *That Was The Week That Was* (1963)

**I won the Beatrice Tunstall Prize for Story Telling** at school. I've always written. In exams I invariably wrote a story, instead of an essay, on a set subject.

In 1962 I bought a house, and it gave me a kitchen table on which to write.

One day Charles Lewsen telephoned me to say he had been given a writing project and hadn't a clue where to start. He was a fearless networker and would ring anybody with whom he had the slightest acquaintance; a quality I admired and envied in him.

I'd been introduced to Charles by ex-Major Toby Wrigley (see Part One). Toby and Charles had both been at Westminster School, though at very different times, and I met Charles while he was at Oxford University. The effect of his performance playing the Fool to Vernon Dobtcheff's Lear wouldn't leave me for some time. While he was still 'up', Charles had strolled me round the city to visit the haunts of some of the would-be luminaries of his era—for example, we exchanged pleasantries with John McGrath (notable left-wing dramatist-to-be) at his outdoor café table.

Charles had approached Ned Sherrin, a very clever and witty man who was about to launch *TW3 (That Was The Week That Was)*, and asked to perform in it. Ned deflected him and—I think because he was also a generous and kind man—said that he needed mountains of writing for such a hungry show, and he wanted someone to write a sketch about religion as if it were a *Which?* report.

Glumly, Charles reported this to me and my immediate response was 'What a wonderful idea. Good luck with it!'

It was then that Charles confessed that he hadn't the slightest notion of where to begin and would I think of joining him to meditate around the proposition. This was how I came to express, before a large public, ideas that had whirled in my mind for many years; ideas that affect most people on our planet and that have changed the direction of history, for good and for ill. Ned's suggested hook meant that it could be done in a few, bold strokes (nothing less than a thousand-page-book would, otherwise, suffice).

Not unexpectedly, Charles demurred at my format and, in the end, seemed inclined to write instead a satire on *Which?* Magazine—not religion itself. So I suggested he write a version, and so would I, and we'd submit both. I went home to that house in Hammersmith I'd bought and, on the table and cloth I still have—finishing at four in the morning—I swept through what was to star as *A Consumer Guide to Religions*. The format I went for was to apply three tests to each religion: 'What do you put into it? What do you get out of it? How much does it cost?'

## A Consumer Guide to Religions

Charles and I had brainstormed on content: I'd thought we should pool what we, as informed lay persons, each knew about religions. We picked six to test. Charles was up on the dietary and culinary sanctions in Judaism etc. etc.… you see how we were thinking. I said we must include Communism since, in its blind doctrine of 'the perfectibility of the human being', it was as remote from the real world as the rest of the major faiths.

TW3 Publication. A Consumer Guide to Religions

# 6 Religion

WHY?  Robert Gillespie & Charles Lewsen

### A Consumer Guide to Religions

THIS WEEK 'Your Consumer Guide' presents its report on Religions. In seeking which was the best buy we first asked ourselves 'What should a good religion do?' And we decided that, ideally, it should offer a way of life, with strong reliable support under all circumstances, culminating in happiness.

Of the dozens of products on the market we investigated the following six:

Judaism, the Roman Catholic Church, the Protestant Church, Islam, Buddhism and Communism.

We ruled out Hinduism. It embodies a caste system which we felt was alien to the British consumer. However, the Hindu does believe that animals have souls, every bit as good as human ones. In this sense it could be said that every Englishman is a Hindu at heart. But we felt that this did not outweigh the main objection.

We began by applying three basic tests:

(a) What do you put into it?
(b) What do you get out of it?
(c) How much does it cost?

*Judaism*—This is the oldest religion we tested. Its small number of users (13 million) is deceptive, since many large and powerful subsidiaries derive from it. (a) What do you put into it? Belief in One Only God. Ten Dos and Don'ts. You must fast severely once a year; pray in Hebrew every morning and every evening; not eat pork or shellfish or dairy produce with your meat; never prepare milk and meat in the same dishes; do no work between sunset on Friday and sunset on Saturday; And you must cut off the foreskins of your male children. (b) What do you get out of it? Membership of the oldest club in the world. A set of simple rules for solving your everyday living and thinking problems, backed by five thousand years of experience and a homely priesthood. Prayers and advice available are tailored to fit most consumer crises and can also be newly bespoke. 'YOU ARE ONE OF THE CHOSEN PEOPLE'—this gives confidence and we particularly liked the guarantee of Eternal Life through the Messiah or Saviour who will take responsibility for all your guilt—when he arrives. (c) What does it cost? In crockery alone the expense is fantastic plus the wages of a reliable Gentile to run the business between sunset on Friday and sunset on Saturday. Infertility is the only grounds for divorce. The vigorous new ideas of this splendid corporation were largely pioneered by the previous Group. But a superb sales organisation has enabled it to far outstrip the parent company with three hundred and forty million

current users. Applying the tests we found: (a) What do yo
Only God-head operating on a Troika basis. Belief that Jes
and working there two thousand years ago, is the Son of Go
Giovanni Battista Montini, now known as Paul the 6th,
organisation in June. We must stress here that the idea th
called) claims infallibility in all matters is a fallacy. The
television set is the best. His infallibility is strictly limited t
tell you which television programme you cannot watch
classical prototypes is Virgin Birth. Most groups have drop
but the testers found it refreshing and it gave no difficulty.
white bulls or fornicating swans to contend with. Freq
attendance at services is required. (b) What do you ge
CHRISTIANITY. This offers a policy of loving kindness,
historically verified Messiah or Christ, in contrast to the
Eye outlook of Judaism. We noted that Jesus Christ
responsibility for the consumer's misdemeanours. This
fessional mechanism is standard; it operates as an adde
mistakes, making Salvation almost foolproof. The rule
confess as soon as possible afterwards. We found th
munications are maintained by using an international
'Life and Death' advisory service is available from a p
ties. It provides high quality blessings, prayer, ritual an
Mass for any occasion. A personal saint or interces
consumer. A built-in Apostolic Succession ensures u
quality by-products such as Madonna on the Rocks
have attracted thousands of new consumers. With Ro
that it is the *only true faith* and exclusive personal s
whole we found this product deeply satisfying. (c) V
very expensive. During a visit to Head Office in
100 lire; a small, votive candle 10 lire; devotional pi
200 lire to see the catacombs; 300 lire to enter the Si
a tour of the ante-rooms of St Peter's Basilica cos
impossible to obtain a divorce.

*Protestantism* is a break-away of the Roman paren
out of divorce proceedings in 1529. Two main br
England or the Non-Conformist Economy Pack. Belief
the Queen should be Head of the Church. Belief
the Archbishop of Canterbury. And belief in Go
you get out of it? Independence. (c) How much d
no difficulty in obtaining a divorce.

We next turned to *Islam* with 270 million users
What do you put into it? It is necessary to belie
Prophet, Mohammed. Kneel down and pray thr
with the Lesser Ablution (Wudu) of face, hands
being required only after Legal Pollution. Recite
your life. Go to Mecca once in your life. When y
do not shave, trim nails or anoint the head. V

Ned, courteously, told us they were accepting my version—it was terrific, just what they wanted—and so it aired on Saturday night, with David Frost performing it. The item created quite a storm: a seventy-year-old clergyman thundered 'if we were true Christians, we would march on Television Centre and burn it down'. There were Questions in the House of Commons about it.

David Frost was so prominent that he was mobbed after the show, and asked searching questions. He never, quite, claimed to have written the piece; he never quite brought himself to credit us, either. I was up and down from rep, and not yet known on TV; Charles was entirely obscure. Writers keep to their burrows. But that item, the *Guide,* is generally acknowledged to be an outstanding piece of the *TW3* enterprise. It's in the *TW3* publication, of course, and extracts from it are trotted out on TV as anniversaries and programmes on satire come around. My brother's favourite bit is in the section on the Catholic Church, which describes virgin birth as a labour-saving device: when Frosty's performance is repeated these days they chop out that little chunk. What's wrong with offending the Catholic Church—it's offended us for long enough?

I wrote six pieces for *TW3* in the end. One week I was given a list of all the naughty words and phrases you can't say in the House of Commons. So I strung them all together and made a single sentence of them. Enjoyed that (see page 224).

Incidentally Charles was to do his best work, I think, devising and performing one-person shows, significantly as Edward Lear in *How Pleasant to Know Mr. Lear.*

Charles had a doctor dad in St. John's Wood with French Impressionist painters on his wall, a mother he fought with and a wild sister. Charles was very open about the years he'd spent in analysis every weekday morning, and I'd often thought that what a patient (really) wanted from a head-doctor was sex. I wrote a stage piece, *Napoleon, Session 2.* It was a tale of a chap talking to a shrink and never getting to that point. How do you say to your analyst, 'can we cut the chat and lie down on this couch together?' Ann Mitchell played the psychiatrist, Tony Webb (a colleague from rep) the patient. Sam Walters accepted the play for the Orange Tree pub theatre—where I'd been directing when Sam first began the enterprise—and we opened the play at lunchtime. Audiences took so well to *Napoleon* that it played in the evenings, too. It even attracted a literary agent, Michael Imison, but he wasn't able to sell it on. I was very pleased with it and still am.

**Do you believe a man's religion should be mocked?**

by DAVID LEWIN

---

# WELL, WAS LEWIN RIGHT ABOUT THIS?

*DAILY EXPRESS 17/1/63*

IN SATURDAY'S B.B.C. TV satire "That Was The Week That Was" one sketch compared religions in shopping-guide style, jokingly analysing them and recommending a "best buy." In Monday's Express David Lewin attacked the programme for mocking religion and declared that TWTWTW men Ned Sherrin and David Frost had shown themselves unfit for the programme. Now Express readers write—

## Now you have your say

**I** THOROUGHLY enjoyed the programme. Why do not the narrow-minded switch off their sets instead of sitting through the whole programme being shocked and offended? I am quite sure Saturday nights at 10.20 sees them firmly glued to their sets.

(Mrs.) SHELAGH THOMPSON,
Brighton-road, Lower Kingswood, Tadworth, Surrey.

**DAVID LEWIN** must be the pen-name of somebody's middle - aged maiden aunt.

ROGER BRUTON,
Priory-close, Dudley, Worcs.

**ALL** decent - minded people—whatever their religion—would be horrified that the B.B.C. should allow such an irreligious item in its programme.

M. M. PEPERELL,
Windermere-avenue, Wembley, Middlesex.

**MY** hearty congratulations to David Lewin. There is very little in this day and age which is personal, and when we reach the point that religion, cannot be personal, then I believe we are nearing the point of no return.

JOHN DAVIS (chairman),
The Rank Organisation Limited,
South-street, London, W.

**C**OME, Mr. Lewin—you know it was funny. I am Church of England, I never took offence, I thought it truthful. Some can take it, some can't.

C. M. WALTERS,
Frobisher-way, Goring-by-Sea, Sussex.

**I** WAS disgusted, although I am not a member of any of the churches mentioned. I am a Latter Day Saint or Mormon.

(Mrs.) ELSIE M. ROCK,
Manor-road, Mitcham, Surrey.

**I** THOUGHT the programme quite revolting. I simply can't imagine what has happened to the B.B.C.

RACHEL BETT,
Fitzroy-avenue, London, W.

**MR.** LEWIN is both stupid and a bully; stupid in his attitude to religion and a bully because he wants to use Mrs. Grundyism to get rid of David Frost. It is high time people were able to mock religion or anything else on the B.B.C. Defending such sacred cows is a sign of decadence.

F. V. WELLS,
West Horsley, Surrey.

**L**IKE Mr. Lewin, I am a Jew, and was under the impression that Jewish people had a sense of humour. It seems I have found the one lacking in this. I found the sketch deliciously funny.

LAURENCE MISENER,
Courtlands, Maidenhead, Berks.

**I** AM a Roman Catholic, by no means a good one, yet on two occasions I felt rather sick at the way this programme mocked at my religion.

(Mrs.) C. F. WARD,
Russell-road, Kensington, London.

**T**HE early Christians had to contend with much more criticism than that meted out by David Frost and yet the creeds survived. The Churches should develop a sense of humour or they will continue to decline.

G. A. WARWICKER,
Angel-road, Edmonton, N.

---

*DAILY MIRROR 14/1/63.*

# TV Show angers Church leaders

By MIRROR REPORTER

THE B.B.C.'s controversial TV satire show plunged into the biggest storm of its eight-week life at the week-end.

One hundred and five angry viewers phoned to ...

---

*EVENING STANDARD. 14/1/63.*

# 190 protests over that BBC show

By RAMSDEN GREIG

The big TV row sparked off on Saturday by the BBC's That Was The Week That Was send-up of religion was still going on today.

Viewers continued to phone the BBC condemning or applauding the programme. By noon today 190 complaints had been logged at Lime Grove. Congratulations were received from 131 viewers.

An inquiry headed by the Assistant Controller of TV Programmes, Mr. Donald Baverstock, was being held today at the TV HQ at the White City. But it is unlikely that the show's "anchor man," 23-year-old Cambridge graduate David Frost, will find himself on the mat.

---

# BISHOP SAYS BBC SATIRE MOCKED RELIGIONS

## CANON CALLS FOR END OF 'HORRIBLE PROGRAMME'

### DAILY TELEGRAPH REPORTER

CLERGYMEN yesterday attacked from their pulpits the Saturday night BBC television broadcast giving a satirical analysis of some religious beliefs. Other clergymen found the programme, "That Was The Week That Was," amusing.

The Bishop of Leicester, Dr. R. R. Williams said: "It seems to be part of the policy of this programme to take all things which normally command respect and reverence and make a mock of them. I do not think it says much for the people who want this form of humour, or those who dispense it." But to take it too seriously would be playing into the hands of the people concerned.

Dr. Williams added that he had not seen the programme. But it appeared to fit in with criticism he had made in his Christmas sermon.

Then he said: "It is not a good sign that the most frequent new form of humour in the Press and on television is what is called satire, but consists of scathing scorn directed against everybody and everything, except those making money and fame by dispensing it."

#### LINES OF "WHICH?"

Religions reviewed

In the broadcast David Frost reviewed Jewish, Roman Catholic, Anglican and Communist beliefs. He did so on the lines of a consumer report as in *Which?*

Canon John Duffield, preaching at St. Peter's, Onchan, Isle of Man, said: "If we were 100 per cent. Christian we would storm the BBC building and make it drop this horrible programme."

He added that the feature had looked at religions and had jeered at the lot.

A well-known London vicar said to me he had been "quite amused." He continued: "Some of the material was grossly unfair, of course, particularly that on the Jewish faith.

"The Church of England is quite accustomed to making fun of itself." He recalled a G. K. Chesterton remark that the only people who can make real jokes about God are believers.

#### "WE MUST LAUGH"

Satire a tonic

A Roman Catholic spokesman said a certain amount of satire on Church and State could be a tonic. "The only thing to do is to laugh," he went on.

But Father Joseph Loran, Roman Catholic priest of St. Edmunds, Little Hulton, Lancs, urged his congregation at Mass to protest to the BBC. He said the broadcast was an insult to all religions.

Viewers made 178 complaints by telephone to the BBC. There were also 131 complimentary calls.

During the feature Roman Catholicism was described as "a cradle-to-grave service from a priesthood unimpeded by family ...

---

*B.B.C. RADIO TIMES. 21/3/63. RELIGIOUS ITEM*

**11.5**

## THAT WAS THE WEEK THAT WAS

It's over, let it go. Whether it's been a sad week, a bad week, or a glorious week, there's no need to respect it. Take it to pieces with ...

# Move over—of course I can drive

Directing

**All actors have opinions about directing,** but few care to try it. I'd tried it once at my grammar school with a very short version of *Hamlet* adapted by a famous critic of the day (Philip Jenkinson played Ophelia).

Later, what deepened my inclination to direct was a growing feeling that not everyone who had the job could find the words to help a particular actor.

Belatedly, Equity had begun to stop seeing directors as arbitrary and capricious controllers of actors' careers, working closely with management: the enemy, almost. Directors had themselves been partly responsible for this stand-off. Gradually, the Union began to think of representing them. As a director I was being regularly reviewed—but I worked both sides of the line, so Equity approached me seeking a detailed description of how directors operated, what characterised them and their methods. I was thrilled to offer them my two cents' worth—be able to help them out…

There are three kinds of director: there is a handful of outstanding people working at any one time who make the miracle happen—between five and ten, say—their work is almost always thrilling to watch; there is a small group of living disasters— wreckers who impose monstrous, mis-interpretive ideas on inoffensive, respectable texts; and there is the vast majority—steady journeymen who have the sense to cast carefully, apply workable stage-craft and wait for a bubbly cast to pour out ideas, editing shrewdly from this wealth of material, till they put together a plausible, good show.

You might care for a couple of examples of the latter. I was once The Player in *Rosencrantz and Guildenstern Are Dead* at the Arcola, just after the venue opened. The play starts with a character tossing a coin and throwing ninety or so heads in a row. This tells us immediately that the laws of the universe have altered (it's statistically not possible for that many tosses to come out anything but roughly equal) and it prepares us for the ideas running through the play: can Rosencrantz and Guildenstern change the outcome of the story? Have they free-will enough to control their own destiny? Is it inevitable that they be killed? How pre-ordained are

*Dan Crawford, Brendan Smith, Diana Fairfax, Tony Doyle, Me*

the play's events? Well, they have an author… can the characters escape the author's mandate (à la Pirandello)? Is the author God? Stoppard—I would have thought any director would know—embeds one or more philosophical ideas in all his plays; it's his stock-in-trade. But our director said *R. and G.* was all related to Music Hall and clowning, and he showed us extracts from silent, slapstick movies. However he listened to the cast, was open to discussion, and when I made the point about the non-random coin-tossing, he asked me 'would I explain that to R and G…' and he got on with something else in the play. A fair and sensible outcome.

Through Neville Teede, my Old Vic colleague and friend, I got to know a part-amateur, part-pro director and administrator called Kay Gardner. She'd been buried deep at the Tower Theatre (a grand north London amateur group full of BBC folk), when unexpectedly she was given the chance to run Lincoln rep. I imposed on personal acquaintance to ask if I could have a shot at directing for her there. After much inner searching, she agreed. The price: I had to play two leads for her, first. So I was Mr. Bates in Tennessee Williams' *A Period of Adjustment* (a play described as

*Checking lines for Rosencrantz, backstage at the Arcola*

his only comedy, that I really fell for and later revived at The King's Head). I played most of the first act with Auriol Smith. Significant, in that her then boyfriend—later husband—Sam Walters popped up from time to time from Oxford and, years later, they were to open the Orange Tree pub theatre in Richmond, London. Another actor member of the company, Brian Tully, also asked to try directing, was offered the Williams play. The first act of *Period of Adjustment* is virtually a two-hander: gradually Brian came to realise that he didn't know how to help his cast interpret the text, and tactfully melted away, leaving Auriol and me to work the scene out together. He gave up immediately after this attempt: said he'd hated the experience, and never wanted to direct again.

After the Williams I was Falk, the rebellious poet lead in *Love's Comedy*, a play in verse by Henrik Ibsen. The Lincoln audience was not drawn to this event. I was allowed to be young, though, and to fall in love…! (see pic page 223). I recall that John Savident (then toying with becoming fully professional) was Guldstad, a merchant, rich and old, who gets the girl. I will never forget that on the first night of this verse play Steven Berkoff came into my dressing room, plonked himself down on a bentwood chair and talked endlessly, relentlessly about some problem he was having with the management about an event of his own; no hint from me could make him aware of how I must be feeling with the verse Ibsen a half hour ahead of me, untried. I ducked out into a corridor to escape him, muttering my text, willing myself to focus on the mountain climb ahead.

After a week's run in Lincoln, so as to make it a fortnightly rep, we had to get on a bus and take each show either to Rotherham or to Loughborough (where some bloke had built an exquisite theatre to show off his beloved). Hard grind.

Then, at last, I directed David Turner's *Semi-Detached*. It was 1963. *Semi-Detached* is a classically structured, sharply satirical look at the corner-cutting, aspiring lower middle classes of the time. Everything's on hire purchase, there's a desperate pushing to acquire a house with air all around it, to display a Rover four-door on your front drive. David named his characters meaningfully—to echo Sheridan: there was a fading upper-ish class lady called Mrs. Hadfield—and so on. The play is extremely witty. The local audience didn't pick up on everything: David explained it to me by saying 'They don't understand; you see Robert, they all come from Devon.'

Lincoln, Semi-Detached with Fred Hall, Auriol Smith and Anna Carteret

Fred Hall played Fred Midway splendidly. Auriol Smith was mum, and I cast a (then) under-appreciated Anna Carteret as Avril: she was the most excruciating, funny, whiny dumb blonde ever. I devised a chase round the stage involving two daughters with their mum bouncing along after them, trying to calm them down; I made Avril tip over a standard lamp and other bits of furniture in the path of her vengeful sister, mother in pursuit, falling over everything, as she tried to stop her daughters killing each other. It wowed the crowd—and Sam Walters confessed he repeated the sequence when he revived the play later. Fred Hall got a shock when I suggested he learn the lines David had written, rather than settle for his version of them, but he was a good-natured man and took it good-humouredly. He struggled, though, and expressed something close to—comic—despair when I pulled him up, yet again, about a mis-reading of David's text. An impossible task, given just a fort-night to learn a huge part.

The play was so good that it attracted fine actors in other productions. Leonard Rossiter created the character of Fred Midway, performed it more than once, and should have come to London with the play. Instead it tempted Laurence Olivier to dip a toe, yet again, into cutting edge theatre of the time. Olivier had gone modern with *The Entertainer* in 1957 and now he tested himself as Fred Midway at the Saville Theatre—I saw it—and it took a dive. It was the only time I ever saw Olivier fluff lines. He apologised to David Turner and (tacitly) to Leonard Rossiter for failing. Interest-ing: great actor as he was, and superb at extreme character work—his Captain Brazen in *The Recruiting Officer* was a towering comic performance; modernist—compared with Gielgud; yet, and yet, he couldn't imagine himself down and ordinary enough to feel natural and truthful and 'common' so as to live the life of vulgar Fred Midway. But Archie Rice in *The Entertainer* is an old theatrical has-been, and Olivier found resonances in Archie that didn't exist for himself in Turner's play.

Besides becoming entirely convinced that I should direct as well as act, my time at Lincoln rep was very much worth my while—in spite of the shattering 'bus-ing' between towns, and not sleeping—because it gave me a climactic experience in English cuisine. The company used to stop the bus just outside Lincoln centre to buy the best fish and chips you can ever hope to imagine existing in the world. Soft, big, juicy shards of spud, divine yielding cod in crispy batter, utterly worth the price of a heavy, though short, sentence in the provinces. How sublime to set a world standard for chips; to know where you are with them forever, after that. It was the same for me with meringues in Dublin.

A footnote for the record; it was drawn to my recollection much later (by himself) that Michael Billington was a young Public Liaison Officer at Lincoln for Kay Gardner.

# Directing in Dublin (from 1972)

**A long-standing mate of mine,** Walter Hall—he had been with me in *Distant Point* at Ipswich—started a lunch time theatre in London's Soho: the Basement Theatre. It was in Greek Street, in a cellar under a Greek restaurant that ran a folk club called Les Cousins in the evenings. Wally said 'Come and direct, if you have something.' So, after Lincoln, I looked for scripts. Rob Walker, then running a studio theatre in Glasgow, magnanimously shoved in my direction a pile of plays that he wasn't interested in himself. I found *Mr. Joyce is Leaving Paris* by Tom Gallacher, a Scottish playwright. It's a brilliant piece about James Joyce confronting his life thus far, as he prepares to escape from Paris at the start of World War II. 'Voices' from his viscous past—significant people from his early time in Dublin—crowd in on him as he sorts through what to leave and what to take: Nora, his wife (Mikel Lambert) is one of them; Tony Doyle played another—highly recommended (I'd never heard of him). We cast it with Robert Bernal playing Joyce—he was superb.

The production got astonishingly good reviews and sold out, and the almost entirely Irish cast said, why don't we take it to Dublin? It turned out that Tony Doyle was already significantly known over there, and he badgered Brendan Smith, the director of the Dublin Theatre Festival, to come over and see the last performance. Brendan came, saw, and said he'd have it. Later, in his Dublin office, he told me that for safety he'd run the text past some local academics—he showed me a lengthy report on the play: they'd condemned it as verbose, untrue and not really theatre—more a dissertation. Fortunately, Brendan had seen the play himself.

Tom Gallacher turned out to have a companion half-hour play (*Mr. Joyce* ran about 75mins), *Trieste,* which featured only the young Joyce and his brother Stanislaus. So we had a full evening—with an interval! The same two actors played their characters both when old and young: we trusted the audience to make the leap of imagination. We rehearsed, flew to Dublin, opened at the Eblana Theatre—and at the first matinée Tony, before his character was due on stage, came on, interrupted the performance and said the High Court of Dublin had put an injunction on us and we had to stop performing immediately. Well…

Walter Hall had got financial support from David Halliwell *(Little Malcolm and his Struggle Against the Eunuchs)* to start up Basement Theatre—to the point that it was first known as Quipu-Basement Theatre. Although I had discovered *Mr. Joyce,* and negotiated directly on all production matters with the author Tom Gallacher, David Halliwell—one of the most pig-headed people that ever lived—decided that he owned the performing rights. No appeal to fairness or reason would shift him. There we were, in Dublin, in limbo with a huge potential theatre success on our hands at an international festival, blocked by this dog-in-the-manger individual. Unfortunately, even though every detail of the process to performance had been negotiated between myself and Tom, he, Gallacher, sat on the fence—in Garelochhead—saying he wasn't able to commit as to who owned the rights to his play: 'there had been a letter between himself and… umm, Halliwell? Was it a David Huh something… ?' This wasn't the last time Tom did something similar to me—and yet we went on speaking. A highly articulate logic-chopper, Tom was; dead now.

So, there we all were at Groome's, Dublin's then political pub, when Brendan Smith suggested we formed what he liked to call a 'consortium' (think of the word in a Dublin accent) to buy the bugger out. Between Brendan and Tony Doyle a telephone negotiation from the bar was conducted, and four of us coughed up a total of £450 to pay Halliwell off—this was 1972, money was worth a lot more then. Robert Bernal was the other backer. Please understand that until we got to Dublin nobody, cast, director, author had been paid a penny.

*Robert Bernal in foreground
in MR. JOYCE IS LEAVING PARIS at the Quipu*

*Once, in a cellar in Soho (Robert Bernal, and the original cast)*

Of course the publicity we got was phenomenal. The case and the outcome were all over every paper. The play did so well that they asked for us at the Gate Theatre—run by Michael MacLiammoir and Hilton Edwards. The show had no set, to speak of—just furniture, a hat stand and a washing line strung from it—so was easy to move.

This production set me directing at five Dublin Festivals in a row—and I had a show at a sixth, much later.

I hadn't been to Dublin since I was groped there in the 50s by the manager of the Olympia Theatre.

This was my reintroduction to the city. Quite innocently, I'd asked Tony if he knew of a good place to stay in town. Solemnly, he thought for a bit and said I might like to stay at Groome's. I booked over the telephone. Looking back, I think I detected a note of surprise at the Dublin end. Yes, they had a room; top floor, sixth floor, would that be okay? Tony met me off the plane and said he must introduce me to the town; we'd end up at Groome's, at my lodgings. So I got to know Mulligan's, Bailey's and at least two other pubs—I've forgotten their names now but they're world famous—and everyone everywhere knew Tony, and at last we were at Groome's.

Extraordinary. Groome's was entirely Victorian, with a vast, open ground floor—occasionally sawdusted—and a prominent pay-telephone that could take incoming calls. As I don't like alcohol, limiting my intake was something of a feat, given the length of the pub crawl, and I may even have taken a tomato juice (with Worcester) or two. Those times, the place was jammed night and day with politicians and folk from the arts; entirely on familiar terms and promiscuously mingled. There was a flight of great stairs leading out of the main bar to the first floor which was a hub, so it was said, for every kind of political machination—'See that feller going up there now? He was De Valera's hatchet man,' someone said to me, nudging.

There were statutory pub hours in Dublin, but some sort of unspoken dispensation meant that the doors of Groome's would be tokenly shut at the correct hour, and after that anyone who tapped would be let in. The crack (the joking and the conversation) went on, sometimes, till four in the morning. I suppose half the judiciary were in there, diverse nights, so there must've been a class of offshore rules in play, I guessed.

At the striking of some unearthly hour I was shown up to my lodgings. Doing a telly up in Manchester for Granada, and saving money, I would sometimes book myself into a grotty pub in Salford; but Groome's sixth floor room was in a category of its own, straight out of Dickens. But no, I didn't walk right out and book into somewhere 20th Century. It was heaven knows what in the morning and I had no idea where I was, anyway. I tried a basin tap: dry as the Gobi desert. The room was autumn icy.

I had a disgusting, greasy bacon-sausage-and-bread breakfast, and complained, faintly, about water in the taps and an acceptable towel. It took me six days of Siberian accommodation Joe Stalin would have been proud of before I realised this was Tony's joke. He was curious to see how long I would stand it. He thought six days was phenomenal—perhaps a record—but he also thought I might soak up a unique essence of Irish political life. Incestuous, poisonous, parochial, drink-soaked, out-of-date and almost entirely male. I went and found a family hotel; good.

I set up *Mr. Joyce…* at the Gate—I think it ran there for five weeks — saw as many shows as I could at the Festival and flew back to London.

*Political powerhouse*

# Another brief detour around family

**At about this time,** the early seventies, at home in London I was contacted by my namesake, 'Lootenant'-General Robert James Gillespie of the US Marines (Reserve).

He was in England running two-day business courses and hoped to contact living members of the Gillespie Clan (a branch of the Clan Macpherson) to record them for his family history project. A Canadian cousin of my father's had got hooked on our genealogy at about this time and had sent us a book of Gillespies—it's how the General tracked us down.

I arranged a meeting at my house in Hammersmith for the few of us stranded in this country. My mum dolled herself up in an embroidered Hungarian blouse, saved from our European wreckage, and showed a strong hint of her youthful gorgeousness. For some reason she'd responded to my news of my namesake's sudden appearance with 'he's a crook'. Curious, but not unlike her. So, one evening, we all sat at one end of my upper room dressed as smart as we could afford, and Robert J. was enthroned between the windows. A big, impressive man, he asked permission to switch on his state-of-the-art mini-recorder. Otherwise he readily forgot stuff, he told us. Of course, we said. I'm always curious about exotic interventions from the gods so I dove in—as they say over there—with some questions.

It appeared that General Robert J. had a courageous son who'd followed him into the Marines—though a pacifist; also a judo black belt, however, so he'd volunteered to join the brave fellows in Vietnam, and set himself to walk into the jungle combat zones, unarmed, and bring out wounded and dead comrades. Robert's son was also a big guy, we were shown pictures; and was on his last trip when he was killed. Lt. Gen. Robert J. 'had built an entire, new, golf clubhouse as a memorial in perpetuity to Robert junior' (I don't remember his rank).

General Robert then told us that there were about thirty-four thousand Gillespies in the States; that he himself regularly wore the kilt and had learned knife-fighting from a last living expert, and expressively told of the ways of the deadly sgian-dubh (the Scottish dirk). Also, how the Gillespies had started in Ireland in the 6th Century, crossed to Scotland, gone back and forth bashing the daylights out of each other, and so on; knew all about my father's farming family in Canada, planted there, via Ulster, in the 18th Century. He asked if we knew the meaning of our name. I said yes, it was 'the Bishop's gamekeeper or landsman': ghillie for huntsman's help, and pie for *episcopus,* Latin for bishop. And I asked about his business courses. They were for a roomful of people at $145 a head to whom he guaranteed he would stimulate five bankable ideas by close of day. Wow.

After some hours, maybe two and a half, he broke off and said, 'Hey, it's happened again.' And picked up his recorder. 'It's going to be mostly me talking on this thing. I find that, I go home and start to run it and—it's me talking'. We murmured politely. He said, 'Thank you so much for arranging this; dammit, there was so much more I wanted to hear.'

I said, genuinely, that I'd been fascinated to dig out some history I could never have known. We hastily filled in a few details about ourselves. Departing, he asked if any of us were aiming to visit America, and that if one or other of us had some idea, some proposal to make, some project in view, to—in the name, I suppose of clan solidarity—not to flinch from contacting him. He went. 'I told you he was a crook,' said my mother.

He hadn't been gone long when… Hang on… here was *Mr. Joyce is Leaving Paris* in Dublin knocking people's socks off, and it occurred to me that the play was perfect for America, given its Irish connection and their scholarly interest in Joyce. So I went to the post office back in Dublin (the battered rebel HQ from the Easter Rising) and spent five pounds on a detailed telegram to Lt. Gen. Robert J Gillespie, telling him of our magnificent Joyce play and could he come to the assistance of his tribe in what might be a glorious addition to the contribution our sub-clan was making to the cultural riches of the New World. Silence. Impenetrable silence. Maybe my mother was right. Oh well; we hadn't parted with any valuables, and we'd learned something—so.

# Directing at The King's Head (1971-1986)

**I can't remember** if it was Dan Crawford who rang me, or his wife Joan (yes, Joan Crawford); she had a degree in English and was a highly educated, cultivated, knowledgeable, beautiful Canadian woman. He and Joan had decided to chance it with pub theatre in London—they managed the King's Head Theatre in Islington—innovative, ground-breaking, the first pub theatre in London. Word had somehow got around that I directed (cheap— I acted, for money), and I was invited to meet them.

Dan Crawford, originally from New Jersey, had been dressed by his mother in black velvet and white lace (so Joan told me). Though I understood that Dan hated his mother, I gather he was, nonetheless, dutiful, visited her, had her over—and got a little bit of cash out of her from time to time; so Joan said. He'd rebelled by hiring himself out as a stage hand in New York, and from that time onward Dan was star-struck and stage-struck. Nevertheless he looked like a bundle of old clothes flung ashore by the tide and dried out in the sun, and—as I later explained to strangers—if you were looking for him in his pub theatre, you searched for the scruffiest, messy corduroyed, paint splattered young guy in back of the bar, half hidden by disreputable cronies—and that would be Dan.

Dan's current show was *Blow Job* (edgy in its day) and he had absolutely nothing to follow it. However he did have about his person a script by an actor, Iain Blair (whom I think I had once met and who may have suggested me), called *The Love Songs of Martha Canary,* which came with Heather Sears attached. That's what turned Dan on: Heather had been the great, ingénue star of British movies—*Room at the Top* etc.—but as she ruefully acknowledged she'd been dropped as soon as she reached…

The Boss, Dan Crawford
"Am I politic?
Am I subtle?
Am I a Machiavel?"

thirty-five? Some age like that. I got to know her a bit—sweet woman. She had this great home-counties house where, as I witnessed when visiting her there, she was called on by other movie has-beens toting block-busting scripts under their arms—scripts that happened to have starring parts for themselves, but couldn't attract a studio that would buy.

So I directed *Love Songs,* and Iain Blair played the lead himself—three linked, short plays I recall; and the show got decent reviews, and of course attracted attention—because of Heather.

I discovered that having nothing to follow a current show was Dan's habitual management state—so it was a fantastic opportunity to throw stuff at the venue if you could find the texts! I and a great cast had just had a big success in Dublin and so I tried *Mr. Joyce* on him. At that time I had an impression that he would read the first ten pages of a script, but that was his limit: what impressed him were our reviews. Joan readily took a script of *Mr. Joyce,* was able to judge it, and liked it.

12  *The Daily Telegraph,*
   *Thursday, December 2, 1971*

*Concerts*

Iain Blair and Heather Sears in " The Love Songs of Martha Canary," a trilogy of one-act plays by Iain Blair, being performed at The King's Head, Islington.

So I brought *Mr. Joyce is Leaving Paris* to the King's Head and it rocked. It was seen by a maverick cameraman, Harry Hart, who leant on Derek Banham to come along: Derek ran The Moving Picture Company (mainly shooting commercials), and a plot was hatched to film *Mr. Joyce* in two days, using a ground-breaking, centrally mounted rig. We did it. The rig, for all its glitchiness, meant we could shoot ten minutes or longer of the play in a single take, in the well-prepared room, and capture the feeling of a live performance. Yes, we did it and I have the thing. Hugely better than filming in the theatre. (Photo and more on page 226). Especially satisfying to have caught five players—Robert Bernal, Tony Doyle, Jim Norton, Mikel Lambert and Alan Barry at the height of their powers.

I started a 'thought-hare' in Part One about self-destructive behaviour, and it happens that I've known or worked with a lot of alcoholics. Robert Bernal (real name O'Shaughnessy) had kicked the booze twice by the time he came to us. Once, he tried to describe the effects of being enveloped by the smell of drink and the sight of seductive rows of many-shaped bottles filled with richly-coloured liquids: how difficult it was, what extraordinary courage it took for him to cross the pub rooms we rehearsed or played in. Responsibly, dutifully he would attend A.A. meetings before coming to rehearsals; partly to help others, partly to keep his own habit in chains. But he hadn't given up smoking: he was on eighty Capstan a day, he said.

Robert's career was blossoming again out of *Mr. Joyce*—his reviews were phenomenal. He bought himself a smart, white, Harold Wilson coat. Then he came to the show one day, having seen his doctor about a back pain, somewhere near a shoulder. Said he would be going to an osteopath: it didn't help. The run of *Mr. Joyce* was over and Robert, unwell, went to hospital. They kept him for a week and, drugged, let

him out. A few days later—I can still hear him—'Robert… the hospital rang me.' He was trying to keep his voice steady and always found a way of making a wry joke of things. 'She went to the wrong cupboard, Robert.' He told me he'd had a startling phone call ordering him straight back to the Oncology wing.

*Dan, wheeling and dealing*

A nurse had given him the wrong drug. He was diagnosed with cancer of the lung and never left hospital. His funeral was bound to be a very jokey affair, lots of mordant Irish laughter. Anna, my partner (we'd met by then), kept wanting to call out 'Stop playing the fool, Robert —come out of that box.'

# Dublin and The King's Head, back and forth (1972-75)

**Dublin again.** Though Tom Gallacher had ratted on me (first occasion), he'd done it with such charm and innocence—and his play had been such a huge success, and he had other plays, after all—that we went on corresponding and speaking and, eventually, meeting. The upshot: we began rehearsals for *Revival!* which is about an actor-manager who decides, while playing Solness in Ibsen's *The Master Builder,* to—actually— jump from the top of Solness' newly built masterpiece tower during a performance of the show. It's a comedy: a Buddhist comedy, as it turned out. Tom was steeped in Kierkegaard, and other Scandinavian influences. In *Revival!,* the actor-manager's conviction that he could hone and polish himself spiritually, could self-improve, Buddhist-style, so virtuosically as to achieve a higher plane of being—beyond conventional death—chimed with a belief of Tom's own.

Julian Somers played the aspiring actor—I'd seen him be magnificent as Iago in Noel Iliffe's company at the Library Theatre, Manchester, when I was a lad of fifteen. Ah, those good-ish old days! Diana Fairfax—very lovely—played the actor-manager's much-tested wife. Diana felt strongly that she'd never been allowed the career she deserved. In life she was married to Derek Godfrey, who could be sublime on his day. Originally I'd offered the leading parts to her and Derek, to cash in on a starry husband-and-wife team, but he said 'no'—though he graciously let Diana come out to play.

We were at the Eblana again—a converted news cinema in the Busaras, Dublin's central bus station; the Eblana was much used by a local outfit called Gemini Productions, run by an elegant, stately, stylish woman *d'un certain âge,* Phyllis Ryan (she did the art), with Brendan Connellan (he was the money).

I don't know if the reviewers ever got the deepest message from the play, but there were lots of lovely, wry observations on show-biz life—a charming daughter, a bull-shitting director, a ruthless, ambitious, rising actress, a quack, philosophising doctor—so the show got decent coverage, and Joan and Dan picked it up for Islington. Everybody from Harold Hobson to Irving Wardle to you-name-them came and reviewed us at the King's Head. We were early, classy London fringe and a huge breath of fresh air from what the guys habitually had to review in the—still—glorious West End.

*Miracles in a bus station*

I noticed, as time passed, a curious tic of Hobson's: because his stuff only appeared at week-ends, it often seemed studiedly not to agree with his weekday colleagues; as if he waited to see what they were saying and then put them sparklingly right on Sundays; often just as complimentary to us—but on different points. Hmm. He was the chap, some will recall, who raved—out of step—about Pinter's *The Birthday Party,* which was about to die at the Lyric Hammersmith— and, you could say, rescued Harold Pinter from years of disappointment; perhaps oblivion?

I got the most amazing people to come and be in shows at the King's Head. Employment in straight plays on television was, then, available: so once you were booked, you knew your engagement dates, and could do other work around them.

*The King's Head today*

It was twenty-five quid a week for the actors—always paid; twenty-five for the production—paid intermittently; but there was good old reliable TV to keep us alive. So I worked with Tony Doyle, Jim Norton, Diana Fairfax, Tom Conti, Jack Shepherd, John Hurt, Robert Bridges, Kevin Stoney, Maggie Shevlin, Nichola McAuliffe and on and on: they 'yessed', because they could play astonishingly good parts in out-of-the-ordinary plays not available to them elsewhere. I focused on world premières or neglected texts—no point in echoing my work as an actor. As performer my rule was 'If it pays, and it's not life-threatening, DO IT'. But, as director, I could see no joy in reviving the standard works, modern or classical, on the King's Head stage; anyway, we didn't have the resources, or the revolve.

Dan's artistic input was lighting—useful. He hired an Irish jobbing builder, John Scully, to construct the sets. Everything was nailed and screwed down, so I daren't leave them to get on with their work: only because I knew the show, and how the actors moved in my productions, could I avoid disasters with trip-ups and blockings and barriers that might make the set unplayable. If a wall was out by even a few inches, you were done. I re-designed the stage so as to give barely, but just enough, acting room and yet leave space to maximise audience numbers. I was amused to see that the same stage lasted there for very many years.

Dan adored all-night get-ins. I aspired to organise to go home at ten-thirty, but I never saw Dan's face glow and his spirits soar around anything else that happened in his theatre the way it did when we stayed up through the night to get the shows in. Sausages and bacon sahnies would be walked in for us. The romance of it all knocked him for six. Hateful, really; unnecessary; exhausting.

I remember much the same thing at the Old Vic when we were ordered taxis at two or four in the morning. Wacky, screwy, baffling, bewildering. Not now, of course, not any more—regs have blocked that, thank… thank lots of things—unions, worry for health, worry for sanity; up to a point, money. Slowly, the operatic habit of creating a false crisis before a theatrical opening by working Herculean hours diminished; and went away for ever. I sometimes think it was a way for everyone to become so exhausted that they were oddly relaxed—only able to muster one last bit of energy for the hideous business of an old-fashioned FIRST NIGHT. Dan had picked up this glamorous hang-up, this absurdity, shifting scenery in New York, and never got over it.

There's another change in theatre practice I support and applaud. Once, the First Night of any production was the night the press came. *All* the press. Pre-opening preparation was in-house, without an audience. Reviewers demanded, and custom backed them, that they should all be present at that first, exemplary, public showing. If one or another couldn't make it, they didn't come at all; there was a slight easing for the Sunday reviewers. The rationale was that if critics all saw the same performance, then their comment would derive from that showing—any variance would arise from a genuine difference in taste or culture, and not because the actors had a flat night.

This was, in most actors' opinions, one of the most unpleasant experiences it was possible to undergo on stage. It produced an artificially induced frenzy that sapped the spirit of many performers—and, I believe, undermined their mental health. You were not being judged on your measured, thought-through craft-iness, but on flash-in-the-pan inspiration; like a matador's one chance to kill his bull. Disgusting.

It suited a minority, and they loved it and could rely on their animal spirits to crack it, most of the time: I'd be curious to know if they died young. However, it reduced first nights in the theatre to a commercial blood sport. Most of all it suited the Gallery First Nighters: a mob of theatre-going hoodlums who infested the gods at every theatre and were supposed—by serious commentators—to be the true arbiters of whether a show should live; or die.

Gradually, critics and actors and producers have killed this pernicious custom and it is acknowledged that we practitioners try to do our best; sometimes on some nights succeed only partially, sometimes fail, and that if a reviewer can't make the official press night he or she will still want to see the show and write about it. Also, we are now allowed our preview performances, because we're not simple machines, and an audience is an integral part of any performance and we can improve! The first-night charade and nightmare still holds on Broadway, I believe. Gamblers cling to it; actors hate it. Sonia Friedman, a West End producer who is an absolute genius in all other ways, also hankers after it. Whoever heard of an F16 flying right the first time you put the bits together?

You have to give Dan and Joan a gold star for courage and enterprise to risk a venture like this at the time, but I found Dan's unhelpfulness a constant puzzle, and it never really changed. He wanted the shows we brought in. He loved the box office queues we began to get for our shows. He loved it when we began to sell out and be booked from America and had people land at Heathrow and come straight to the theatre. But there was a constant, wearing, undermining struggle with his arty bohemianism. Dan insisted on still using pounds shillings and pence at the bar and box office—quirky; and he liked to pay in guineas.

Dan and Joan had got the public spaces, the bar and auditorium, marginally usable; he sanded the floor and put a band in the corner of the bar (that was good). But sanding and sealing the floor became one of his obsessions: took priority way over finding somewhere for the actors to change without breaking their shins against clobber piled up on the middle floor of the pub.

At any theatre you hope there'll be a consensus about essentials. If you have costumes you need to park them somewhere on the premises, rather than make the actors bring them in every evening. Same with props. And they need to be there every night the show is on—and findable. The sort of actors I was bringing in didn't fancy changing on the stairs, or on a landing, or in the middle of a pile of junk.

Once, looking for them early one morning, I found Joan and Dan asleep, charmingly entwined on the—partially cleaned up—top floor. The middle floor stored the rubble and the spares and the half smashed doors—but that's where the actors and the costumes had to go. Mostly, the women preferred not to strip in the presence of the men. Dan slung up a blanket and a sheet or two, to divide the space, to begin with. Some minimal cleaning was done.

We were shown a possible back-stage 'dressing room'. It had the feel of a Neolithic cave hacked straight out of the earth. My first cast looked: was it any better than preparing on the middle floor? I explained that actors needed more than just two rickety chairs, and was there a mirror they could have? Of course, there was no loo, back stage: so once the audience was in there was no escape—till the interval, or the end of the show. Pissing in a bucket, possibly, was mentioned. Not on. Dan said you could get to a

*Payment for Productions*
*at King's Head*

| | £ | p |
|---|---|---|
| Sept. 1976 – "Spokesong" | 126 | =00 |
| 21.7.77 – "Da" | 126 | =00 |
| | +126 | =00 |
| 21.9.77 – "Oedipus at the C." | 17 | =00 |
| 17.2.78 – "Oedipus at the C." | 15 | =00 |
| March 1978 – "Des Keogh show" | 27 | =00 |
| 27.4.79 – "Fearless Frank" | 52 | =50 |
| 8.5.79 – "Fearless Frank" | 52 | =50 |
| 11.5.79 – "Fearless Frank" | 52 | =50 |
| 19.6.79 – "Fearless Frank" | 110 | =00 |

loo by climbing over the partially-glazed roof and going front of house. He found a ladder. Some people, mainly blokes, used it. The actresses nipped through the audience at the interval. When I worked in Israel—more of this later—I taught myself to shout to get things done, but here it wouldn't do: I learned to quietly, steadily, persistently ask for things. I counted. It took ten, polite, courteous, requests to get Dan to do anything that was practical and vital for the show—just good housekeeping, I mean; nothing extravagant, but absolutely necessary. Suggesting that the band couldn't play in the bar while actors were speaking lines in straight plays in the theatre took a bit of doing.

The politics of power apply everywhere, and it's wise to be in a state of readiness. *Blow Job* actors put up with anything, but mine wouldn't: when we came back from Dublin with Tom Gallacher's *Revival!* and my cast were re-rehearsing to open at the King's Head, out of the blue I received an urgent deputation about the lack of a

back-stage bog. Diana led this; she was unexpectedly, surprisingly firm; she spoke of first-night nerves… I had, of course, brought it up with Dan a number of times but nothing had happened. I said I would try again.

By then there were rudimentary dressing tables and mirrors, some lighting. But it really wasn't easy to organise yourself for a full length play and manipulate or time your bodily functions to avoid acute discomfort: some actors would 'go' at the last moment, and then dash back through the audience; players had to decide whether to be in costume, or to change very fast as soon as they got back stage; if you weren't entirely well, or had drunk a fair bit, or were just caught short… Of course I was sympathetic, but my rule of ten requests with Dan wasn't working. Lack of drainage was threatening our art. Very hesitantly, very reluctantly, Dan conceded that there were the remains of a drain back-stage that could, in principle, perhaps, be re-instated.

We all went and stood around it and had a good look—at this broken end of pottery flue. Still nothing happened. Then national politics of the time inspired me: I explained to my actors that I was quite unable to move Dan, but if they would agree to threaten me with strike action, with a refusal to perform until they had a workable crapper back stage, I would happily go to Dan and say matters were out of control and there would be no *Revival!* without a viable lavatory back-stage. It brought him down to meet the company. They were all sitting at a table by the main entrance to the theatre and very calmly, very politely, explained that they could not go on working in these conditions. Dan got hold of John Scully and within twelve hours they'd installed an operable loo and made a few other improvements and the cast was happy and the show opened on time. Solidarity, deployed serenely and with discretion, can work.

Once more a show finished with nothing to follow it. Dan's incorrigible lack of organisation continued to give me an unimaginably wonderful opportunity to put on plays. I came up with the writers, Joan checked them out, we happily dramaturged together, we cast, then I rehearsed them. Swiftly, Joan and I began to think ahead and, as the place's reputation grew, it became possible to butt-on shows, end to end. We tended to go for a four-week run, but the management's unconventional way of working meant that when we had a success the show could run as long as there was an audience—sometimes we even had to re-cast. Programming was super fluid, we could turn on a sixpence, change our minds and no one would sue because no one had any money.

*The Wednesday Play* was the rage on telly and I suggested a text by David Mercer, who was huge on TV at the time—*Let's Murder Vivaldi*—to Dan and Joan. It wasn't full-length theatre, so Joan drew my attention to the work of an American writer called A.R. Gurney. Scripts had begun to come in from every direction, including agents, and I went through the vast pile of unread texts that Dan and Joan handed me. I read anything. Gurney's short play called *The Problem* turned out to be one of the funniest things I've ever seen or heard. Gurney was an academic, very prolific, but with a variable output. It helped me to learn a universal truth. Deep reflection had suggested to me that Mercer's play—a bitter, sarcastic, tragic story of the linked relationship of an older and a younger married couple—given its seriousness and weight, should climax the evening. Kevin Stoney and Diana Fairfax were in both the Gurney and the Mercer, so we started the evening with the side-splitting Gurney. Mistake. It was impossible, after the helpless laughter provoked by *The Problem,* to pay attention to the serious Mercer play. I switched them after the first performance and the show was a wow.

Lesson never to be forgot. Something to do with the human psyche. Silly me: of course—the Greeks did it this way round, and so did Shakespeare.

Jack Shepherd couldn't do the whole run playing the younger husband, so Tom Conti took over for a week. Amazing. The guys were supposed to play the violin (badly), but still play. They got away with it: devotion; application; terrific.

In the Mercer, at the end of the older couple's story, fed-up with being nagged the husband stabs his wife. I pointed out to Dan, right at the beginning, that we had to get a plausible, retractable knife from somewhere—the action couldn't be faked as it had been on TV. All through rehearsals I kept asking if he had sorted this. I said that we couldn't really do the play to a live audience unless we could make the stabbing reasonably believable. Nothing appeared, and on the night before we opened, I brought it up again. For the first time, he seemed to cotton on. He rooted among some of his office clobber and found—a wooden pencil box with a sliding lid in a groove: it was his best effort. I took it home and worked on it after supper, into the morning, shaping the lid to look like a knife blade and strapping the box to look—ludicrous—like a huge handle. The actors, till then, had worked with nothing. The 'knife' looked absurd, but the doctored lid slid into its groove, and in the climate of the time and the brilliance of the playing and the texts, it meant that we weren't hammered for this risible prop.

*A very English murder;*
*Mercer's Vivaldi*

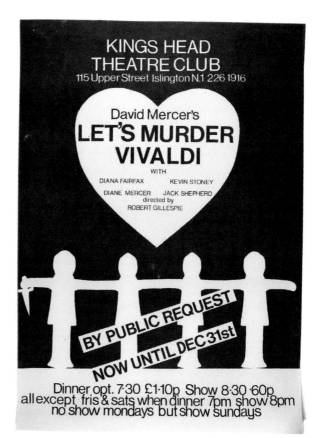

Another road block, at times, at the King's Head was the quality of the stage management. For a while, a great young bloke called Peter Stephenson was in place: he was a pleasure to work with, punctilious and wondrously protesting at, and irritated by, Dan's messiness. His sanity and hard work helped keep us incomers happy. But he had a degree in something interesting and eventually became a major wheel in animal rights campaigning. After Peter, things weren't so good.

Thick and fast, the plays of Tom Gallacher rolled towards us. *Schellenbrack* was next: an Ibsenite dark-secret play with a journalist nosing out 'the truth'. All about personality and privacy. Not half bad, did O.K. Wolfe Morris, excellent character actor, played the lead; Alan Barry, the journalist. Wolfe (whose brother Aubrey was with me at the Vic) challenged me when I said I never read through a play with the cast at the beginning of rehearsals. He said it was an integral element of his approach to a part. I argued that it was pointless and a waste of time, because the play changed so much once the actors voiced it and moved it. We compromised. I conceded that we'd sit and read *Schellenbrack* after two weeks' rehearsal. Of course, we never did— we attempted a few pages, but adhering to the punctuation on the page was, by then, so ridiculous that Wolfe saw my point: the play was soaring in a different medium, by then; autonomous. At the RSC, sit-down cast readings can make sense with a difficult, archaic text to clarify, and learned background information to absorb.

Writer Tom Gallacher tenaciously maintained his mystery. For years while I directed his plays he was just a voice at the end of a telephone. He'd spent some years in Denmark, birth nation of his guru, Kierkegaard; there was hint of oil industry, and time on seven-sea tankers. He had a strong connection with Pitlochry—in fact, he later showed me a very silly play about the comic adventures of a man knocked out by a blow on the head: apparently a riot in Pitlochry; perhaps the Buddhist dimension licensed him to take this school play seriously. He confessed to me that he didn't speak to his family: sometimes he visited his mother; once while he was there he looked out the window, saw his brother approaching the house—the brother spotted Tom's car parked outside and turned round and went away to avoid meeting. We wondered if the family was darkly Catholic. Nothing ever was, quite, confirmed.

Then one day Tom Gallacher materialised. Success tempted him to London and, suddenly, he was real enough to have dinner with Anna and me in Hammersmith by the romantic light of an old oil lamp. Faced with corn on the cob, he asked how it was eaten. Writers are different.

Jeremy Kingston, a distinguished critic at *Punch* for ten years and then *The Times* so, essentially, a journalist, didn't bat an eyelid if you suggested a possible re-write in one of his plays—as long as he saw the point; and he worked very fast. Gallacher's stance, in contrast, was polar: once he had finished a play to his own satisfaction, he maintained it was complete. The act of handing it over for production meant loss of sovereignty—it was now in our hands, a different animal, we could do what we liked. He claimed never—or hardly ever—to attend performances of his plays. At first I interpreted this as some sort of purist philosophical position (perhaps linked to the shade of Buddhism he was drawn to). After a while, though, I reckoned that he had in his head some perfect performance of what he'd written, and dreaded to see it mauled by fluffing, sweating, live actors. At last, I persuaded him to see a King's Head show. And… he seemed pleased.

By then, Michael Imison, a junior at a top literary agency, was sniffing around (I'd first known Michael from his interest in my play *Napoleon Session 2* at the Orange Tree). Agent Michael took on Tom.

I still can't quite figure why we went on speaking after the second time Tom ratted on me. *Revival!* did so well that director Patrick Garland came and sat in the front row to take notes of my production… I'm quite sure that if Tom had been firm, he could have attached me to the play as director. And there were no contracts at the King's Head, so I was helpless. The word was that someone, Imison, a management, I'm not certain, had spotted a possible role for Ralph Richardson as the suicidal actor-manager. But life is stranger than fiction, isn't it, and next thing Dan told me was that Richardson insisted on meeting me. He'd snuck in to see the production and had read the text. We sat on bentwoods in the cursorily cleaned-up middle floor at the King's Head and chatted.

Of course Sir Ralph Richardson was one of our stratospherically eminent stage stars; up there with Olivier, Michael Redgrave, Alec Guinness and Gielgud. Richardson wanted to know—above all—what the devil Gallacher was on about with Bernard's (the actor-manager in the play) fixation about 'improving himself in order to move on' and 'reach a higher state of being'. After he'd jumped off his own building, where was he in Act III—alive? Dead? Could I explain it: was it some sort of 'New Age' trip? And who was this special 'teacher' feller of Bernard's—and Gallacher's—the feller Kierke… what… gore… yes Kierkegaard? Who was he? What had he done? Would the audience know, or care?

I explained; and soon I sensed that Richardson believed his followers might not wish to 'bother with it' if he took on this play. So that was that. And then we got talking about his present head-scratching dilemma. I'd gone specially to see him in William Douglas-Home's play, *Lloyd George Knew My Father,* co-starring Celia Johnson. Sir Ralph had been in it for fifteen months, from the opening. The latest fad—infuriating, he thought it—was for leading players to wish to do no more than three months in a play; Celia Johnson was his current leading lady and she was about to leave. 'It's right there on the Strand,' he said. 'People like it; they're coming. I've spoken to her… "Won't you do another three months?" "No." I asked her very nicely. I can't understand it—can you? I mean… it's work.'

I can truthfully say that I never expected to hear Sir Ralph Richardson say that he was just glad to be in work. He meant it though. Old School.

Sir Ralph didn't do *Revival!.* Tom explained away his readiness to dump me—dump, well, anyone—by implying that he was in other people's hands. Once commerce was king you had to bend to its imperatives—something like that. And however he danced around this state of mind, it was adroitly phrased and plausibly argued, and done with such modest charm that it was impossible to get angry with him. I learned, slowly, that writers will ruthlessly double-cross anyone if it helps get their babies promoted on stage or screen. Only writers have ever cheated on me.

Brendan Smith, still Director of the Dublin Theatre Festival, took up the fourth play of Tom's I was prepared to direct. Called *The Only Street* it was the strangest, so far. There were two stunning parts for brothers. Tony Doyle agreed to play one; the other was John Hurt. John came to us, ruefully, saying he kept being 'discovered'—and then dropped—and hoped it wasn't going to happen again. The Fates took care of that.

*The Only Street* is about a family splitting. One of the brothers must go on a journey—he is convinced. His brother and mother and girl-friend can't see why. They are a close, tight group; can the young man explain the sense of what he wants to do?

At this distance, I can see a version of the actor-manager in *Revival!,* who wants to slough off his current bodily burden and—move up: to somewhere. This time, the brother wants to move—on—to somewhere. Because Tom wouldn't be explicit in the text and tell us he was writing a version of a devout Buddhist's experimental journey towards that old elusive higher state, the audiences and critics were a bit nonplussed. I only picked up the message from hints that Tom let fall—and from one, tuned-in, Dublin reviewer, who spotted the inferences. The play worked at the level of family splintering, of course, and was well acted, but almost all the audience missed a crucial element to the tale—a kind of spiritual, a believer's, obsessive fixation, I suppose— which could have made it really fascinating for them, if they'd been helped. Tom wouldn't change a line, couldn't see the problem: stubborn as ever, in his exquisitely measured, civil way. There was a curious sequel, which I'll come to.

John Hurt in a scene from "The Only Street."

'I keep being discovered,' he said to me. 'If it happens again, I hope it sticks.' (It did)

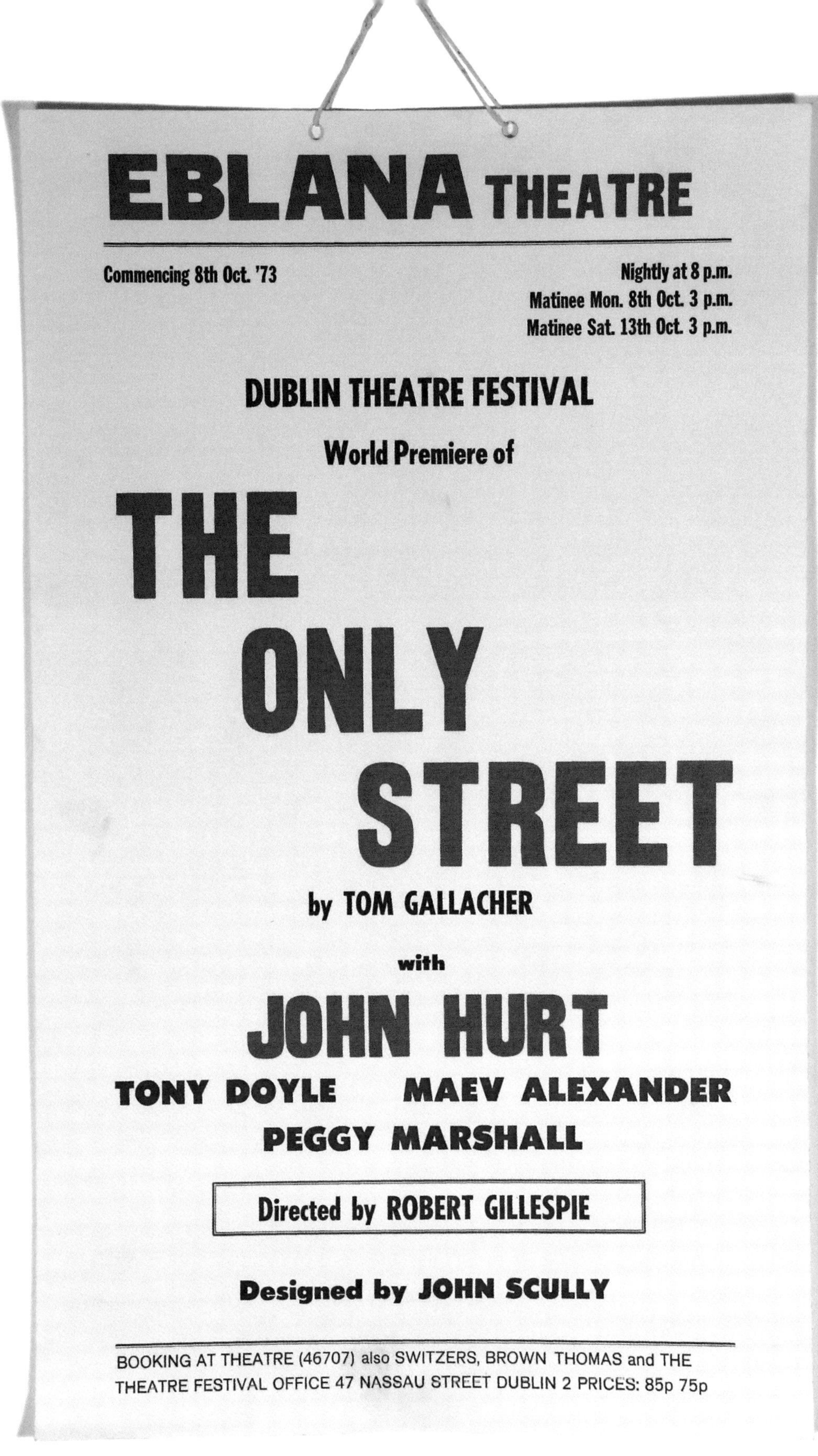

# EBLANA THEATRE

Commencing 8th Oct. '73

Nightly at 8 p.m.
Matinee Mon. 8th Oct. 3 p.m.
Matinee Sat. 13th Oct. 3 p.m.

## DUBLIN THEATRE FESTIVAL

World Premiere of

# THE
# ONLY
# STREET

by TOM GALLACHER

with

# JOHN HURT

## TONY DOYLE    MAEV ALEXANDER
## PEGGY MARSHALL

Directed by ROBERT GILLESPIE

Designed by JOHN SCULLY

BOOKING AT THEATRE (46707) also SWITZERS, BROWN THOMAS and THE
THEATRE FESTIVAL OFFICE 47 NASSAU STREET DUBLIN 2 PRICES: 85p 75p

Working with Brendan Smith was always a singular treat. Later, I discovered that he had in fact founded the Dublin Theatre Festival (back in 1957) and had something of an international reputation. I knew he ran the Brendan Smith Academy of Acting which many locals thought a bit of a joke.

You have to imagine a small, bearded man with an archetypal Dublin honk to his way of speaking. He approached every visiting director with a plea for them to audition some of the queue of mendicant Dublin-based actors who saw the Festival as a rare chance in the year to work. Brendan quickly cottoned on that he could trust me to be discreet, and said to me, 'To be frank with you, Robert, I call them the un-employables, but if you meet them they'll stop badgering me.' I see everybody: the actor's trade is even more part-time in Ireland than it is here. He was right and I never cast them. He also, regularly, offered me his wife, Beryl. She was a forceful woman of middle age and not, so the word went, hugely talented, but Brendan indicated that his home life would hardly be bearable if his wife wasn't hawked round the visiting Festival directors. She, also, with a knowing smile, described the rag-tag crew as 'the unemployables'. I never used her either. I saw her play once: I've seen worse; but there was nothing in my shows to offer.

After every opening, the director and some of the cast would appear the next morning before a roomful of press; not a thing I was used to. Tony Doyle warned me it was a small city, everybody in the swim knew everybody else; we quickly got on first name terms with leading critics. We ran into them in pubs, on the street, had chats with them. Having Tony around was a boon: he was already celebrated as a regular on a Dublin soap *The Riordans,* so we were hailed and fêted everywhere. Idly, I wondered what this regular time away was doing to his marriage. He rang Sue, his ex-model wife back in London, without fail every early evening.

Incidentally, in Dublin a thing that shook me was the begging. Women in shawls, with small children and what looked like dirtied-up faces, sat on bridges and minor but busy roads, in some numbers. I couldn't remember when I'd last seen people begging like that on a European street. Not till it happened one day on the Shepherd's Bush triangle. In the Thatcher years, a perfectly decently dressed, but worn-looking woman with a buggy and three kids accosted me. I was shocked; she didn't look as if made up for a disaster movie, the children weren't dirtied up, as they seemed in

Dublin. It stayed very rare, in England—but I saw the same thing on every trip to Ireland (it may be different now).

An eccentric Irish bi-sexual chap name of Alan McLelland who'd been in my Basement production of *Mr. Joyce is Leaving Paris* (playing Stannie, Joyce's brother) asked me to direct him in a rehearsed reading of *Albert Nobbs*—one of the short stories from George Moore's *Celibates;* it was a scandalous—and risky—account of a cross-dressing waiter. Brendan Smith found him a venue, and at that venue I saw a musical by Stewart Parker called *Spokesong* which ran just one week; but from which hangs a tale—more on this later.

We brought *The Only Street* back from Dublin to the King's Head in 1973. By then we were getting requests for full press publicity calls, up to a dozen guys with cameras wanting pictures for their papers, or freelancing—I got to know quite a few of them, because they came and they came, show on show; and by now folks were booking to see what we did just because it was the King's Head. It was all interesting.

But *The Only Street* again bamboozled the reviewers: to the point that Tom was provoked to write, at lightning speed, a dramatic riposte *à la* 18th Century: this play was nearly a masterpiece—but you had to have seen *The Only Street* and have read its reviews to get the full whack out of attending this scintillating reply. I couldn't persuade Tom to lace it with enough references to help the virgin viewer get full value from it. Once again, Tom's inflexibility torpedoed a potentially exhilarating enterprise. And of course the script dated with every hour that *The Only Street* was history. Wonderful to think that you might be able to revive this kind of responsive theatre, where a writer could push a point, have it mauled and savaged and praised by society and then reply on the instant with a brilliant defence. I nearly put it on—but London, the world, was too big by then—it would have missed most people. Never mind.

About this time came the big crisis at The King's Head. It seemed to centre on ordering booze and therefore meant money. Aside from all the frayed edges everyone who tried to work at the King's Head had to cope with, the enterprise could not continue—I was told—if there wasn't enough money to order the minimum amount of drink from the brewers that they'd stipulated in their opening deal with Dan and Joan. Dan's opposition to methodical—anything—book keeping, cash tracking, and so on, meant that the brewers threatened to end his lease.

Joan had come to me one day and said Dan had told her he was, 'Sick of all this "good work" we are doing'. I'd wondered: what did Dan like? What did he enjoy? He loved the place to be full. He loved gossiping with cronies. But what was he getting out of what was happening in the theatre? There came a make-or-break meeting with the brewers at which—if Dan didn't come up with the cash to pay for the next booze order—he was out. By then, the atmosphere between Dan and Joan was strained. The long-anticipated power-struggle had begun. Many around the theatre thought that Joan could run the place more tightly than Dan. She told us that, on deep reflection, despite the agro, she would take on the King's Head, solo. The brewers had settled for this. Many of us methodical people quietly supported her because she was competent. As far as anybody knew, Dan was skint. So—came the big day and the meeting with the bosses and we all expected Dan to be chucked. No. Joan told me, after, that Dan talked a blinder, fished out some coins (Mummy again?) and jaw-jawed the brewers round. He kept the running of the King's Head.

So Joan split. I had a last conversation with her: she was immensely relieved. Dan's screwing around was a factor in their distancing, but not critical—she herself engaged with women in some weathers. It was his refusal to create any sort of system or order that finished her: it was wasteful; it lost a lot of box office money. I remember well, after months, years, of virtually full houses, show after show, saying to Dan—surely, by now, we could afford a little more on the set, a little more for the actors. Cash wasn't regularly rescued from the till. One day, I came in, there'd been a burglary: Scully's brother, Charlie—wearing a Harold Wilson coat (but grubby) had snatched three hundred quid from the till—said it was money owed him for work sanding the floor, or something. So we were suddenly short of whatever for our next show. That's what finished Joan. She went into publishing—and a clean house, I imagine.

Shows by other directors were scoring, filling the gaps in the schedule by that time; *Kennedy's Children* by Robert Patrick was a wow. But soon, Dan was stuck again; some half-expected project had fallen through.

Within hours I found a play, written for radio, but with an excellent story, and I blocked it at lightning speed—to Dan's wonder and admiration as he watched. It had sixty sound cues—and that's where the stage management hazard really hit. To get over the nightmare of a tale told in many short scenes (fine on the wireless, not ideal for the stage) I arranged for the chairs and table to be tubular steel and very slidable and, to keep the scene-change black-outs very brief, I had the actors move everything short, but significant, distances in the pitch dark to achieve the change of location. Provided the furniture didn't have to move too far, it could be done. We rehearsed and rehearsed it. To cover the lightning changes I used sound.

But the delicate, new, stage manager couldn't hack the sound. The King's Head system wasn't marvellous, but functional. I just kept quietly, steadily working over and over the cues with her. She got in a terrible muddle. It went on so long that Dan approached me. Awkwardly, diffidently, he implied that I was upsetting her.

I said the show would be shit if it wasn't technically faultless—the piece wasn't meant for the stage and only technical sleight-of-hand could crack it; it had a good story and that was all. The stage manager was out of her depth and weepy. I questioned whether this was the best we could get at the King's Head, given the clout we now had in the biz. It was only years later that I learned she was there 'because Dan was knocking her off'. Odd, because Dan was a handsome guy and could pull the best and she didn't accord with the house profile; with Joan gone, passing ladies were an extra rock on the road for us hardworking pros. Years further on I was in the BBC canteen and there she was—she was now a proper BBC trainee—and she came up to my table: and apologised. She said I must have thought she was a walking show-crew disaster—I agreed.

By then, I'd discovered that Dan didn't read a line of any script that came in. Sometimes he handed me fifty scripts to read and one of the few we ever produced off the pile was by Mike Jackson. It was seriously offensive, in places, given the epoch. *The Man Who Knew He Was Jesus Christ* was about a TV show host who got so above and beyond he began to think he had a mission for putting the world right; an early stab from Jackson at deflating celebrity culture. Trouble was, the last twenty minutes didn't work. Mike freely said he hadn't known how to finish the piece. We talked. He wasn't resisting: just couldn't get back into the story and revive the original drive, the flow. However, it was too good to pass up altogether, so I cobbled together a wrap-up from ideas he'd laid down in the text and that just about held together without spoiling the rest of the evening. Another slant on how writers are, or can be. Early Jerry Springer. There were some wonderfully filthy performances from Tony Doyle and Robert Bridges, and from an outrageous Jewish actress called Linda Polan. Brave Americans came off their planes and said they liked it—breath of fresh air. So that was all right.

My mate Walter Hall (Basement Theatre) took on lunch time productions at the King's Head. I'd just read a script that had come in from Jeremy Kingston telling the 'real' story behind the tale of Oedipus the luckless King—*Oedipus At The Crossroads*, he called it. Jeremy had reviewed us for *The Times,* was an important man, and this was an honour. It was a smashing script. Strange thing, I'd just begun thinking along similar lines, wondering why a sane royal couple, ruling in Thebes, might expose their baby son to die, just because some fortune teller had told them it would cause them problems later in life. I came to the conclusion that the fault lay in listening to Oracles, and I thought there should be an enquiry: I began a dramatised judicial review. Then Kingston's script landed, with the same core idea, but a different treatment.

His *Oedipus* ran just an hour (like the Sophocles tragedy from which it's derived) and so not quite an evening. Which meant that we could do it at lunch-time and offer leading parts to members of the RSC, then in town playing at the

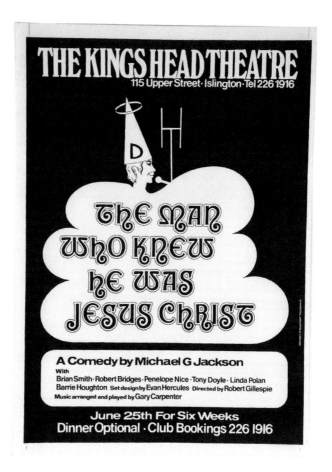

Piccadilly. Nicky Henson was Oedipus, Raymond Westwell played Laius, his dad, and John Bott spooked as Tiresias. The show got rave reviews and sold out (from this, I conceived the notion of making a full evening by matching it with the original Greek tragedy—but that was later). The only review that knocked the play came from Bernard Levin—though that's the review Jeremy remembers after fifty years…

I'd caught Jeremy at the end of a spiky divorce from his wife; he was prepared to be movingly open about it and we shared thoughts on the perplexities of trying to breathe unremittingly the same air as another human being, the closeness offering hell and heaven in unpredictable dollops. We both agreed that Iris Murdoch's *The Black Prince* didn't cut it on erotic love.

Working in Dublin had deepened my knowledge of Irish drama. It led to my putting on Hugh Leonard's *Da* at the King's Head; Leonard is a sort of Irish Alan Ayckbourn, and *Da* is probably his best play. *Da* is a funny and moving evocation of Ireland's conflicted past, played out among family and friends. I had a superb cast: Tony Doyle as Charlie Now and Mike McCabe as Charlie Then. But the coup for the show was to have got Eamon Kelly over from Ireland to be *Da*. Controversy: he was from Cork and Da is out and out Dublin. But, what a wonderful actor! Hugh Leonard fretted, but by now I knew better than to sacrifice a real actor for a genuine accent and what did London know? I'd seen Eamon in Dublin telling stories—one of the funniest character men ever. The show packed, and Eamon did fine out of it (adventure for him, coming over to London for not much money). It was pleasant to be able to cast my friend Anne Robson (from Vic days) in the part of the awful, English ascendancy woman, a condescending snob. Anne, with her Imperial Indian background, understood this woman's attitude to the 'natives', perfectly. *Da* went to Greenwich for a spell, but was frozen out by the vast, clanging playing space and poor local marketing.

Michael Codron, celebrated independent entrepreneur, came to see our shows regularly, and after a characteristic smoky and wine-soaked night at the King's Head, said to me, 'I don't think I'd ever transfer anything from here. I just couldn't re-create the atmosphere; it's half the show, isn't it?' Right. He was right. Dan served full meals pre-show in the auditorium and jammed in as many tables (each seating up to eight) as he could. Everyone sat on bentwood chairs. Serving food and drink— moving around at all—needed some skill and suppleness; we sometimes wondered about fires. You were allowed to sit on at your table with your liquor for the show. I imagined the Elizabethan theatre to have felt something like this: people pressed together, inescapably aware of each other's sweating bodies and ceasing to care. It was wonderfully liberating; you couldn't fret on about your mortgage or the price of bread in this unlaced, promiscuous atmosphere. Strangers talked to each other and forgot about to-morrow and opened themselves to story-telling. The invention of this seductive refuge, not tangible, not plannable, an 'emergent property' as the scientists have it, was, I think, Joan and Dan's best achievement.

There was a great night when Tennessee Williams came to see my production of his own play—that's how famous we got! Ever since my first brush with his *Period of Adjustment* at Lincoln I'd wanted to re-visit it. Supposedly it was Tennessee's only comedy: according to the pundits, especially according to Elia Kazan. I blame Kazan for misguiding a generation: by then I'd begun to have some sense that his defining of Williams' plays as poetic, domestic tragedies was mistaken; and he seemed to think *Period* was a flawed aberration. Well, I'll tell you what happened. Tennessee was shown to his seat, accompanied by his self-appointed minder Lady Maria St. Just (previously Maria Britneva), a chunky lady without whom, I was told, he didn't move an inch, and who vetted anyone and anything that might bother him.

The house lights went down and the show started. It begins with one of those standard, small-town American local radio broadcasts detailing—rapid-fire—the weather, the traffic, shop-openings and so on. From the back of the house came this thin, high-pitched laugh… 'Hih…hih…hih…hih…': Tennessee. It got the whole audience going. That night, the show was a smash: Tennessee had given the audience permission to laugh—at a Tennessee Williams play. Till then, because Kazan and Co had fixed in audiences' and directors' and managements' minds that Williams' plays were pain-soaked, psychological dramas, the King's Head cast had found it uphill work stimulating the laughter clearly present in the dialogue. The play is about a very young woman, just-married—and still a virgin (Holly Palance), whose cowboy husband dumps her with a friend they are visiting (Tony Doyle) and drives off, supposedly to get some beer. There is a queasy feeling that he may not come back. The friend, Mr. Bates, has just had his wife walk out on him. Good situation, eh? Tony—a superb, thinking actor—reckoned Williams' name for his character was

# THEATRE ROYAL Norwich

in association with the Arts Council of Great Britain presents for Norfolk & Norwich Triennial Festival

**ANNE ROGERS**  **MICHAEL BILLINGTON**  **HOLLY PALANCE**  **LEON GREENE**

in Tennessee Williams
Pulitzer Prize Winning Masterpiece

# A STREETCAR NAMED DESIRE

STEPHEN TURNER   JUDITH ORBACH

FRANK CODA   BILL REIMBOLD   LORNA ROSSLYN

STEPHEN LESTER   QUEENIE CAVETTE

directed by Robert Gillespie

in the award winning set by Patrick Robertson
lighting by Molly Friedel

designed and printed by studios, norwich tel 26538

## From Tuesday 19th October For One Week

NIGHTLY at 7·30pm   WEDNESDAY 2·30pm   SATURDAY 4·30 & 8·15pm

Prices 90p, 1·20, 1·60, 2·00, 2·50  Wed. & Sat. Mat. 80p, 1·10, 1·50, 1·70, 2·10 loaded—Mister Bates, Mastur-Bates?

I was introduced to Tennessee after. He was very pleasant, relaxed and kind. Looked worn and lived-in with long, thin, greying straggly hair. He loved the show. Very nice about us and everybody. A great evening.

One other thing about *Period of Adjustment,* and casting: you can still, sometimes, get it wrong. Bates' wife, Dorothy is a miserable woman, mostly weepy; very hard to play. A semi-professional actress, Frances Martin, read for it—and was brilliant. Just the right note of pathos with self-pity very well controlled. Then, at rehearsals, she could never repeat her audition performance. I've had this happen perhaps three or four times; it's strange, odd; how do you avoid it? Impossible, I guess. She knew she couldn't find her way back to where she'd been, emotionally, technically, and was very unhappy with herself—upsetting. In the end, she was so off-beam that we agreed to call it a day. She left the cast, late, and I recruited Anne Robson at short notice. Dorothy, as described by the author, is always close to tears, brimming with complaint, in a failing marriage and often, from the stage directions, breaks down. Anne did this, I supported her, encouraged her and many of the reviewers slammed her. My fault; but I thought she was exactly right and brave and rather wonderful. Funny old trade.

Further to my point on Williams: I'd directed *A Streetcar Named Desire* at the Theatre Royal, Norwich: Richard Condon had taken over this vast, magnificent provincial theatre, and he knew my work well. A fugitive from the Dublin Theatre Festival—where he'd served as number two to Brendan Smith—Richard ran Norwich with great imagination, offering a mix of world class plays and popular potboilers. We had a superb cast for *Streetcar*—except for Anne Rogers who couldn't believe that Blanche Dubois was pathetically funny—as well as very sad. At one or two rehearsals she let herself be drawn into the comic pathos of the character—but finally settled for tragedy queen: and so helped deaden the show; she made it heavy, even though everyone on stage with her was getting delicious, bitter-sweet laughs by playing their parts as written. It meant that Dick Condon's brave sally at tempting a provincial audience to enjoy a great modern drama (rather than an Agatha Christie) was lamed. Blanche, after all, carries a lot of the action, and to hear someone whine in self-pity half the night isn't enjoyable.

The rest of the cast hit exactly the right balance between tears and laughter. Sadly,

Anne helped limit our tour to just one other date; the Arts Council couldn't see us filling vast provincial receiving houses with her turgid moan; sad, as it had meant so much to Anne—she'd imagined re-booting her career with this performance.

Richard Condon was admirably full of ideas—and Dublin cheek. He had me coach a local actor in his solo performance as Richard Burbage. He also convinced me that I was the only director who could train his girlfriend to act. She came, specially, to my house in Hammersmith for her alchemical transformation and I found her very endearing. 'Robert,' she said, 'I'm sorry about this, but Dick is certain you can magick me into a competent actress—he has an extraordinarily high opinion of you as a director and, well, you know how macho he can be... while somehow maintaining his Irish charm. Robert, the thing is, I'm not sure he's right.' 'O.K.' I said, 'This won't be painful; let's try a few things.' She spoke some texts. I got her to improvise. 'You're right,' I said. 'Dick's wrong. But *you* will have to tell him.' She was so relieved, and she left the house, head high.

One day, suddenly, Richard dropped dead. A pleasure-giver much missed.

One more reflection on Williams: in 1991 I was cast in Peter Hall's production of *The Rose Tattoo,* and it was the final break-through, for me, on how to approach this writer. First, Peter cut it ruthlessly, cut the fat and waffle; daring—and dead right. Then, he took on Julie Walters (as Serafina) and Ken Stott (Alvaro). If Julie's on stage she's going to make you laugh as well as cry. The iron corset of tragedy constraining poor Tennessee's plays was at last smashed to scrap for good! Since then I've seen many revivals of different Williams plays and, thank goodness, the ashy grasp of Kazan has gone. If you think about it, the centre of just about every Tennessee Williams play is sexual frustration. From having the privilege of his presence at a show of mine, I realise that Tennessee has always found sexual frustration funny. Which is why he has always said that ALL his plays are comedies. If the man says it, perhaps he'd like you to believe it.

My exposure as a director was beginning to get me offers in commercial theatre. In Dublin a big wheel, Noel Pearson, wanted to put on an American piece by George Furth called *Twigs.* It hailed from Broadway and is an odd evening of four linked one-act plays. Directing for money was a new experience, but there was enough acute observation in the writing to help me summon the will to do it. Anna Manahan

The Rose Tattoo, Julie Walters, RG;
Playhouse Theatre, London

was to star, playing all four—very different—women, young and old. And I was told Niall Toibin (a very fine character actor and story teller, with a huge local reputation) would also be in the show and—of course—Des Keogh. Here's what's interesting: I'd seen Des in something and he was a face-puller. His fans loved it. Characterisation, then, to him was out and out mugging: he didn't merely make his point in a part once; he made it at least three times, just in case you'd missed it. The last time I'd seen anything as coarse as this was in the amateur theatre—but Des was a local star. He was tall, blond, personable and very charming. And that's commercial theatre, folks: it was take him or leave it, for me. Des was (local) box office.

One of the characters Des had to play was a lugubrious American guy of Swedish descent whose chief topic of conversation was describing his drive to meet his friends. Des, at the start, didn't trust his text, and did double takes on himself supported by facial contortions—awful, embarrassing. I thought, well, nothing to lose, so I began, very tactfully, gently, to speak to him. First, I tried to sell him the idea that the humour in his text lay in the timing: because his character's pronouncements were superbly banal, if Des waited a moment and then came out with his description of stopping at traffic lights as if he were announcing World War Three, it would be funny. Also, I pointed out that with his Scandinavian looks, he was very right for the part and needn't help it along with mouth chewing and hand flapping; just rely on his real, solemn self, but with monumentally uninteresting things to say: he'd get laughs. Des struggled to believe me, kept trying what I suggested, kept looking my way for reassurance, kept looking at Anna and Niall (who both, fortunately, nodded with approval at him and at me) and on the first night he risked it; he held his nerve and triumphed. He found me later and confessed something: told me that till then in his career he'd been so nervous before an opening performance that he'd invariably gone to the lavatory and vomited before going on. *Twigs* was the first time it hadn't happened, and he'd gone on stage feeling, calm, secure and in control of his material. He never vomited or was scared again.

After—in the late 70s—because he adored Noel Coward, he got Gemini Productions to put on *Private Lives* for him at the Eblana and I directed; Des was excellent. Later he came to the King's Head in London with an evening of Coward songs and stories that I staged for him.

Anna Manahan had a reputation and a following for being a 'heavyweight' performer—I think she thought she was an Irish Anna Magnani—but was capable of much greater delicacy, on stage, if only she dared risk it. In *Twigs* I tempted her to deploy her sweeter side (she was a very sweet woman). And that worked too, later, when she starred in *The Sea Horse,* an American two-hander by Edward J. Moore, which I also directed. Gentler, kinder, quieter—good.

Back at the King's Head, one of my regular appeals to Dan had been to try to get a press rep on board, or find a way to do marketing methodically—posters, outreach. I tried to explain to him that we couldn't rely on getting good reviews for everything —some day, something would divide opinion enough to put off some people from coming, in spite of the tremendous goodwill the place had now built up. I remembered the extraordinary effect Gerald Frow had achieved at the Mermaid, often rescuing indifferent shows. By this time we were attracting organisations that wanted to be associated with the brand we were making, and the full houses we were getting: a marketing firm offered to produce classy posters for us at their expense.

At the time, I was directing *Chocolate Cake.* The playwright, Nick Wood, was a curious, very quiet young man—he should have been one of our landmark playwrights, in the absurdist vein, treating 'Englishness' like a mild ailment. *Chocolate Cake* was engagingly bizarre in its squinted view of—everything. It sticks in the mind because it required a live goat to be led across the stage. (Dan Crawford could organise goats: they were non-routine enough to appeal to him. Almost invariably, the goat stopped to piss on stage: which was a treat for some...)

The poster design produced for *Chocolate Cake* was unusually stylish (see page 248); a significant advance on some of the scrawlier stuff we'd lived with till then. On my way in to work I looked out for our new posters—in shops, on walls, in pubs. At the end of the run of *Chocolate Cake* I asked Dan what had happened to the beautiful posters we'd had provided for us by the marketing co: I hadn't seen more than a couple around. Dan was behind the bar. He looked down—and fished out a completely unopened roll of *Chocolate Cake* A2 sheets.

After that, for my next shows, Anna and I would take a bunch of show bills, get in the car and trawl round hotels in various well-heeled parts of—especially tourist —London; I stayed in the car while Anna went up to the desk, batting her eyelashes at the staff, asking if they'd put up a poster or two. Almost no one refused; we got through about fifty at a time like this.

This, and all the other irritations about 'not putting costumes there, please' and 'that's got to be left clear for the cook' and 'yes the water will be on again, the lights will be fixed in the dressing room to-morrow or maybe the next day' etc. led me to ask Dan, one fine day, what he wanted out of the King's Head for himself: I couldn't figure out what turned Dan on about running this pub theatre. Did he want to direct, to try to write, to act? What was he getting out of it? I've always believed that when people are not doing something for money (the usual reason) they should be getting some sort of emotional or professional hit—if they didn't, they'd become discontented—surely?

A side of Dan was oddly diffident, almost shy and indecisive. But eventually, eventually he said to me, 'I like Noel Coward, I like Somerset Maugham… in America, I loved the English, upper class, clipped, formal, light comedy manner of being alive.' Whew. I confessed that Noel Coward was not my favourite dramatist, though I thought *Private Lives* was a masterpiece. And, on the strength of this conversation, one day Dan asked me if I would direct Coward's *The Vortex,* if he could get Paul Scofield to be in it. You'd never have guessed on first meeting him, but it's the sort of thing Dan could bring himself to try on. I was in the office when Dan called Scofield's agent, explained the engagement, the dates, (the pay!) and then, on request, passed the receiver to me. No one was giggling, it was all taken seriously and the agent undertook to pass our message on. I think it was a day or two later that Dan told me that the agent had rung back to say that Mr. Scofield was pleased to have been approached but that, given his commitments, he didn't think he would be able to fit *The Vortex* at the King's Head pub theatre into his plans.

So, we were discussing what else we might put on and suddenly I recalled seeing *Spokesong* in Dublin and said, so far as I knew, it had played for a week and then sunk without trace; pity. With the same effrontery Dan 'got on his bike': he phoned and phoned and eventually discovered that the Royal Court had been sitting on it for three years, but the rights were up for renewal and the Court was wondering whether to bother, ever. Dan was now in his element. After a few nail-biting days, days that seemed to thrill Dan, the Court relinquished the rights and Dan got them. *Spokesong* ran at the King's Head for six months!

*Spokesong* was an acerbic play by Stewart Parker with music by the great Jimmy Kennedy *(Red Sails In The Sunset,* etc.). Stewart was from Belfast and is, in the piece, peering into the guts of the Protestant-Catholic cat-and-dog fight, using a couple as a metaphor. A Protestant dame with a broken bike comes into a not-really-that-young Catholic guy's bicycle shop to have it fixed. And guess what happens? There's a wonderfully menacing Unionist thug in the piece, played by hugely overweight but very funny Robert Bridges—meant to ride a unicycle (and almost did). I hoped to cast it Irish throughout—one of the people I read was a very young Mary Tamm; she asked me if any of the events in the story had really happened anywhere … I didn't cast her—she was too young. When I did—later—work with her she solidly denied her astonishing ignorance of UK politics (but actors can be magnificently out of touch). Only a couple of the cast ended up Irish, including the not-so-young bicycle shop owner: this actor had enormous, vulnerable charm on stage and his lady customer was suitably tough and direct. They start as strangers and in three scenes, carefully progressed by the author, get to know each other well enough to try to share the shop, and life. The whole delight of that part of the story is to watch the metaphor worked out—see the wary Protestant and Catholic find a means of—co-habiting. On the first night, and for many performances, this getting to know each other, scene by scene, in stages, worked dreamily. Audiences loved it. Then it became clear, as you watched the woman enter the bicycle shop for the first time, that they knew each other, must have met before; they were far too comfortable and familiar. The actors were jumping several stages in the progress of the play. I pointed this out: they paid heed for a while and restored the early tension in their relationship. But, sadly, they lapsed; permanently. They were the two leads in the show, they ran lines and socialised together and, eventually, they split the company, shutting out the rest of what was otherwise a delightful cast. They just knew better, and stopped listening. Shame. I consulted Dan. The play was still packing, but mainly on reputation, I thought—though it still half-worked. We tried various things: Dan suggested treating the actress to tea and a talk at Fortnum and Mason's. But it was like talking to Ghengis Khan about seeing the other chap's point of view—and pointlessly expensive, too.

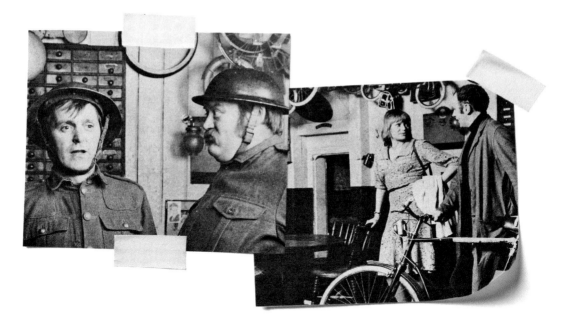

*Spokesong; Bikes, bombs and blarney*

The possibility arose of transferring *Spokesong*: this was misguided; it had worked to perfection in the steamy back room of a pub… But, there you go, one gets trundled along by the momentum of these things. We ended up at the Vaudeville (a West End venue, the wrong shape for intimate theatre) without a proper set and with bolshie, time-serving musicians. But then the ultimate disaster arose out of the leading performance.

The success of the bicycle shop owner's stage persona derives from his diffident, charming, self-deprecating, modest approach to his customers and his audience. But on the first night at the Vaudeville the leading actor bid for stardom. He lost all his shy humour and oblique, wise, commonsensical attractiveness—and belted his lines at the audience at the top of his voice. He was auditioning for Hamlet, Richard III and Arturo Ui all at the same time. It was very sad and deeply embarrassing. Not a shred of humour remained in the character. He was never that bad again—but still not properly receptive to comment and, given the stand-or-fall-on-the-first-night custom still in force in theatre at that time, the show didn't get business-friendly reviews—not enough of them. It got what, on the night, it deserved. It was a relief to see the back of such a warped and spoiled 'product'.

A footnote to *Spokesong's* long run at The King's Head: the show had blocked the theatre; there was nothing else we could do all that time. We had no alternative space to go on producing shows. And it was round about this time—1976—Dan told me about the Almeida. He'd found this locked up Victorian lecture theatre a stone's throw from the King's Head, and he took me to look at it.

A stage-manager friend of mine, who works there often, has just written a slim vol. about the building. I've just started to read it. And, whereas the Literary Society began its activities around 1834, apparently the BUILDING was not realised till 1837. Dan wanted to turn it into a funky dinner theatre on a newly stepped, platformed auditorium; it was (is) a lovely, slender-pillared place. Great idea, I thought, we could transfer shows like *Spokesong*, let them run their natural span—take the money—and keep trying whatever we fancied back at the pub. He said he'd be looking round to raise the money. I've never wanted to run a building, and—Dan didn't make it, just didn't quite make it. Brilliant idea, though; and Pierre Audi got there in the end.

By the mid-'70s, in Dublin, my Festival productions, and *Twigs, The Sea Horse*, et al had produced sufficient clout for me to be invited to direct a Brian Friel world première at the Abbey Theatre. I knew enough to understand that I'd been handed a chalice with a doubtful mix of good and bad medicine. The play was *Volunteers!* It takes place on an archaeological excavation and I assume the metaphor is clear. The play had two very good acts and one dud one, and Brian Friel, utterly delightful man that he was, wouldn't alter a comma, never mind a word: he was that kind of writer.

Now, *Volunteers!* has key parts for old men…

I'd seen shows at the Abbey and I'd watched the old actors. Two of them were brothers. The difficulty was that there wafted from the stage of the Abbey a mist of imprecision and woolliness, a fitful, only-sometimes focused energy of purpose, sense of story-telling direction. On the other hand, the younger members of the company were full of beans, up for anything. I auditioned a number of people and debated for a while and discussed with Brian—should we take a flyer and ask the young, hungry actors to age up and give us the economy and force of effort needed to tell the story? It was still the time (unthinkable now) when young performers went on stage and played forty years adrift from their own age. But the old-timer stalwarts of the Abbey company were such juicy, fruity individuals, it seemed to me insulting to pass them over and hand their perfect roles to whipper-snappers. Perhaps I could cajole and drill the old guard into learning their lines and coming in on cue? So I cast them and tried—and I couldn't.

People like Eddy Golden and Geoffrey Golden—especially Geoffrey—came to me and said 'We've been spoiled, Robert. You have to understand that for years we've been asked to learn *King Lear* in a fortnight. Your four-week rehearsal is a luxury to us: we hardly know what to do with the time. All us senior actors got used to faking major dramas, year after year, because we were never given the time to do them properly. Now things are changing but we're in a pattern, have habits, and we're older and not so agile, flexible, up here, anywhere. Sorry.' Endearing, moving, but a pain in the butt. Because what you saw on stage, depending on which night you came, was an old boy mooning through a speech not sure exactly where it ended, and his fellow actor, with the next line, also not sure whether his interlocutor had finished and therefore when to come in.

So, the old guys had devised a technique—and this is difficult to convey on paper —of rounding off their speeches with a reflective sigh—a kind of 'a-hummm'—slightly

musical and poetic. And the chap receiving the cue would also preface his speech with a pensive 'a-huh-hmmm', just in case the other guy hadn't finished and so as not to tread on his fellow actor's words. And suddenly you'd see an actor who seemed to have finished speaking, burst into life with another line or two, which he'd hastily recalled and which might be the very key idea to the speech and on no account to be missed out… and then the 'a-huh-hmmm' came in very handy, because it sounded like a bit of character embellishment and not as if you were fluffing and drying all night.

I was very, very encouraging and told them how wonderful they were when they got the text right and came in sharp on cue and got a bit of pace on the show. And, in the end, they sort of alternated. On a sharp night, the show took off pretty well (no one could do anything about the dud middle act). But on an 'a-huh-hmmm' night, well… I leave it to your imagination.

The play has a trap for a young actor playing a revolutionary: Friel has given him an inflammatory speech which becomes intolerable if it's screamed throughout. It was helpful that I'd played a similar agitator at RADA and my teacher, Hugh Miller, warned me then not to think I could screech throughout a long rant—like a piece of music, he said, it had to be modulated. You had to find effective lows and select just one or two climactic highs for best effect and save the hottest for the very end— perhaps. My *Volunteers!* actor battled, hit then missed the note, and suffered at the hands of some reviewers. So hard to do. There's exactly the same conundrum—at the other end of the age range—for an actor playing Sir Anthony Absolute in Sheridan's *The Rivals*. Sir Anthony is a very, very angry man. Unbearable, unplayable, some have said—till you hit on the trick: which is to play him as if he is constantly on the verge of exploding and allow yourself, perhaps, two proper shouts in your entire performance. Fascinating.

Another conundrum: because archaeological sites are inherently fairly static for tens of minutes at a time, I had to decide whether to be 'accurate' or keep it interesting: in the end, it wasn't difficult to find reasons for the trowellers to fetch things or keep having to measure things, and on a good night the piece worked rather well. The play got mixed reviews, and that was about right—it looked very good.

Working in Ireland was uncannily similar to working in Israel (page 98), in that the cast spent a great deal of time at funerals, and also were always asking for leave to go to unmissable weddings or family events. And, unless you made your position very clear, Israeli actors were as cavalier about accurately learning the text as Dublin ones. The Dublin actors had a better excuse, though, because Israeli actors rehearsed for ever. Perhaps over-rehearsal and under-rehearsal come to the same fluffy end.

Incidentally, it rained heavily throughout our rehearsals. Often, bedraggled, we'd be in Brian Friel's hotel bedroom working on the production. So Brian gave me a fold-away umbrella to get me there from my digs, which I kept and cherished for many years, and then decided to bring out and use: I put it on the back window ledge of my car (I was in a theatre, seeing a show) and some young thugs broke the rear window and pinched it (took nothing else) just because it was wet—bastards.

In 1979, again at the King's Head, an irresistible script turned up. Andrew Davies, who has become immensely celebrated for his TV period adaptations, had submitted a sublimely scurrilous life of Frank Harris—*Fearless Frank*—with lyrics. Frank Harris

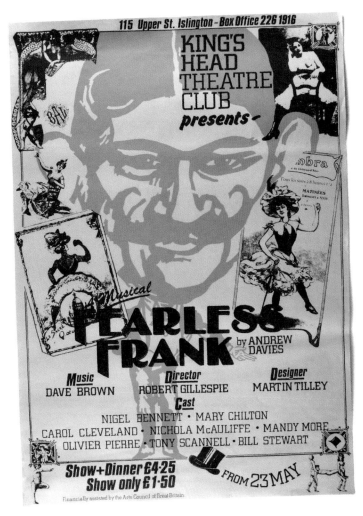

(1855-1931) was a highly influential Irish editor, journalist and publisher, and, when he tried to recover his fortunes, became a high end pornographer: he was a connoisseur of female flesh, and best known for his racy memoir *My Life and Loves.* Harris, according to himself, had been a cowboy among other trades but his chief talent was self-advertisement. George Bernard Shaw said of him 'He is neither first rate, nor second rate, nor tenth rate. He is just his horrible unique self.' Early in the play Harris begins an address to the audience… 'How to get women…! Look them straight in the eye and put a stiff cock in their hand.' I realise, now, how many of the shows I directed had music: this was yet another, and there was a brilliant song from Olivier Pierre playing Guy de Maupassant who 'had syphilis, but it went away…' The show fitted in very well with the rising trend of modernism and idol-smashing. We revelled in spectacular dance numbers from Fred Peters; a cast of eight hoofing it on that tiny platform. It was a delicious gallop and a fair old riot.

After that there was another Stewart Parker: *Catchpenny Twist.* Very cleverly, he'd wrapped the same old Northern Ireland tragedy into a story of four young ex-teachers, two men and two women, who were trying to make it in the music industry— apart from one of the girls, who when the friends meet again, discloses herself to be a republican terrorist: a killer. Maggie Shevlin as this character gave the most wonderfully chilling performance. But Maggie couldn't finish the run and I had to recast. Although the dramatic function of this revolutionary was entirely clear—she genuinely frightened the other three teacher friends with her murderous, activist views—once the replacement actress got through her first two or three performances, she began to soften her persona: she began to want to be liked. The other members of the company were desperate. They had nothing to fight, on-stage: their terrors seemed absurd. Anna Keaveney was the actress and nothing I said would make her play what she'd rehearsed. She wanted to be sympathetic and wouldn't budge. It was a perfect lesson on how the imbalance in one part of a drama can wreck the whole.

Fortunately there were some excellent songs in the show, but because of this destructive element—it was a quarter of the narrative and the driver of the story's engine—the rest of the run became a pleasant, innocuous caprice with music. Tony Doyle was in the cast and we discussed what might be behind it: insecurity about self? Or was it about advertising yourself to the profession for parts you'd rather be

# KINGS HEAD THEATRE CLUB
### 115 Upper Street, Islington, N1. 01- 226 1916

CATCHPENNY TWIST

BY STEWART PARKER

Music By SHAUN DAVEY

Director
ROBERT GILLESPIE

Musical Director DAVE BROWN

Choreography FRED PETERS                    Designer MARTIN TILLEY

With

TONY DOYLE          SALLY HUGHES          ANNA KEAVENEY

NICHOLA McAULIFFE          BRYAN MURRAY          LINDA POLAN

TONY SCANNELL

FROM 16th. FEBRUARY          DINNER 7.00pm. SHOW 8.00 pm.

Financially assisted by the Arts Council of Great Britain

cast in? Mystery. But very damaging. Nichola McAuliffe was lovely (sang tremendously) as one of the non-violent ex-chalkies. It was hard on Stewart who, sadly, didn't have so much longer to live. He already limped, and he died, so I understand, of cancer—very young; a missed talent.

I began to be offered so much TV sit-com, also some film work, that directing in the theatre for no money—but lots of satisfaction—started to slide. The uphill struggle at the King's Head to get things right—overcoming the unchanging messiness, Dan's inclination to block things—steadily palled. The reluctance was deepened by the arrival of yet another woman partner on the scene. Dan became—a surprise to us—hen-pecked, for the first time; and more inclined than ever to deny us space to store costumes or props or let us be around back-stage much at all. I kept checking: yes, he still wanted the shows but, now, someone was shouting at him from another room; it was wearying for us.

Also, in Dublin, my digs slowly declined: from a pleasant private hotel with good service and a beautiful daughter, and a most interesting grandmother who told me how she'd been harassed and chivvied by the Black-and-Tans on her way to school when she was a kid, it withered to a place that stopped giving steady hot water or decent breakfasts, and with that I began to think my times there were on the wane.

This feeling was underlined by the last show I directed at the Eblana for Gemini, called *Bonfire*. The writer, Joe O'Donnell, had recently had a play on at the Gate: at first it hadn't done well. When the local critics turned up and decided that it was immoral, filthy, disgusting and so on, the show immediately sold out. Our play, *Bonfire*, by the same author, was about the Dublin upwardly mobile almost-glitterati, experimenting, co-habiting, wheeling, dealing and divorcing. It was a more astringent and accurate picture of the city scene than Hugh Leonard ever risked writing about. It trumpeted the beginning of modernity in Ireland—the latent, shocking air of promiscuity, actual drunkenness and threat of social change. All in the context of a venal, self-serving political elite. There was, for instance, a bare-toe-fighting scene in which Dearbhla Molloy challenged the guys to strip off their footwear down to their naked feet, get themselves down on the rug, and do battle with her, toe to toe. The men wagered money; she offered—herself. In the Dublin of that day, it made a difference whether the men who took her on were married or unmarried. On our stage, all the men's wives or girl-friends were onlookers—cheering on the combatants or clucking ruefully in disapproval—and much of the audience of that time experienced a potent sexual frisson.

It really was a rather good play, fairly tough, entertaining, uncomfortable and racy for its time. The audience responded exceptionally well on press night, with enormous laughter and huge approval. Clearly, Dublin was in a mood to move on.

I had already noticed a significant amount of male sexual frustration, habitually dissipated with alcohol, in the tight circle of people I kept company with. The iron grip of the Catholic Church was only just showing hints of slipping and a deadening hypocrisy reigned among public men. This mealy-mouthed line was often pursued by many reviewers. Collectively they'd realised that, by drawing attention to the 'immorality' of Joe O'Donnell's first play, they had made it a significant success. Having learnt this lesson, they got their revenge. Next day, with two exceptions, they told their readers just how flat and boring *Bonfire* had been.

One hack, in particular, stated that the 'usual claque' had been hired by the management to give the impression that the audience was enjoying the show. They all wrote that the play was immoral, filthy, disgusting just like the previous one by the same author: but this time killed it by saying it was—dull.

The journalist who led the lies, Con Houlihan, was a most peculiar individual. I saw him often at Groome's and conversed with him. He was a large man with a floppy mane of hair, and when he spoke to you he held one hand directly in front of his face, edge on, but masking most of it; always. He had a local reputation as a lyrical, poetic scribbler, but from this mannerism and the deliberate, published lie, I'd say he was disturbed; and he hated the show. He insisted it sent him to sleep and invented this stuff about the paid-for applause. I wonder what the bare toes had really done to his head.

Many people I came across in Ireland were trying to live sane, modern lives. But, in the 1970s and early '80s, the time I was there, the Catholic Church still had a profound influence on most minds. I've found it barely believable to hear, recently and at last, the once Taoiseach Enda Kenny talk straight about the Catholic Church. When I was working there hundreds of men and women were still signing up to be nuns and priests. Many of the actors I worked with, but especially Robert Bernal and Jim Norton, had been brought up or educated by the Christian Brothers. Both actors, at

*Dublin Festival: Bonfire, setting for a toe-fighting contest*

one time or another, began describing his experiences to me and then each found he had to stop, could not go on, for fear of unsettling his present balanced life. Especially Robert, who got as far as talking about the beatings, and then… I knew I must not press him further.

A religion has to be judged by the way it is practised. A religion IS what is practised. I remember at school, all that time ago, hearing jokes about priests and choir-boys. I don't think any of us understood precisely what was meant—merely that it was something naughty, but amusing; nothing too serious, and then you got over it and forgot about it. Anyone can write an idealised description of the aims and aspirations of a religion; but every religion is a human invention. Ian Paisley's dad invented an entire Protestant variant of his own. You can write down on paper that every human life is sacred, precious and inviolate. You can sing and chant it. But if you use another's life for forced sex and the sharp pleasure of physical violence, then that is your religion: not the never-practised, imaginary, sanctimonious garbage you write or preach about; that is merely your cover for what you really want to do.

I wondered, for a while, whether Gemini Productions would sue the press for its fabrication; I don't think they had the money. And Dublin is a small town: everybody knows everybody and they meet each other all the time, whether they hate or no. It left a sour taste and I began to think I'd had enough.

One wholesome thing came out of *Bonfire*. Dearbhla, the female lead, was very good, but very quiet. I persuaded and persuaded, and worked with her to help her believe she wasn't shouting when, in point of fact, her voice was comfortably pitched for the audience's enjoyment. She pretty well got there in the end for this production. And many years later I got a message back from Dearbhla through my daughter: Lucy was producing a show in Edinburgh, and there was Dearbhla too, saying 'thanks' for what I'd said in Dublin: 'I was the only director, who…' Very soon after, I saw her at the Gate Theatre in London being terrific in *The Trojan Women* as Hecuba. We spoke after the show and she was looking wonderfully gorgeous, given the water that's passed down the Liffey in all that time.

# Directing in the West End (1981-2)

**Limping round England** was a production of J.B. Priestley's *Dangerous Corner*. At that time Peter Bridge was one of the last independent producers in the biz. Peter had heard of my work at the King's Head and asked if I would take over this show, which he believed would work in town, but was wrongly directed. There was a complication: two prominent members of the company each stated that if the other remained in the cast, he wouldn't come into London. So I spent a long time on the telephone to Peter Dennis (celebrated for his Montgomery imitations) and Anthony Daniels (celebrated for being C-3PO in *Star Wars*). The difficulty was that Peter Dennis insisted on giving the other cast members acting notes—especially to Anthony. It took hours and hours and hours to persuade them to give it a try, to attend at least a few re-rehearsals. I vehemently assured them that—as director—all ideas and instructions would come from me or be channelled through me. I had only two weeks to re-direct the play, and I can tell you there were some hairy rehearsal moments. Both guys were very charming and good in their parts, but could hardly bear to be in the same town, never mind on stage together.

The thing is that Peter Dennis had the curious idea that theatre was some sort of collective enterprise whereby everyone's ideas on the subject of everyone else's performances were equally valid, and should be discussed and considered, even if not taken up. But we were in the West End! So far as I knew, Peter had never been a member of the Communist Party, nor The Berliner Ensemble, nor worked for Joan Littlewood. Peter Dennis—whom I went on knowing personally and professionally—was in the wrong, really, but he had a generally odd cast of mind and, I fear, frightened so many theatre practitioners that he never had the career he deserved; yet an utterly innocuous and non-dangerous bloke—just talked too much.

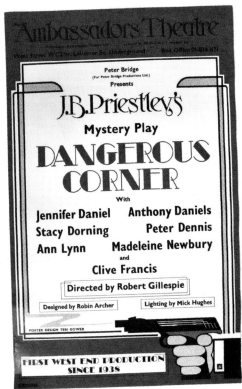

AMENDED DESIGN. "DANGEROUS CORNER!"

3'0

## OBSERVER REVIEW

# Sharp bends

### Theatre

by VICTORIA RADIN

J. B. PRIESTLEY'S first play, Dangerous Corner, written in 1932 and now revived with awesome credibility at the Ambassadors, is not about the collision of vehicular traffic.

Dangerous corners, for Priestley, are those hairpin conversational turns where a chance remark meets a fact—or, as Priestley would have it, a Truth. Truth, in the sort of softly-spoken lives he is talking about, is to be avoided. Better, far better, to realise the social mask and continue the quiet desperation.

Why did Martin, charming cad beloved by all, kill himself? Or did he? Who stole the £500 (this was 1932) from the office? And who was the last to see him before he died, and why, indeed, were all these people pouring in and out of his house?

Martin, it transpires, had been a bisexual and drug addict, as well as a collector of 'beastly Belgian paintings' and magnetically at-

'Time' pieces, closes with an alternative version of its opening sequence, which shows what would have happened if the perilous bend in question had been rounded with fiction rather than fact. Left to their masks, his char-

child-like and helpless. Kitchen is also haunted by the memory of 'somewhere else I can never recall' and the fact that his children remember his earlier years better than he can.

A falling-away, the swift

poet?)—are not people, but sounding-boards for Mr Richardson and Mr Storey's thoughts. They appear to speak a different language; or at any rate Lindsay Anderson, who directs, has ensured that they all declaim with

clinging frocks which show off her nobbles, ribs, elbows and knees to best advantage.

Cinderella's Dad (Arthur Cox) has immensely high padded hips, and his bride, the wicked stepmother (Ali-

**Anthony Daniels and Stacy Dorning in J. B. Priestley's 'Dangerous Corner.'** NOBBY CLARK

Dangerous Corner;
Anthony Daniels (C-3PO
without his armour)

Peter Bridge also wanted to re-cast a couple of the parts. We cast Stacy Dorning —playing my younger daughter in *Keep It in the Family* at the time—to replace the juvenile lead. She was excellent.

No one had warned me what it would be like working with Peter Bridge. I had noticed that he talked a long time to me on the telephone, but I just assumed he was thorough. When I was in his office, the conversation would start with his being edgy, abrupt— almost rude—to me and to anyone who phoned him. But then he would reach for a glass of water, take a pill; and as the medicine worked, he became steadily coherent, normal, courteous, efficient, business-like. He didn't like to let me go, and as he kept on—going over the same points, often many times—I thought 'surely, we've done all we can, this evening?' Apparently not. And I would watch Peter begin to slow down, slur his words, often stop and gaze around, lost. Gradually, I realised he was suffering from some condition—nobody on his staff or his family had warned me; I had no name for it.

Once I was in Al Parker's office. Parker was the grandest agent of the day and an ex-Hollywood movie director, with an office in Mayfair. I was with his side-kick, Ronnie Waters, when the phone rang. It was Peter Bridge. Ronnie raised his eye-brows but spoke to Peter courteously. It was clear from the side of the conversation I could hear that Peter was being long-winded. After a few minutes, Ronnie opened a drawer of his desk and put the telephone receiver inside it, closing it as far as the wire would allow. I said I could wait, but Ronnie waved me aside and we continued our discussion. It took about half an hour; then Ronnie opened the drawer and took out the phone: Peter was still speaking. Ronnie listened for a minute or two and then said 'That's all very interesting, Peter, but I have some business to attend to. Thanks very much for calling and we'll be in touch.' And he put the receiver down.

Peter Bridge's sons, eventually, let me in on the family secret. They implied he had some variant of bipolar disease. Clearly distressed, they were gradually taking over from their father and, with difficulty, prising him away from his beloved business. Peter was a very well-meaning fellow and had been a brave manager in his day. Sad.

*Dangerous Corner* ran for ten months at the Ambassadors and in the last week was visited by Tiki Dayan, young star of the Israeli theatre. She was so taken with the show that she bullied her boss, Uri Ofer, into seeing it; thought it would be a play for them, back home.

# Directing in Israel (1982-4)

**Uri Ofer was the artistic director** of the Cameri Theatre in Tel Aviv. He was an Ashkenazi Jew (from Poland) and very energetic. He got in touch, arranged to meet me at 9a.m. (a good sign) downstairs at a small hotel in Leicester Square. He approached me, hand stretched out and, with a strong Israeli accent said, 'I am Uri Ofer. Zey will try not to learn zere lines.' Here was a man who wanted changes made.

I was hired to direct *Dangerous Corner* in Hebrew and told that it would be a ten-week rehearsal. Why? In London we put on major shows in four. 'That's why I've engaged you. That's why I'm getting English and American directors out there. Our actors, well… Our people, as you know, have been through—a lot. Everyone is very careful not to push, not to ask too much. But the result is—not good. The result I want cannot be achieved by our directors—everybody knows everybody, meets everybody; they take no notice. For example, our actors never learn the author's lines. It's terrible. They learn the story and they invent on the basis of the text.'

This took me straight back to my time at the Abbey Theatre, Dublin—but there, it was because they habitually put on *Lear* in two weeks. 'Discipline. Get the company to learn the lines as written. They will take it from you. They don't take it even from me.' I soon learnt what he meant.

I was given a translator, Rivkah Meshullah, to sit with me at rehearsals, and Uri, before the entire cast, told us that he had asked Rivkah to stop on (or write down) every single misquoted word; that he had instructed me to refer constantly to Rivkah to ask if the actors were learning their text accurately. Orders! From him, Uri, the boss. I didn't speak a word of Hebrew, though, amazingly, all my cast spoke more or less passable English so they could take direction. I had some of their best loved stars in the show. There were two actors called Itzhak Hischiar—one old, one young-ish; and of course, Tiki Dayan. They absolutely loved playing smart-arse English people—uptight, formal, understated; loved trying to quell their Mediterranean exuberance and hand-waving. But on the opening night they were all coming up to me and telling me they were 'excited'. They meant (I discovered) 'nervous'. They had never known what it was to feel nervous going on stage. Astonishing. They had felt so free to make up their own stories round the texts they performed, that they had never believed it was

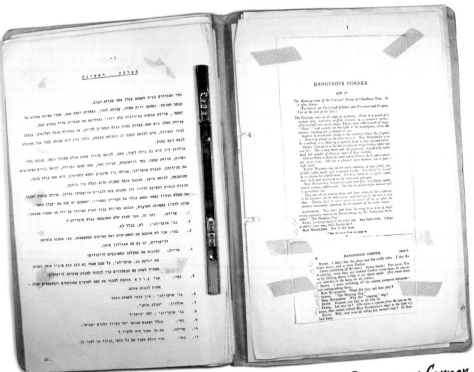

*Prompt copy, Dangerous Corner*

**DANGEROUS CORNER** Directed by **ROBERT GILLESPIE**
First performance at the Cameri Theatre 14th January 1982

possible to go wrong. So for the first time there was a pace and precision and variety of emphasis in the performance they'd not known before—but found exhilarating.

I found out why we had ten weeks' rehearsal: I discovered that at the HaBima (the National Theatre) no play was ever rehearsed under three months—and half the productions never opened; they gave themselves an easy time. No one rehearsed Saturday or Sunday; there was a half day, mid-week break, too (Wednesday, I think); everyone was let go to attend funerals. I've never known so many people pop their clogs during rehearsals. I discovered that, unlike England, where time off would apply if a very close relative died, in Israel you had to be there if a friend's or neighbour's third cousin had gone; so I was told.

The outcome of this relaxed near-Eastern schedule was that I hired a car and drove everywhere. So much of the history that has affected all of us has happened on that bit of the Earth. I used to come back and meet the cast on a Monday and they'd say, 'You've been to Nablus (old Neapolis). Goodness, we'd never dare.' I twigged, after a bit, that I'd been to a Palestinian town in an Israeli registered hire car, and in fact leaving Nablus was the only time an old guy stepped half into the road in front of me and spat. That's all that ever happened, then. It was the 1980s. I wouldn't go now. In fact I'd parked in Nablus and been up on the Tel, the ancient settlement mound, and collected a few—probably modern—pottery sherds. No problem. Any site you can think of, I've visited; even the underground barrel-vaulted halls at Tyre —there in Richard I's time. Perhaps the loveliest thing I ever saw was the slow descent into Hebron.

Arabs build their dwellings of stone and fit them into the shoulder of slopes; they don't let them break the skyline. Israelis shove everything up vertically, dominating. The most hideous example of this is the university building on top of Mount Carmel: it destroys one of the most beautiful contours in the land. The only exception has been Jerusalem, where strict rules about use of materials and height has meant the old city still retains its ancient loveliness—though constantly renewed. On the twisting road into Hebron each dwelling had a walled garden and orchard, all different, a ravishing visual treat. It was an almost entirely Arab town and at the bottom of the valley there was a large throng of people, trading, roving. I was approached and offered a glass of very sweet tea at my car window, which I took. I'd been told that a residual Jewish enclave hung on, desperately, in a part of Hebron. I saw some boarded-up shops. The main reason for visiting was to see The Cave of Machpelah or Tomb of the Patriarchs—sacred to Jew and Arab: Abraham, Isaac, Jacob, Sarah, Rebecca and Leah are all supposed to be buried there. Even then, it wasn't possible to get in due to the tension between the two opposed nations, and later there were horrors there. I went to Har Megiddo, the prophesied site of the 'final war'—Armageddon; and the Sea of Galilee, where archaeologists have found a circular stone base on the shore, which could have supported Peter's fishing hut…

As I drove all over Israel, I noticed that the narrow roads were strangely empty. Something else, very striking: as I motored out of undisputed Israeli territory into the chiefly Arab countryside, there immediately appeared, carefully placed along both edges of each road, mile after mile, rubbish dumped from refuse collecting vehicles. It was carefully dumped. All of it was non-perishable—presumably the rotting garbage was disposed of hygienically. These planted items were battered cooking pots, old fridges, heaters, kitchen utensils, a chamber pot I spotted, battered metal ornaments, lamps… anything and everything you can think of. It was the most powerful, unspoken gesture of colonialist contempt I had ever experienced. Idly, I mentioned this to one or two of the cast. They were completely unaware of it, they said. I wonder when the policy changed.

It was noticeable how disparate the people who called themselves Jews, in Israel, were. The younger Itzhak, for example, had his roots in 15th Century Spain, his ancestors re-locating to Turkey after the fall of Granada, but he still spoke the language of Cervantes: I found that amazing. However there were two main groups: one came from every part of Europe, Ashkenazim—immediately, comfortably, recognisable in terms of culture and outlook and tending to be socialist (like Uri). The other were eastern Jews, Sephardim, very used for centuries to living under Moslem domination, and as a reaction, tending to the political Right. The Sephardim have been in charge for years now, but Israel was very liberal when I was there. There were also outliers: for instance, I regularly ran into a group of Jews from Ethiopia who looked African—'Falasha', Rivkah Meshullah called them. She turned to me, as we passed them in the street and said 'Are these my people? I can't get used to it'. Now they're known as 'Beta Israel'.

I did two more productions for Uri. He got me back to direct Michael Frayn's

I can't read it either

Set of 'Night Mother

*Noises Off*; the young lead was a Yemeni Jew. The second act of the play is about a theatre company observed back stage in the middle of a show, performing a very technical, proppy play, trying to keep it humming on cue and trying to avoid screw-ups while their personal battles and rivalries are kept on the boil, in parallel. It needs exquisite timing, total precision and consistency of playing: otherwise it's heavy and obvious and boring. The Yemeni lad, who untypically had little English and had to have things translated for him, was always a half second behind in his responses. I was taken aside to have it explained: 'the Yemenis, you see, they all come from (the Near-Eastern equivalent of) Devon; a bit slow; what can you do?' A similar rationalisation to David Turner's in Lincoln.

I remember we rehearsed for twelve weeks, this time, but I still thought the show would be hit or miss. Some days, Act II would take off for fifteen, twenty minutes at a time, and then there'd be a hiatus—if only for a split second—and the ball would be dropped, the thinness of the device exposed. I have to say that Uri came to rehearsals more than he'd ever done for the Priestley, and sat at the back of the stalls with tears of laughter streaming down his face watching the antics of his cast.

Uri decided to tour the play for a fortnight before letting the critics in. I'd kept being asked to stay on: why not wander round the country, follow my show, what was there for me in England? Stay, enjoy yourself. I thought about it and declined. Back in London, I received a letter and a packet of reviews. They'd let the critics see the show in—I can't remember which city—and every single gag had worked that night. The tour was selling out—we'd got rave reviews: I have them; they're in Hebrew and I still haven't read them.

The third play I was asked to direct for Uri was Marsha Norman's *'Night Mother*. It's about a daughter trying to persuade her mother, who's had enough of life, not to commit suicide. I thought—and some Tel Aviv friends thought—it was an odd choice for Israelis: they were very touchy about despair. They wanted so much to live in hope, at last. Never again, they kept saying, would they fall into the great trap of the fugitives on the high plateau of Masada when, besieged by the Romans, they'd preferred mass suicide to slavery. But the play offered star parts for Tiki Dayan (daughter) and for Orna Porat (mother). Orna was German, but had married a Jew. I suggested that, as there were just two of them, how about trying a four-week, concentrated rehearsal? It scared them, but they agreed. I realised just how unused they were to giving up the hours in the day needed for this intensity of work. Perfectly routine for English actors with a big role to study. I thought it an essential part of Uri Ofer's bid to professionalise his players.

Gradually, I also realised that the people I was spending time with were a thin stratum of highly educated, sensitive, warm, broad-minded… yes, an elite, you had to call them that. Often, they asked me how the argy-bargy in Northern Ireland compared with theirs? It's easy to nit-pick at differences but, in the end, I said it's about two peoples claiming the same piece of land and refusing to share it: that part of it is universal. The Israelis I was speaking to were all so—sounded so—generous. I said to them, you have to imagine living pleasantly in a tree-lined street, serene, comfortable and at ease with the people around you, with the culture you know— and one day a family of twelve moves in next door, living at the tops of their voices, all day, in Arabic. How does that make you feel? After years, if you could put up with it, you'd probably find a way of rubbing down each other's rough edges, a middle way to tolerate each other's style of life, but you wouldn't give it the time, you'd move —wouldn't you? Long before you found a way of living together. The differences are superficial: 'If you prick us, do we not bleed?' But crucial—culture is superficial, learned at birth, re-learnt in a generation, but critical; we kill in its name. I've often thought, if I'd been adopted at the age of six months by a middle-income family in Beijing, I'd be Chinese. My appearance might be a minor talking point, but my behaviour would fit in with the people around me—they would find nothing 'different' to react against, or fight. Supposing Shylock, in Shakespeare's play, had been orphaned at the age of six months and adopted by Antonio's family and raised and educated as one of themselves? He'd have grown up with the manners and habits of an upper class Venetian, there'd be nothing to resent—and we wouldn't have a play.

Most people, the stage management and especially crew were… not quite as honed, as polished as my actor friends; not entirely couth. Routinely, I would ask for substitute props, furniture for the rehearsal room: they wouldn't appear. The cast and I would have to hastily scavenge nearby rooms, offices, for something to use. 'Sorry, they'll be here to-morrow.' They weren't. I thought, I can't bother Uri all the time for stuff as trivial and basic as rehearsal gear. So very early on I tried shouting.

It worked like magic; depressing. Quickly, I learned that as soon as I heard waffle like 'So-and-so was meant to do that this morning, but his aunt is sick, so...' I'd bellow 'Get me a table, get me four chairs (not broken), get me something to use as a dinner set, something to stand in for an axe!!! No-o-ow...!!!!' and my interlocutor instantly became submissive and said 'Yes, now, I'll get it, we'll get it for you. Sorry.' Unimaginable to behave like this, to treat anyone like this in England. It was quite horrible to have to do it, but quickly the staff became used to anticipating what the production wanted (as good stage management always does) and word got round that I expected this level of service on my shows. Why was it like this? European Israelis told me that something like a Near-Eastern mañana was very catching and that it took a guy like Uri to resist this slow-spreading, seductive, insidious affliction and reverse it back to efficiency, smartness and a good outcome.

I worked out my own, unscientific, rationale. If, for hundreds of years, your survival trick was to thwart overwhelming authority by slyly never doing what it wanted... seeming to carry out orders, but actually sabotaging the ascendancy in very subtle ways that wouldn't, quite, get you into trouble, then this is how you operated. Very infectious. And difficult to get out of the habit. I'd have done exactly the same. People are wonderfully resourceful at finding ways to stay alive.

Another curious thing: wherever I went in the street, people bumped into me. For a few days, I thought it was chance, or I was unlucky—or invisible. But it happened so often that I devised a counter-measure. Many of the footpaths were narrow: I would spot someone, alone, coming towards me and it was clear that—to this man—I didn't exist; so, instead of stepping into the gutter, I stopped walking, braced myself for the collision and waited. I shall never forget one instance of this: the guy came within a few inches of me and as I readied myself for the bump, he stopped, his face only centimetres from mine and leapt back; looking as astonished and startled as if I'd materialised out of smoke. With a grunt, he backed away looking at me as if I were completely demented, very, very wary, stepped into the road, stepped back on the pavement and, never letting his gaze shift, walked round me, staring, edging past me as if I were a dangerous zoo animal, and then very gingerly walked on his way, looking back at me from time to time as if I were from a different planet.

I realised that apart from the kind of people I spent time with, the large majority didn't 'see' each other: they jostled and banged and walked through one another. You had to watch out on buses in the scramble for seats. Nobody queues in Israel—they didn't then, anyway. If you didn't catch on, you'd miss out getting in to whatever it was you were supposed to be queuing for. Or, perhaps, getting a loaf—when there weren't enough in the shop to go round. That's another rationalisation, unscientific, I made about this behavioural symptom. The not-seeing people made sense if you are an under-privileged person in hostile surroundings. Catching someone's eye brings on trouble; it provokes challenge and possible aggression. Wise adults everywhere teach teenage boys not to eye-up dangerous rivals. If you don't see people, with luck, they overlook you. Darwinian survival mechanism, and of course if you stand patiently in a queue and there's only enough bread for the first thirty people—you go home hungry.

I thought this was curious and interesting and a vivid study in the effects of insecurity, and I wanted to discuss it with Alfred Burke when I found we were both in the RSC company at Stratford in 1994: I knew he went to Israel a lot with his wife, so as a conversation starter I mentioned that I still remembered a line he'd spoken as a bishop on the Old Vic stage in 1952 ('Rome shall remedy this…!'). However when I began on the general shoving and bumping and shouting that happened everywhere in Israeli society, he looked blank; hadn't noticed it himself. He said he wondered whom I'd associated with.

Anna came over to join me for a while in Israel in 1983, and we were treated to a visit to Eilat, at the company's expense, a reward for good work. They were just putting Eilat together, then—I believe it's Blackpool on the Red Sea, now. We went for a fabulous under-water experience in a glass-sided observation bubble. And just in case the wild creatures had been shy that day and hadn't given us our money's worth, they'd built a gallery with a sample of fabulous creatures in individual display tanks. In one, there was a spectacular octopus, doing a sinuous dance. Two French girls were gazing at it. As we passed, I heard one of them say *'Ça mange très bien.'* And that's all you need to know about the French…

The Israelis were immensely generous to me and I was given beautiful albums of my production photographs, and of the Negev and Sinai. And it was a wonderful prize to see the Greek, Roman, Egyptian, Assyrian, Hebrew, Canaanite, Crusader—and so many other—resonant historical relics, and watch the hyraxes (like prairie dogs) come out to sun themselves on the rocks in the early morning, and hear very honest local archaeologists say they'd found no evidence to back up the Joshua story; nor, for that matter, the Exodus from Egypt story. But I must say something about Jericho.

I was on top of the old city, the oldest walled city in the world, when I saw a large, open-topped car—looked like something out of P.G. Wodehouse—roll up with seven people in it; sort of thing you could hire from Tel Aviv to save money, if you were able to drum up fellow travellers going your way. The passengers began to clamber out of this jalopy when one of them (a young bloke) suddenly looked up at me and beckoned to the others… ' 'Ere, it's Dudley Rush from *Keep It in the Family*. 'Ow are you? Can I have your…?' It's happened to me in a Neapolitan slum, in the Rockefeller Building in New York… all over, it's happened.

I remember Israel for jokes about inflation—about the bus fare going up between the time you got on, and walked to the driver's end to pay; and for visiting kibbutzim, plain or glitzy—adventures in living together. But Israel wasn't home. And getting fabulous reviews over there, was—like winning the mile on Mars. A terrific experience, but it was about the right time to leave.

# The great seductress

## America and Broadway (1980)

**Over the years** I've known actors and directors who'd taken themselves to New York or Hollywood on spec, hoping to hustle a ticket to stardom. I'd always vowed that the US would *pay me* to go; I sensed that it would happen some time and that they could afford it. It did happen, in what proved to be a Mephisthelean bargain.

If you'd had (once again) a resounding success with a show on the fashionable fringe, and a gleeful, hand-rubbing foreigner came to you with an offer to take your wicked show to Broadway, wouldn't you be scared of feeling, looking back, a right twerp for refusing: for turning the opportunity down?

It fell out like this: the unsound David Black (an American 'Angel') saw *Fearless Frank* at the King's Head and wanted to pick it up for a showing in New York. David's record as entrepreneur was indeterminate, but he had a superlative talent for talking money out of people to back shows. *Fearless Frank* was shocking to Americans (we know how delicate their sensibilities can be) but David thought that it was just the moment to get away with a provocative, stimulating—challenging—high-octane presentation. He believed he could bring off a *succès de scandale* and make his name in the big league. He had his eye on the old Latin Quarter nightspot (renamed The Princess Theatre), a four-hundred-seater with a chequered history but RIGHT IN THE MIDDLE OF BROADWAY. Problem: American Equity absolutely forbade our bringing a single member of the English cast to the States. I knew the soreness around the Brits' invasion because my dear American friend Linda Barrett, fellow student at RADA and New York based actress, constantly moaned about the parts denied her by directors importing English actors. Linda is a true WASP and prided herself on her near-perfect English accent.

Now, Frank Harris in the play has roughly eighty per cent of the text, and must be able to dance and, especially, sing. What to do? We nearly lassoed Milo O'Shea for the part but he wouldn't budge unless we cast his wife as Frank's secretary. We read her and she was frightfully bad. I should have cast her: I was still too young to get that message. It takes till you're about fifty to know that you have to go along with those little bits of corrupt behaviour that lets things happen and makes the wheels go round. Impasse. Till we heard that American Equity would accept Niall Tóibín (sympathetically Irish) as a compromise, because he'd already starred in Brendan Behan's *Borstal Boy* and scored with the critics in a short run on Broadway at the Lyceum. I'd worked with Niall so I asked him if he could dance and sing. He said 'Um yes, of course'. And he lied. He drove our musical director insane trying to keep him to rhythm, never mind in tune.

Poor Dave Brown the musical director; we nearly lost him from the show, he was so despairing. Casting in New York was an eye-opener. I was inundated with thanks by actors when I let them get beyond the first three lines of their audition. They described what they were used to, 'Some enchanted evening, you will see a…' 'Thank you very much Mr. Burkheim. O.K. Fine…' and they would pick up their sheet music and exit the room. It was unthinkable, for me, to give them less than ten or fifteen minutes to show what they could do. Whenever an actor had a chance of getting it

*Became the Princess Theatre…*

right, I gave him or her some direction. So I would get little packets of scribbled notes sent up to me from reception, expressing effusive thanks for letting them breathe before they were dismissed. I was mildly ticked off by the theatre establishment for taking longer to see people than the locals were used to. But by giving actors an insulting bum's rush, how would we use the time we saved, I wondered?

The system of theatre proprietorship is quite different, on Broadway, from ours. Every venue is presented to an incoming management stripped of all equipment, and unpainted. They have to tart up the building to whatever degree they can stretch to—and that will depend on their hopes for the show's outcome. As a result, when I was first there, the theatres I attended smelt damp, were peeling and strangely seedy; there was no maintenance budget, and two thirds of them were dark. Melancholy; an example of extreme market forces at work.

I would spend hour after hour carefully enthusing, rallying, coaxing and encouraging Niall to pitch his performance of Frank Harris at the right mischievous, arrogant, defiant level. David Black's investors, especially one guy, would sit at the back (praying, I shouldn't be surprised). As we broke for lunch I would pass his gloomy face and slumped body; he wouldn't catch my eye. But then, round about four in the afternoon, Tóibín would get some way on his sluggish craft, would begin to show a promising sliver of Harris' sparkle and I would pass the same backer, beaming now. Hey, we might have a show. No such thing. I would get phone calls from Niall later at night, in my pleasant apartment, expressing his misery, his loneliness. By next morning, he was as flat and doleful and dreary in the role as ever. And he never got to keep time in his numbers or sang in tune; ever, ever.

David Black and I, rightly, had regular meetings and I advised him that we should pause rehearsals and try to re-cast, or not open the show. With Niall Tóibín, the piece would be just—mediocre at the very best—possibly dire. David would lose his investors' money.

It's odd about momentum. Is it possible that those famous woolly mammoths, pursued by Neanderthal hunters, really could not see the edge of the cliff ahead of them? Or were they just not able to bring themselves to swerve because they were paralysed by fear and custom and routine? Yes, fellow tuskers, we can all see the edge approaching, but is the drop really so steep—and at the speed we are going, with so much tonnage on board—that dodging about, changing one's direction of travel was, is impossible; unthinkable, surely? But why?

This propensity in us, this inability we have to change direction even when we see disaster clearly looming, fascinates me. I had a similar experience in 1988 when working with Richard Jackson (who hired me to direct a number of the shows he produced). He asked me to talk to his friend Susan Hampshire.

Richard's heart was never fully engaged in his theatrical agency, but he was a very adventurous producer. He seemed to have a large-ish sum of his own money to chuck about, and a smart pad in Knightsbridge, and was never seen at first nights without a stunning female star, or aspiring, rising beauty, on his arm. Richard deployed an old-school courtesy that never, never flagged: even when he was implying something negative or crooked about someone, or some event, it was done with a deprecating, philosophical chuckle as if to say, 'I believe it happened in such a way and it's regrettable, perhaps deplorable, but so is the reality of life, heigh-ho!' He met you, unfailingly, with a little bow.

When Susan Hampshire came to him with a problem, Richard contacted me. Susan was playing the lead in a show dear to her heart: about Marie Stopes. She and I share a profound concern about the greatest threat to our long-term survival on this finite planet: human over-population. Marie Stopes was an early pioneer of universal contraception and women's rights, and Susan had persuaded her husband (Eddie Kulukundis, the theatre angel) to back this play which featured the life of her heroine. It was called *Married Love* after Stopes' seminal book. I went to see the production on its way to town. Unfortunately Joan Plowright, directing for her first (and I believe last) time, was not effectively in control of her material: and a discontented cast had ganged up on the leading lady, Susan Hampshire; who was of course also wife of the backer of their show! John Moffat—playing Bernard Shaw—was especially cantankerous: talk about biting the hand that feeds you…

On seeing the production, I thought Susan was being very badly treated: she absolutely was not responsible for what was going wrong with the show. We talked about it over dinner. We discovered our shared interest in the ecology of Mother Earth and she made me laugh when she pointed out that we were the first species to transform sex from procreation to recreation. Neither of us, then, had caught up with the practice of the Bonobos: they're are a kind of chimpanzee, and they use every variant of a sexual encounter to soften the enormous difficulties of living in family groups, in tribal groups. Sex, for them, has begun to replace fighting as a solution to day to day living. There's always something or someone ahead of you with a big idea…

But to the play… I asked Susan if it was feasible to break its tour and re-rehearse it entirely, possibly with changes of supporting cast?—I thought there might be a chance to rescue it. She didn't think that would be possible. Would I, alternatively, think about sitting, unobtrusively, at the back during any further rehearsals, and of attending performances, surreptitiously, then giving her notes? I said I didn't think she was the problem; and were Joan to catch sight of me, lurking about, it would be embarrassing

*Broadway glamour: Fearless Frank in rehearsal*

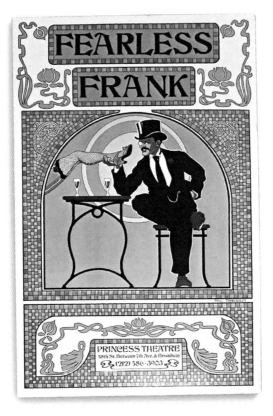

for everyone. And I added, significantly, that I feared that if the play came into town as seen, she would lose Eddie all his money (about a hundred grand); better to stop now and re-think. Changing direction couldn't be thought of, she said. It's as if, having assembled a large army, it becomes impossible not to send it into battle—however dire its prospects of success. Pleasant evening, nice conversation. The show came in to Wyndham's and lasted two weeks.

On Broadway the same, sad, inadequate, lame but crucial portrayal of the monumental starring role of Frank Harris was limping towards opening night.

There were some entertaining moments on the way. A particularly hard-bitten forty-year old New York actress in the cast had a song in the show that used the word 'pussy'. No one had batted an eyelid about this in London, but she kept stumbling over it and stopping in mid-song and, eventually, she asked me if she could replace it with another word. We had long talks about it, but I insisted 'no'. The show was the show—a crucial part of the project David Black was backing. Later, during the run, the same woman was flashing small glass tubes of white stuff around the company, asking if anyone wanted some. Innocent me wondered, idly, what it could be. Later, it dawned on me that this lady was able to offer small phials of cocaine to her mates, but couldn't bring herself to say the word 'pussy' on stage.

I saw as many shows as I could while in New York, and there was a Bob Fosse dance night I attended. In one of his creations a lithe young lead dancer pinned a luscious young prima ballerina against the proscenium arch and gave her a good shagging. There wasn't a whisper of protest from the audience. I listened out, at the end, as we streamed from the auditorium—nothing but warm appreciation; no shock. I realised why: provided that no one had actually spoken a naughty word in your hearing when in the company of your mum, or grandmum—or whichever kind of family party you'd attended the show with—that was O.K. In 'respectable' company— even to your wife—no American would say, 'Hey folks, hey darling, did you see the way that young guy was screwing that leading lady up against the wall of the theatre; there was energy there, goddamit, he was giving her some…' No: as long as it wasn't mentioned, it wasn't seen; didn't happen.

America wafts over on trade winds and soaks into your being, especially if you speak English. From an early age if I heard 'Tucson' I could follow it with 'Arizona';

'Dayton' with 'Ohio'. The one thing about America that I had no idea was so prominent—and that nobody had ever even hinted at—was the most striking characteristic to hit me smack between my eyes when I was there: hypocrisy. It reigned everywhere, supreme. It was almost tangible; you could carve it with a knife. The chasm between how people claimed they conducted themselves and what they actually did was enormous. The violence and coarseness of private conversations between men was astonishing: in front of auntie, they became different people—old-world courteous, deferential—wowie! Not far from Times Square, in 42nd Street, in those days, there were street machines into which you could slip a quarter and watch—so I was assured—short film clips of women being, actually, murdered. I was told, quietly, privately, with a chuckle, that you could get somebody snuffed out for between five and ten thousand dollars. I really wasn't being sent up, I really don't think so. One night in my apartment I heard a distinct gunshot, quite close. I asked about it: shrugs.

Also, I'd expected super-efficiency in business and workaday practice from our transatlantic cousins, but nobody liaised with anybody else enough. They worked very hard, and made up for messes by labouring into the night, catching up, and throwing money at a problem. Wearing.

So: we had our first performance and wended our way to traditional Sardi's for the critics' verdict. David Black collected the huge bundle of first editions, and he interrupted the party and began to read the reviews—selectively (as I was to learn). What we all heard sounded… good. Later, he took me aside and told it to me for real. By and large, on the whole, with some supportive qualifications, we'd been given the thumbs down.

Then a curious thing happened. David Black changed his name and disappeared. He'd had some sort of panic attack and submerged. I got a call, eventually, telling me to go to a suite at the Waldorf-Astoria (that's an expensive hang-out, trust me) and ask for Mr _ _ _ at reception (I can't remember the name he'd assumed). ON NO ACCOUNT was I to reveal his new identity or location to anyone. Well, David was sitting up in bed and all set for an hours-long, post-mortal recrimination about our stuttering show. He was looking for a fall guy, but I could only, patiently, go over the inadequacies I had already flagged up, starting with Equity's obstruction to quality casting—only an English 'star' would have been admitted under American rules, and we'd been conned by poor, Broadway-struck Niall Tóibín.

I reminded David that I'd tried several times to warn him: we simply shouldn't have opened with a third-rate leading performance. The fellow could act in straight plays and he could tell stories; the end. No use to our enterprise. And then, David began to get a little Himmler-ish, not attractive for a Jew, and tried to off-load his angst, ponderously, onto me. He didn't call in the guards—he didn't have any—but the atmosphere began, steadily, to be quite menacing. I looked round the room: I realised that no one else knew I was there. I'd heard of autocratic, heavyweight star producers tongue-lashing their subordinates; it had never happened to me before. Was he threatening to sue me or even physically assault me? I recall describing it all to Tony Doyle, weeks later, back home; eerie. Pity I didn't write it down, then, in detail, for the Hammer Films aspect of the narrative.

The phone went beside David; someone asked permission to come up. The guy walked into the room, greeted David kindly and then asked to speak to me alone. Graciously, David conceded.

It was his shrink! What was my opinion? Did *Fearless Frank* have a future? Should David raise more money to nurse its run? Tense, tight-lipped, the shrink revealed to me that David had been schmoozing his backers to invest even more dollars in *Fearless Frank*. What did I think?

'No-o-o', I said. 'All too late: good money after bad. Crazy idea'. Immediate relaxation: the shrink had been given the impression that I was looking to Black for continued financial support for the show. The professional brow cleared, his relief was palpable. We became allies. Would I support him in getting David to give up the nutty idea of seeking fantasy future success for the show? Black, the shrink said, was terrified of losing his already fairly rocky reputation as a producer, finally. I explained to him, the shrink, that from way back I'd been trying to limit the angels' losses by aborting our wobbly enterprise: it was clearly not going to match the punch of the London version by a long mile—had been utterly clear after two weeks of rehearsals. So, everything after that turned into a kind of Tolstoyan plot to get David to accept reality—and treatment. The hotel room—just that—was costing a fortune. Then from the skies, his lady arrived. By complex and devious means, she'd managed to track him down. She was a delightful, vividly attractive woman and completely sane. She told me David had suddenly vanished out of her life. I never knew, for sure, if the men in white coats were ever called but, leaving him safely in the hands of his analyst and his family, I got out of town. Odd thing: Andrew Davies was never funded to see his own piece; just as well, perhaps. And David Black refused to pay for Dan Crawford to be around. I understood Dan got himself over there later—after all, he was an American. Something tells me he caught the performance: it limped along for a bit. I do know that a cyclist—racing the wrong way up a one-way Avenue—seriously injured Dan.

Here's an extra dash of sauce, ref. David Black. One day we were deep into the show, walking New York, talking, and passed close to scaffolding. Something, some speck, fell and caught in David's eye. Immediately he dropped everything, got the number of the construction company, called his lawyer and we lost the rest of that day while he went to his physician and checked out if he should begin legal action at once. His eye went red and it hurt, for a bit. He told me of some other case where a 'victim' had failed to act instantaneously. David was genuinely concerned and pretty shaky; but can you imagine a response like this in London? No NHS, of course.

Many years later, in London, I got a card asking me to—an art show. Black had become an abstract painter (not great) and had engineered some exhibition he wanted people to attend. Insisted on meeting; cheerful, wacky; his lady, looking older and a little battered, but just as pleasant. I did not feel hugely hospitable. Not directly the poor sap's fault, but his Broadway brainwave had cost me my second West End production.

Here's how. Everybody came to my King's Head shows, and so I was approached by Bill Freedman and Howard Panter (of Freedman-Panter Ltd and Namara Ltd) to direct J.P. Donleavy's *The Beastly Beatitudes Of Balthazar B*, featuring Simon Callow and Patrick Ryecart at the Duke of York's. Simon and Co. said O.K. and then—Donleavy asked to see my track record. He picked up on the Broadway production of *Fearless Frank;* studiedly ignored the raves for the London showing—and all my other work—and, self-protectively, said 'no'. The guys in London—Bill and Howard—tried to make my case; the writer was adamant. *Beastly…* was not a bad play, not a bad show, and ran for a bit. Someone told me, not so long after, 'Donleavy's snuffed it'. How do these stories start? It wasn't true, of course. Now it is, so I'll never get the chance to … meet him at a party and gently, courteously ask him how—with a body of evidence before him—he came to his decision. Reminds me, though, of Jeremy Kingston's response to his Levin review—it's the one that stuck in his head.

David Black and the Fates had done me in, but I wonder who, with this fair prospect of changing opinions and provoking laughter—of putting a cat among the local pigeons so far from home—would have turned his back on that American adventure?

At the time, it was just one happening among many. I was doing plenty of TV, and more than once I was beckoned to run some outfit as artistic director (be 'boss of an establishment'…?). I was asked to direct, out of London, the first revival of the whole of Ayckbourn's *The Norman Conquests*: I turned it down. I tell myself that if I'd wanted, principally, to direct, I'd have done the trilogy. But I never directed for the money: I was interested in new or neglected writing, and saw it as a balancing activity to performing. As an actor, if the money is right, I am anybody's: I couldn't see the point of living like that as a director. I'd seen the *Conquests*—they were fine—but essentially safe stuff with just enough edge (but not too much) to make the thrusting middle class of the day believe they were immersing in transgressive drama.

117

# The odd couple

The King's Head, Leo Rost & Florida (1986)

**So I was working steadily,** being funny as an actor on TV, when the phone rang: Dan Crawford. I had promised myself never to work within Dan's ambit again. He ran a proposal past me and I said 'No'. Dan rang again: I said 'No'. He rang a third time: Dan was like that—it was one of his admirable qualities—persistence.

A some-time London backer—he'd hit pay-dirt with his production of *Sleuth*—had written a musical about Christopher Marlowe: the text needed work; Dan kept thinking of me. I kept thinking of the all-over booby-trapped experience on Upper Street. If I gave in, this would be my seventeenth production at the King's Head! Would I, Dan asked, at least meet the author? Well, O.K.

I can't remember where it was, I think it was in some hotel room, and there was Leo Rost. Leo was a huge man with a Russian orthodox beard. He'd run a club in Nassau in the Bahamas for ten years—and stayed alive. He might have been Ernest Hemingway and had, indeed, won the Look-Alike competition in Key West, one time. Rost was a foreshortening of some Russian-Jewish moniker and Leo's family had come out of an eastern European fastness, first to Canada, then the States; and not so long ago he'd gambled his fortune in show biz in our West End. He admitted to playing in a minor league compared with Kulukundis, Codron and others, but his triumph with Anthony Shaffer's *Sleuth* led to a friendship with him (Peter Shaffer's less famous twin): he expressed great affection for Anthony as a person and especially admired him—in fact preferred him—as a writer. Leo had aspirations to write. He was a seductive fellow, generous. I read his script.

Extraordinary: it was half a powerful work. Rost told me Dan had recommended me because I worked so much with writers and Leo knew the script needed attention. What also became clear is that we'd have a budget. For the first time ever at the King's Head we'd all be paid. I said nothing about Dan's standard deal—£25 per week for the actors and I got £25 for the production (not always). In the end, Leo lashed out twenty-five grand on his show; I got a £1,000 fee and the actors got Equity minimum. Big time! But it was his personality that won me to working with Leo—funny, warm,

*Steve Harley. Hemingway (Leo Rost look-alike?)*

119

easy and open-handed. In conscience, I had to warn him why I'd resisted working with Dan one more time and, regrettably, I didn't get that wrong: Dan wasn't able to change too much.

Steve Harley, lead singer of *Steve Harley & Cockney Rebel,* was a mate of Leo's—only God knows why—and it may have been something to do with unexpected Englishness and backing dark horses, but *Marlowe* had been promised to Steve: Steve himself was a Look, a logo, a banner that rang a good many people's bells; so we had a name, of sorts. But Steve's clangour of popular music was opaque to me. I was introduced to the composer Jimmy Horowitz: the music he gave us was decent, tuneful enough, and we auditioned for singer-actors.

Exceptional was Martin George, who shattered us all and threatened nearby wine glasses with a thrilling, tenor voice—why wasn't this guy training for opera? Extremely bizarre was Steve himself. He had a limp, a bowed leg—the result of lengthy childhood surgery (reminded me of Stewart Parker), and it made his stage presence singular: for all the world like an unmeant parody of Olivier as Richard III. His singing voice was astonishing, smoky, as if produced through a cheese grater, moderated with rough sand paper—but in tune. His acting—it's hard to find words to describe it—was appalling: try to think of the most extreme, hammed up, over-expressed amateur delivery you can conjure up and you will be only half way there. But he was a nice, amenable fellow. As a result, we had the most outlandish mix of theatrical elements I've ever been associated with, to offer to a curious and perplexed public.

There was a particular, key, scene we handed back and forth, and by the time it was re-written Leo claimed to the world, to his dying day, that it was the best scene he'd ever penned. We improved the rest of the text here and there, tightened it some notches.

In addition to the 'great scene', the end of the show was extremely atmospheric, a fugue with candles and a long descending cadence: strangely gripping.

And we survived Dan. However, having pursued me so avidly to direct the show, it was puzzling that I should still be fighting for costume fitting time, and space, and places to store our props and bits—and on and on. I was most grateful to be able to share half the aggro with Leo who, innocently, tried to negotiate and reason sweetly with Dan, apply logic and common-sense, find out why he was obstructing so much of what we were trying to achieve together. Just as an example: we had a failure of the

# THE KINGS HEAD THEATRE CLUB
### 115 UPPER STREET, ISLINGTON, LONDON N.1.  TEL: 226 1916

## Leo Rost and Kings Head Productions present

## STEVE HARLEY in

## Marlowe

**Aug 19th - Sept 27th Dinner 7.00pm
Show 8.00pm**

Music, Lyrics and Book by Leo Rost and Jimmy Horowitz

Directed by Robert Gillespie  Designed by David Blight
Choreography by Joe Hayes  Musical Director James Hallawell
Cast - Terence Conoley, Martin George,
         Seeta Indrani, Aidan James,
         Frank Kovacs, Pauline Munro,
         Ray Sharples.

lighting on one occasion. Leo reacted as visiting producer—the investor, the money man: 'Could Dan explain why he wasn't getting minimum service like, the lights coming on with the right colours in the right order when the cue came?' I left them to it. I got that miffed head shake from Leo that communicated everything I already knew: 'Yeah, you said...' he said. 'Does he want the show? I thought he wanted the show.' We shrugged together.

The musical baffled the reviewers, but sufficient people came. No one had a standard of comparison for Steve's performance. It hit people like an early Damien Hirst. Nobody could place it, it wasn't on any art spectrum that fellow humans could recognise or place in a category. Out of that arose a new thing that bugged Dan; hugely, disproportionately, I thought. The innovative mix of unheard-of sound and ludicrous speaking and posturing led to a table in the house being regularly booked by the same party. This made Dan twitchy: noticeably, so I asked Dan what was eating him. 'Those people... on that table.' 'What's wrong with them?' I enquired. Well, this party turned up fairly often (all blokes) and ordered a good amount of booze, and early in the run Dan marched up to them all and asked them to be quiet. I'd never seen him so agitated before. 'What's up, Dan?' 'They're here all the time, they're...' 'Isn't that good, Dan? They're paying, they're buying drinks...?' 'I'm going to throw them out...' and Dan again stomped up

to the guys and had words; but they stayed. Finally, he came out with it: Cameron Mackintosh plus friends were booking this table and he—Dan—was sure they were coming to make fun of him. He was shaking with frustration and impotent rage: not usually on show; I left them to it.

*Marlowe* was my last production at the King's Head. Distanced from that abrasive alchemy, I was consciously pleased to be working in clean studios, with a well-conducted management. But there's been nothing like Dan's King's Head: it was far richer, artistically, than Joan Littlewood's Workshop; fascinatingly messier and generous, a stirred pot full of every kind of living—hateful and ecstatic; it had range, it had reach.

And yet… Dan didn't seem to leave anything substantial or viable after himself; perhaps his illness caught him out (he died of cancer aged only 62). By this I mean he left no definable method of approaching theatre, or even management, that has survived or been taken up by others. At the Royal Court Theatre George Devine has left a very precious legacy, guaranteeing the ever-renewing vigour of new writing and modern drama. Sam Walters at the Orange Tree has taken care to hand on a vibrant, varied theatre enterprise—in stark contrast to Bernard Miles and his buccaneering Mermaid outfit, which died with him; almost no one I talk to has ever heard of his beautiful Mermaid with her tail in the Thames, though she was very lively while she lasted.

Truly, the King's Head was magicked into existence by all the various ideas for plays and musicals and comedy shows that directors and writers and actors and managers brought to Dan from outside. I directed 17 shows there. Visiting the pub I've noticed photographs of Tom Conti and Jack Shepherd and John Hurt on the wall; their names are there but not a hint of the productions they were in—I tempted all three to work at the King's Head for me. Nor—until recently—were there posters up of any of the shows which featured so many of the visiting artists who gave their time and talent to magnificently putting the King's Head on the theatre map.

Once Dan spoke to me of Noel Coward's *Cavalcade*. Ambitious, certainly. Later I heard that he got it on, in association with Bill Kenwright—pursuing his love for British things, and West End glory. Did he direct? Did he find the words to help actors solve their complex and subtle problems of interpretation? Maybe?

Dan left… an atmosphere and a pub with an extraordinary reputation; and for many years desultory, passing theatre-makers took advantage of its profile on the Brewer's tough terms. But it was only when Adam Spreadbury-Maher took the place on that something solid, something potentially lasting has come alive. He has promised a kind of continuity for Dan's enterprise—but with a completely different programme—it's now a lively, largely gay scene. I would dearly love to see Dan's face, if only he could come back, and watch as he takes a look at what's been thriving and pulling in audiences in his pub. Spreadbury-Maher's project has attracted funds to move to new, modern, custom-built premises, nearby—but he's stepping down. And we are living in interesting times.

# Leo Rost and Florida

The amazing Leo Rost had an idea a day. The upshot of this was that he flew me out to Florida to sit and write with him: he wanted to work on a thriller movie, set in Key West, around the Hemingway Look-Alike Contest. He'd bought himself an Apple computer and as we beavered away to get down a few lines for a possible scene, lunch came and—to my astonishment—Leo shut down the machine. 'Why didn't you save the scene…? Now we'll have to start all over again.' Leo didn't know how to save, didn't want to learn how to save, was pretty intimidated by this new-fangled device—but, as a concession, was prepared to print the paragraph we'd put together; finis. Swiftly, in imagination, I was transported back to Lancashire, into the presence of the first black-leg operative who, breaking ranks with his Luddite comrades, timidly tinkered with the first mechanised weaving machine. America liked to surprise.

Leo had rescued Margo, the wife of an alcoholic acquaintance, and married her—and also took on her entire family. Margo was adorable; his fairly grown-up stepkids were a band calling themselves *The Rising Tide*. He built a Roman-like villa for them all: grapefruit grew on his territory; the central dwelling was a mix of Saxon great hall and Yellowstone-style wooden folk ranch, enormous, tall; and all around the central courtyard Leo had added habitations as the kids got married and the babies came. He was *paterfamilias,* big time: benefactor *in excelsis;* but never had a kid of his own.

He was inherently impatient with the idea of dramatic structure, of shaping a script: instead, impressions and effects and explosive moments, characters and ambiences and atmosphere filled his imagination. We got as far as bullet points scrawled on paper; he was completely uninterested in learning even the basics of word processing and then, typically, switched track. Said he'd been to Key West so many times, it would be a bore for him to go yet again: but why didn't I go alone? The brief was to check it out, get a flavour of the setting for his thriller. So, I was trusted with this enormous Hummer-like vehicle (he had two—one for him, one for her) that did about eight miles to the gallon. When I mildly commented on how uneconomical that was, he rounded on me to say that we Brits, we Europeans, were just envious of the abundant life Americans had worked hard to hand themselves, and anyway, gasoline was a derisory figure per gallon and screw you all, covetous bastards.

It was comfy for Leo to get up into the vehicle, but for me—I practically needed steps.

From Leo's place just inland of Palm Beach, north of Miami, the drive to Key West is along a road forced across a chain of what used to be an exquisite string of Bay of Mexico islands. Many years later, I read Jared Diamond's book *Collapse: How Societies Choose to Fail or Survive*; he's a biogeographer concerned for the healthy survival of the planet, and he described making this same trip, but only just after the road had been slammed down. He knew the islands before they were linked up, and as he approached one of them in his car he braked and stopped, appalled. What he remembered as one of the most lush, bio-diverse, vibrantly alive habitats he knew on earth was now—a car park. He burst into tears.

Very soon, I discovered another common characteristic of the natives (white). I set out on a three-lane (each way) highway with a forty-mile-an-hour limit. I was inclined to try forty-two, maybe forty-three, but for mile after mile, right ahead of me were three old boys in similar sit-up-and-beg machines, dead in line across the road and refusing to change lane, whichever I tried. I could feel the self-righteous emotional posturing streaming out of them and wafting back in their exhausts as they imposed their LAW on me and on everybody else. It wasn't till I got past Miami that the silly buggers peeled off.

Key West was colourful, animated and pleasant to be in. Lots of fishing and holiday craft, full of locals as well as tourists; low rise, and a mix of seedy run-down and gaudily painted-up architecture, full of eateries and references to Ernest Hemingway. I checked out some of his haunts, including the venue for the Look-Alike Contest. I watched the sunset at the harbour—very fine—an obligatory activity, with crowds of others. I was told that the local ecology, the very thing people came for, was under threat because a developer wanted to chuck concrete down alongside the key to extend the money-making platform. I stayed the night in some unmemorable, small hostelry— and drove back. I had no idea what I was doing there—in terms of writing a script. I realised that Leo was hopping around in his head and that I was in Florida to keep him company, really, and because I could talk deep stuff with him. Once, he told me, in his Nassau Club days he'd dealt in ancient coins, and he and some associates had tried to corner the world market in old Roman money. He said it nearly came off. Using various ploys they'd concentrated heaps of the metal in certain locations, then claimed exclusive ownership. Only, something upset the game. A key player stopped co-operating and the enterprise sprang a leak, I think he told me.

He owned a boat and told me about a conversation he'd had with two friends, also with boats, neighbours: they were evaluating themselves; comparing craft and the rest. Two million described Friend 1; one million rated Friend 2; Leo hit out at half a million. Remember this is the 1980s—I don't know what the multiplier is, but considerable.

Florida is built on sand: it's an arid place; there were restrictions on lawn watering. Water was diverted from the Everglades, and they were drying up; yet people went on building. I crossed a nearby patch of remaining wilderness and came across a fast-moving black-brown snake—not poisonous, I was told. I expressed an interest in the Everglades. 'In God's name, why? It's just mosquitos,' says Leo. To him, nature was a darned nuisance: utterly useless; 'but go if you want.'

I went. Saw the caymans; the anhingas—magnificent cormorant-like birds—perched on a branch, spreading out their wide, silvery wings in the sun to dry; listened to the wardens explain how the whole area was threatened by water extraction for unlimited housing and hotels, for the showers and the gardens planted with thirsty

*Hemingway look-alikes*

European exotics: everyone wanted their English roses. 'We're trying', said the wardens, 'to persuade the incomers to fill their gardens with the local, drought-resistant flora. Just as beautiful and interesting, if you can switch your state of mind. Hard job, persuading people; we're trying.' And they're still trying in California, right now. But time is running out… I got to walk around Palm Beach and see the Fitzgerald-style mansions—urban castles from film sets, stupendously expensive-looking.

One morning, very early, a guy Leo knew called. He drove a truck towing a very long vehicle, something like a film location trailer, with 'Gardening Services and Supplies' painted on it. The fellow who owned this rig, fairly young, hopped out and he and Leo exchanged pleasantries—I didn't catch what they said. I was briefly introduced; the vehicles pulled away. 'That's his front,' said Leo. 'He does gardening—some… but at this hour, it's his morning drop off of drugs round the Park; that's what he's doing.' Chuckle. 'I don't do it; haven't for a long while. That's it, though.'

We never got far with the thriller. I went to *The Rising Tide's* gig one time; flew home. Leo popped up from time to time: he had an American friend in London who, having made his money at something, now wrought exquisite, jokey, objects from found timber; polished them up, put eyes on them, tails, horns—a kind of sculpture. 'I want to find a way we can use his things—they're beautiful, aren't they?—in a show; maybe if we…'. And he had Victor Spinetti on the phone—I met him, once, with Leo—some scheme for Victor to play Shylock in a bullring on skates, inside a hologram of Gina Lollobrigida, or something like that, I can't remember. Victor reared and bucked like a very startled mustang, laughed, and changed the subject.

I still have a pair of Walmart, all-purpose shorts Leo bought me, as soon as I turned up, 'You can't wear what you're wearing in this climate', and he climbed us into the Hummer and we shopped—yes, generous. Last I heard, his prostate was playing up. Told me his physician recommended sex—if he could manage it. Leo could arrange anything like that and he arranged it: not bad, he told me; not great, but… His final story: he needed to go to the toilet and the nearest place was his bank. He padded in, went up to the counter and asked the teller if he might use their bathroom. Teller said, sorry, only available to staff. So Leo said 'Look, if this bank don't let me use your john, I shall make a deposit right here on your carpet. Which would you prefer?' Well, they opened up and let him use the loo.

# Hollywood, you'll never know what you missed

Film (1958 and on...)

**I've observed that everywhere** associated with me has been pulled down. I don't know what to make of that. It can't be personal? My grammar school—Sale County Grammar School for Boys—has been obliterated: it is now a housing estate. It's merged with the Girls' School: and girls are a good thing, I'm sure you'll agree; they may save the world. Whew. So that's O.K.

They also pulled down Lime Grove Studios—a good bit of my early history was tied up there. Not a crumb left: it's a residential block. Until very recently, Television Centre was going to go, too. Then I'd have been wiped out. But they're keeping the shell—the question mark bit—and the naked golden man that my friend Rosemary Hill used to stare out of her office at, and that Anna used to walk around and admire. That's a relief. A few studios have been saved.

My life in movies! Very limited. But I hit a sort of a peak playing the AA Man in *The Magnificent Seven Deadly Sins* directed by—almost as eccentric as Spike Milligan—Graham Stark, and it was pleasant to be in something with Alfie Bass and Ian Carmichael. It's that story where the jalopy meets the Rolls in a narrow lane… Click and you'll find it on YouTube. Sin of Pride it illustrates, I think.

In my very first film I said the Lord's Prayer in German on the Titanic as it was sinking at Pinewood Studios—*A Night to Remember*—starring Kenneth More. And, yes, I scammed George Devine at the Royal Court when the old swine wouldn't let me off matinée days to do one of my very first film jobs: as soon as we broke for lunch at Pinewood, I leapt in my car and drove like a lunatic to Sloane Square, strolled in at the stage door, made myself known and tore back to Pinewood. I was understudying, that's all. No one ever knew. The film was *The Square Peg*, with Norman Wisdom as a fake German officer ('fraid I never thought he was funny—but very popular). I was in a scene with Peter Sellers in *The Prisoner of Zenda*: interesting to watch him operate—quiet, slightly giggly, floaty, drifting—brilliant. *Force 10 From Navarone*: I had a scene with Robert Shaw in that, on Jersey, while he was fighting the drink; so getting a good take out of him was a bit like playing roulette.

Hammer Films worked like a Toyota production line: barely believably, I was on the set within four hours of parking my car. *Frankenstein Must Be Destroyed* was the film; populated with the politest, most courteous, soft-spoken bunch of fiends I've ever worked with. Peter Cushing—a heart-throb of my mother's—utterly charming; the director economical in movement and just audible as he comfortingly smiled and arranged success. There was only one rule: NO RETAKES under any circumstance whatever, heart attacks included. Achieved by rehearsing four or five times, checking if everyone was truly ready, evoking a hospital surgical hush and then, you just heard it, *ACTION!* That day, momentously, one of the cast said he thought he'd—very slight-ly—slurred a word. It was talked over in subdued tones— and accepted and left in. The system could not be broken. (Why not watch the movie and see if you can spot

*My ma collected this — her heartthrob*

the fluff?). I said good-bye to everyone and quietly left the set, tiptoeing from the hallowed precincts of a temple to low-budget moneymaking.

I winked at Ian Holm in *A Severed Head*. And I took a couple of *The Thirty-Nine Steps*. I'd warned the company that I was booked on another movie, but they got behind and someone took over the rest of my part; I still got invited to the big John Buchan celebration not long ago!

And then one day I was flown to Nice: to be a waiter on a movie called *Picasso Summer*. The script was about a couple chasing round the Côte d'Azur and just missing Picasso (starring Albert Finney—and Michael Medwin from *The Army Game*). No one met me at the airport; fine. I took a cab to the Negresco Hotel—and asked the driver to wait while I went in to find someone to pay him, because I'd been caught like that before. At long last the location accountant turned up (young man), settled the fare, and yes, there was a room booked for me—and he disappeared. I was shown upstairs by a footman, in striped livery with tight white stockings and breeches, into a courtesan's palace of a room with a silk swag over this enormous bed. The whole place is marble and columns and carved wood and—Google it, check it out. There was no shot list, no call sheet, no communication; I had some script pages. I ate, slept, looked at the revellers on the beach; no one on Reception could tell me anything. Got through to an office and was told to take the day off. Did some sightseeing, ate, watched two cracking young women guests negotiate with a very fit young holidaymaker guy—and take him upstairs to share. Next day still no crew, but the accountant came out, handed me some francs and said 'Why don't you go to Monaco for the day.' I took a bus there: it was fascinating. The steep climbs, narrow roads (murder for the Grand Prix drivers) were surprising. I saw the Rainier palace, the exquisite casino, the million dollar yachts. And I felt privileged to watch an ancient entertainment in the square: travelling show-people had semi-circled their caged lions, a tiger, monkeys (the cages were on wheels) to make an amphitheatre, and I saw a grown man dressed as a baby, in white, wearing a tight baby's cap and sucking a dummy, lying in a pram. Round him two other characters, perhaps mother and a priest, were waving slender palm fronds over him. Survival of a rite stretching back to the Middle Ages it seemed, or earlier? The players were collecting from the steadily growing crowd. I hadn't the slightest idea what it meant, but I felt that it might improve your day or, perhaps, your whole life, to be around it. Good; a thrill.

*The Magnificent 7 Deadly Sins: Pride, with Alfie Bass and Ian Carmichael*

Still no call sheet at the Negresco, but next morning there were Albert Finney and Michael Medwin on the terrace with coffee—laughing. They hadn't done a stroke, either, and I remarked that I had a deadline—the company knew I had to be on a plane, Sunday, to go to another job. Albert's deadline was Monday: if they didn't finish, he was gone. And, at last, staff appeared. Apart from the American producer and director the entire production crew was French. Light shone in a dark place. I was fitted with my waiter's gear. Next morning we all piled into company cars and were driven to the location—the very, very grand holiday retreat of Lord somebody or other—on the coast. The very first thing the French crew did on arrival was strip to their bathing costumes and start farting about in his Lordship's pool. I could see the director and producer earnestly talking to each other, entirely alone—no support offered of any kind. I felt sorry for these Yanks; they were being taken for a First Class ride by these French clowns. When the director tentatively approached the

woman who, I gathered, was First Assistant he was greeted with breathtaking rudeness. The French were taking the money and doing nothing. By exerting extreme pressure, I had a flight out booked for me and a car to take me to the airport. I got into my costume, and mid-afternoon I got out of my costume, and left the location. I heard, later, that the director put on my waiter's kit and played me. Film buffs will find clips (1969). The animated sequence is worth a look—Picasso come alive.

The only way home was through Geneva (annoying) but it gave me a chance to see my Hungarian friend Andrea. Because she was very blonde, it was she, the innocuous fourteen-year-old, who was sent out to find food by the other Jews hiding in Budapest, once the Germans there got nasty in 1944-5. Her mother told her to clear off as soon as the war ended; she got as far as Zürich and was taken in by a Jewish family—who had a son, José Berlinka. He got in to RADA—brought Andrea with him—was in my class and he gave far and away the best parties; never more than eight people, and distinguished by very high-class conversation. Every other party at RADA was a typical English drunken brawl, punctuated by vomiting, desperate sexual groping and a certain amount of opportunistic copulation, if the hosts hadn't a lock on their bedroom door. But, at José's parties, I kept hearing a baby crying. I knew nothing, then, of Andrea's story, but I looked around for infant things.

I asked her straight. 'I can hear a baby… I can, can't I?' 'You're hallucinating,' she said. But no, I wasn't. All through RADA they'd locked this kid up and, whenever they had visitors, tidied away all trace of him.

Andrea left for Switzerland with the child, José stayed to 'make it' in England; he worked with Charles Lewsen—Orchard Theatre, I believe, in Devon; fell flat on his face and ran out of money. Hard-lucked me at the Arts Theatre Club and I lent him twenty-six quid—plus a few pence—to get home; said his dad would send me the money. I'm still waiting for it; he's dead now. So…

Another time I was in Zürich on a film with George Pravda—*Inspector Clouseau* —and from breakfast till supper we would ramble around the town while George told stories: for five days he never repeated a single one—he reckoned he knew about three thousand. We had a highly technical discussion about how to deliver the pay-off of a joke about a bloke who kept a million bees. It goes like this:

| | |
|---|---|
| <u>Curious layman:</u> | You're a beekeeper? |
| <u>Beekeeper:</u> | Yes. |
| <u>Curious layman:</u> | I see that you only possess one hive? |
| <u>Beekeeper:</u> | That's right. |
| <u>Curious layman:</u> | That can't produce much honey. |
| <u>Beekeeper:</u> | I do all right. |
| <u>Curious layman:</u> | And how many bees are there in your hive? |
| <u>Beekeeper:</u> | A million. |
| <u>Curious layman:</u> | A million! |
| <u>Beekeeper:</u> | That's right. |
| <u>Curious layman:</u> | Oh, but that's awful. A million bees trying to work and eat and make honey and keep healthy in that one rather small hive. Isn't that cruel? Wouldn't it be better to acquire another hive or two and offer them the choice of moving in there? I know they're only insects and probably don't have exactly the same feelings as we do, but seriously, deep down, what do you think about this? |
| <u>Beekeeper:</u> | Fuck 'em. |

*Outpleasencing Pleasence*

Now, should you pause before the killer line, or slam straight in. I said I preferred to leave a brief pause before the pay-off. George said he always came straight in on cue.

Eventually, we got on the film set: I was Schell, a Swiss banker and George played Wulf.

Then I was cast in *Barry McKenzie Holds His Own*. It was an attempt to capture Barry Humphries' cartoon strip on celluloid. I think Barry and Bruce Beresford knew it was going to be dire as they were shooting it but, too late, they couldn't stop: and we all knew—at the moment in *Barry McKenzie* when the meant-to-be sinister cut-out bat jerked across the set unhappily on its wire, and froze. As Barry said, 'I think this bat's trying to tell us something.' Barry and Bruce were trying to make a virtue of having no money. They were also trying to parody Hammer Films, I can't imagine why; Donald Pleasence was, of course, the horror. Even this kind of movie usually has an internal logic, but inexplicably I was playing Dorothy, a vaguely mediaeval, deformed character with a hideously dropped eye; I was described as Donald Pleasence's catamite.

Fellow Aussie Dick Bentley was also in the show, and having lunch with the cast and sitting next to Dick spinning yarns was the chief pleasure. He was almost as fecund as George Pravda. One story of his I remember: 'I was visiting my friend Trev the other day... he's done terribly well, you know... "Dick..." he was saying to me "Dick, remember the old days... how we used to eat our meals indoors and crap out-side in the yard. Now, I've got all this money... we crap in the house and eat outside. I guess that's progress."' A moment later he turned to me and said 'Are you on the nest to-night?' I'd never heard this expression before and wondered, for a moment, if this was a personal enquiry—or an offer... Then Dick roared with laughter and explained he had another friend who solemnly would ask his mates if they expected to be 'en-gaging' with their wives, or whoever, later that evening.

I'd worked with Bruce at the British Film Institute—and I'd started his car for him once. Barry Humphries was interesting to be around, and watch. He was curiously soft and bendy for a big man and a bit like Milligan, but not off his rocker. He had a strong, silent, large, attractive young woman always there, fetching and carrying for him. And I remember he talked about his missis.

And then TV took over.

# Bread, butter & the first hint of Jam

## Television before sit-com (1962–1968)

**In Part One I describe my introduction to TV** in *Jesus of Nazareth,* which went out live. I write of my unforgettable walk down Bond Street, dressed as a woman, in *Mary's Wife.* They are vivid examples of the medium in which I have worked most of all.

The first time I was on a set with Mike Leigh was 1962 when he was—briefly—an actor, playing an 'idiot boy' (see page 10), in an episode of *Maigret* starring Rupert Davies. I was playing a local criminal suspect, and I was invited to breakfast with the great inspector. At rehearsal, Rupert timed his searching questions exquisitely, with breaking his bread roll, pouring his coffee, sipping it and glancing—or not glancing— at me. All without a single prop—substitute or real. On the second day, he began to ask the staff if they could supply him with something to work with—it didn't need to be the real items. Blank: nothing. He kept asking. The floor-staff raised eyebrows, were blatant and rude. Rupert kept his temper; his series was, after all, a raging hit. He asked me if I thought he was being unreasonable.

He explained to me how he liked to make his character put suspects at ease: ordinary life seeming to go on—while at the same time pointing his questions with careful pauses between prop use and ruminative chewings. I was in the presence of a real craftsman. And none of the ignorant creeps supposed to be working on the show to make it a success seemed to understand this—not even the director—'Eating a roll is just eating a roll, isn't it? Sipping coffee is just…' Rupert didn't get his props till we were in the studio. He brought the odd thing in himself to work with—even screwed up a page of script to stand for the bread roll. It was a bad case of crew rudeness to a meticulous performer. This has got better now: more crews understand how actors work.

Mike Leigh tells me he still has a copy of that Maigret. I must check it out.

Strangers remind me that I was in *The New Avengers;* all that sticks is a faint recollection of something mechanical nastily doing me in. Different strangers say I was in the old *Avengers,* too. Hmmm. I was all over *Survivors*—well, three of them: I do remember that. I have spotty recollections of being near an overwhelming turbine in a real power station; and being slightly wicked. Also, we were in Wales, so I visited a dead coal mine and went down in a cage, and was told by the operator that he'd worked at the mine when it was privately owned, and that in bad times the posh family on the hill simply closed the mine for ten years and concentrated on making chocolate, till the price of coal could support their life style once more. It's why Socialism happened, and nationalisation, and so on. I also picked up a wonderful chunk of Welsh ironstone and used it as a doorstop, till some effing builder nicked it; now I use a piece of chalky flint which looks like a stranded seal.

I was in two episodes of *The Professionals*. In one I was bumped off pre-title—false beard and all. In *Rogue* I was yet another one of my petty criminals, though this shoot will be scorched in my mind forever. I was leading the stars, Bodie and Doyle, towards their target, a secluded mansion, when the director suggested that—for extra excitement—we perform what I thought was a highly dangerous leap. At once, in my mind, arose the standard actors' question 'do I want to go on working, or do I make a fuss and get a reputation for being difficult?' It's astonishing what the industry felt it could, not so long ago, impose on its actors. And I can't help thinking of my classmate Roy Kinnear's dilemma faced with getting on a horse out in Spain shooting *The Last of the Musketeers*. Roy didn't ride. Was an obliging guy; hated making a fuss. Got up on the beast. Came off, fractured pelvis, heart attack and died. He was 54.

After many sharp, quick, energetic bursts of TV I remember the strange sinking feeling I suffered when I was offered the whole of *Midnight Is a Place,* for Southern Television. It would tie me up for a whole ten weeks. Think of what I might miss from signing such an enormously long contract! This was a seriously weird response… but I'd got so used to being on call at three hours' notice, that to be stuck in a series felt like an indeterminate sentence—what if Hollywood rang? I took the job! I think it's called 'being turned around' in the intelligence world.

Chris McMaster—who directed *Midnight Is a Place*—was emperor of kids' TV at Southern, and he went on to cast me as a smart baddie—with Neil McCarthy as the heavy—in his flagship children's adventure series, *Freewheelers*. We were on an extended shoot in the south of France, which Chris ran like a Napoleonic campaign. He often stood like Napoleon, with one hand inside the breast of his coat—even if he wasn't wearing one. He compulsively drew maps of the boundaries of 18th Century Europe and then asked you to name which year the nations were configured like that.

Once we arrived in several cars at a location which turned out to be unsuitable, whereupon Chris leapt into his own car, crying 'Follow me'. We tried. Neil McArthy had been allowed to bring his personal motor provided he also used it as a company car. So, with four crucial members of the cast in his vehicle, Neil put his foot down and tore after Chris. Along winding roads, negotiating rural hazards. Before long, we'd lost him. At junctions, we had to use our limited military skills to try to guess which direction Chris had taken. We drove on; for hours; expecting to find him stopped at the side of the road to guide us. We debated where, logically, he would be heading for (no mobiles, no radios).

At last, we reached Les Saintes Maries de la Mer. Nothing. We decided to stay still and wait. Ages later, a crew vehicle turned up. Finally, Chris. 'What happened to you?' he demanded. Neil asked, politely, whether or not Chris had thought of checking in his mirror to see if we were behind him, visible? (Was this how Napoleon lost Europe? Was this why the actor-manager system collapsed?) We lost a day's filming.

On another day, the light was failing, with the canoe chase still to do. Leave it till the morning? No chance. Chris hurried us down to the river… 'That's your canoe…' he pointed to the young hero and heroine of the series. 'This is yours'—indicating the baddies' boat for myself and Neil McCarthy. 'The young people will set off and then I'll count, let's say, to thirty and then you two paddle after them. As you pass the camera—it'll be on the bank there—you stand up in your canoe, Robert, pistol in hand and fire at the young people. This will cause you to over-balance, upsetting the canoe, and you will fall into the water, followed by Neil. We'll hold for a moment and that'll be the end of the shot; and we'll come and help you out of the river. All right?'

'But Chris, don't you think…?' 'No time for rehearsal… if we don't do it now, I'm going to have to cut the sequence. But it's very important—and exciting.'

Some of the staff quietly asked me if I'd ever, er, done anything like this? I said 'No, but I could swim—it should be fine.' The props man came up: 'Would you like me to attach the gun to your pocket on a long wire—in case you happen to let go of it; no one'll see the wire in the long shot?' 'That's O.K.' I said. Then, at the very last moment, I said, 'Yes, why not. Might as well.'

So, as these things sometimes do, everything went according to plan. Except… that I had no idea how quickly clothing soaks up water, and how incredibly difficult it

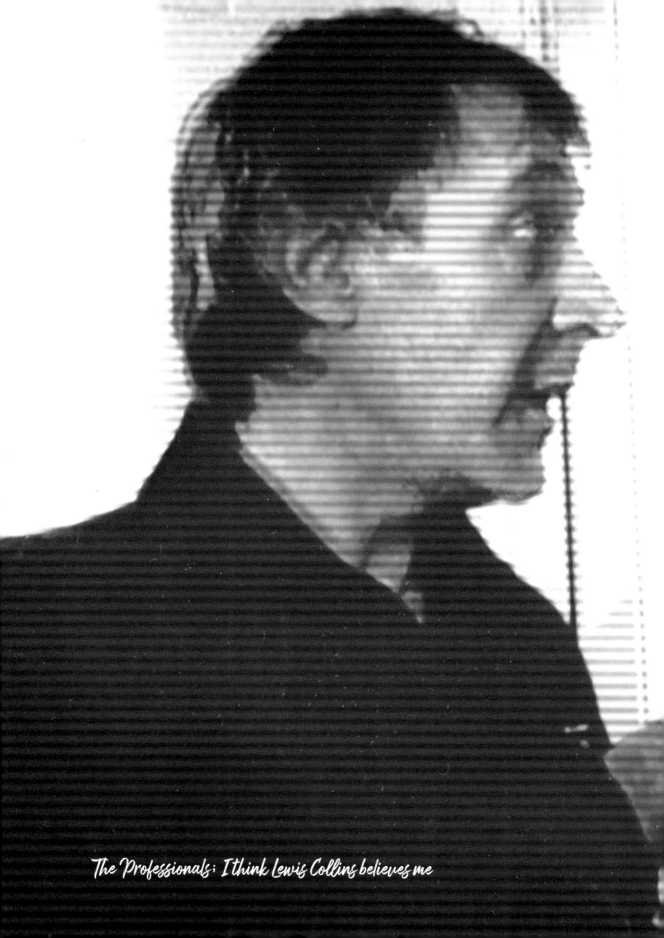

The Professionals; I think Lewis Collins believes me

is to swim fully clothed. I tried swimming with one hand, panicked, let go of the gun and fought to make sure this wasn't the end of my life in show business. The friendly staff hauled us out, reeling in the revolver like an iron fish. 'Thank you. That's a wrap,' said Chris. 'See you at supper.'

I like to think that this kind of thing is pretty rare, now, in the film industry—but I still sometimes wonder…

I found it impossible not to like Chris. There's a sad—or is it sad?—story about Chris (a small man—his father, Anew, was very tall). His sweet wife would go up to London, Thursdays, and we heard it was part of their deal: so as not to lose her, he accepted that she met another love of her life; Chris saved his family life with this arrangement. I wondered also if, for her, this was a break from living with Napoleon. Chris was an engaging chap, but always on show, performing. Only once did I ever have an unadorned conversation with him: you felt he couldn't bear it for long— a hidden hurt? Reminded me of Kenneth Williams.

I'd always dreaded being typecast: already on TV, in 'serious' drama, it began to look as if I was fated to play small time crooks. Typecasting was supposed to be how you made it, big time: got yourself a profile and proper money. That's the way Donald Pleasence invented the Donald Pleasence persona. Now I look back, in sitcom, perhaps I also got myself 'typecast'—but not for the characters I played: I was everything from pebble-blind nutters, to dentists, to Charles Boyer as Napoleon, to cops; joyous. The only consistent thing was—I heard it back from some kind director—that 'Robert never misses a laugh'. It's why the telephone kept ringing.

*Survivors; a conflicted villain*

*Maigret; young French villain*

*The Professionals; pre-title villain*

*The Avengers; part-time villain*

# The sort of big time

## Situation comedy (1968–1993)

**Sitcom: it's what I'm best known for.** For a number of years I was public property—some days more than others. I was accosted in the street, hailed from passing vans, interrupted strolling in Italian slums, button-holed on the site of ancient cities: and I have David Croft to thank for setting me off in the only branch of show-business where that happened.

*Keep It in the Family* was written for me—but that was later. On the way, I worked a fair bit for David. And by gum you learn as you go.

It all started with *Hugh And I Spy*. BBC Light Entertainment decided to liven up Terry Scott and Hugh Lloyd's domestic scrapes with foreign adventures. The episode I was called in for happened in 'Morocco' and I was there because I could do a French accent. I was asked to read for the part of a police sergeant: he was dry, downbeat, behind a desk, long-suffering and patient with idiots. And he was the first version of a character I was to play many times afterwards (he has a wonderful reincarnation in *Whatever Happened to the Likely Lads* when Bob and Terry are moving house, and come in to report the loss of their toys: I noted down 'one rabbit, luminous'—I can still hear the laughter).

David Croft, the director, explained the intention to go exotic, hence the Morocco setting: 'it's a very good year for camels,' he remarked. The script was excellent, coarse, broad comedy; some of Terry Scott's signing and mouthing sequences when trying to speak a foreign language were inspired.

In *Up Pompeii!* (1969-70) I was part of a sequence of four actors who each had a single line that built up to Frankie's Howerd's pay-off. One of us, a lost soul, decorated his sentence—he tried to make it tell, give it content, complex meaning. Frankie's professional distress was clear. He didn't get angry: he tried to illustrate, without words, by making a simple sound, pointing at each of us 'Deh… deh… deh… deh… and then it's me; my line; and a laugh… we hope.'

He reminded me so much of Hugh Miller at RADA. As a young actor Miller worked with an American star and had sought to embellish his small part with a complex and heightened delivery plus some gestures. He'd driven the great man mad. All the star wanted was simple cues 'For Christ's sake, Hughie, give me the straight,' the star actor screamed, vividly illustrating the vital, straight feed necessary for a comic's pay-off line to score. It must be biological, this obligatory pattern: for getting laughs. Has anyone done a neurological study of why? I went in homage to see Howerd at the Palladium, towards the end of his career. Mostly the same old material (the three little fishes song), but he was so relaxed, and endearing and so—seemingly—spontaneous that there came waves of pure love from the audience. Frankie Howerd, in my opinion, could have been the greatest comic of his generation if he'd had quality material, consistently. He might have matched Sid Field? Frankie, let loose on *That Was The Week That Was,* was glorious—talking about 'adultery on the front bench… have you seen the width of it? I mean… no, seriously… how would they do it…?' If only he could have found a top writer who suited his style; oh well.

David Croft being David, *Up Pompeii!* gave him the chance to cast six or seven model girls for the series to play—I'm not sure what they were meant to be, really, but they evoked those popular 19th century paintings of exotic eastern harems. It seriously was unusual to see that many exceedingly lovely young females in a scratchy sit-com setting. I had never before seen a professional model ready herself for her public: as soon as a camera was pointed, I saw one girl literally arrange the muscles of her face and mouth, her throat, brow; flick her hair and lie back as if each item had been on a separate little motor, independently controllable for max pulling power. Ve-e-ry professional. Ve-e-ry impressive.

For some people Diana Dors walked on water. I arrived at the studio on the fourth floor at the BBC building in Acton to rehearse the only episode of *All Our Saturdays* that I was in, and before we'd even all said hullo, a voice called out 'Knicker inspection!' And Tony Caunter and Doug Fisher and the young director started undoing their belts and their flies, and tugging out sample pinches of their Y-fronts and boxers. Dors hoicked up her own skirt, flashed her fashionable drawers—can't remember the shade—and then went round commenting on everyone's colours, and oohing. Pass: I wouldn't play. She scanned me: I looked back. Curious, that moment when you know the brain wheels are working in the other person. Should she pull rank, should she schmooze me into joining in? 'Who are you…? Robert… come on, it's only fun.'

*Whatever Happened to the Likely Lads?*

Curious, the profound awkwardness in a minor player—me—before a 'star'—of sorts. Is this part of the climb up the greasy pole? She didn't push it. But every day started with 'KNICKER INSPECTION!!!' She got used to my dissidence and stopped seeing me. The only other cast member who didn't play ball was John Comer. She didn't try it on with him. Echoes, for me, of Joan Littlewood and her careful political judgement of whom she could browbeat and who not.

We hardly rehearsed at all. The young director was obsequious to the point of declining into the babbling state of a fifteen-year-old schoolboy. Chaos. There was a bit of location filming in which Diana wore a pink sweater. Came the studio recording day: we stumbled through the episode and someone noticed that Diana was in a blue sweater, in the studio. Couldn't change the film, so there was a chase round the building to find the pink sweater—so they could re-take the studio sequence where she'd worn the blue one. Wardrobe could not find the pink sweater—anywhere. So, there was shrugging and everyone went to the bar. If you watch that episode, you'll see D.D. come off film and walk into the studio set, with her top miraculously changing colour. This is pretty well a hanging matter in the trade. I suppose it was the closest thing I've known, in Britain, to the contempt the Spanish National Theatre lot displayed for their audience (see Part One). Way beyond the foolery at the Old Vic. Only time I ever saw it. Alan Lake, her husband, seemed a pleasant fellow; weighed down with gold danglers, frequently showing us his watch.

Most of the people I worked with in sitcom were unfailingly pleasant and generous—except one.

The only performer who ever tried to get the director to change the way I was playing a part was Harry Worth. I was a clerk at a post office window and the director knew exactly why he'd cast me and what he wanted from the scene. I'd played—many times—long-suffering, patient officials who had to deal with flowery, expressive, rambling individuals who wanted something. Anyone who knows Harry's work will understand at once how I would be the straight foil to his exuberant, waffling persona.

For some reason Harry tried to get me to be huffy, cross, answer back and—decorate what I was doing. It meant so much to him that he went to the director and asked him to speak to me and make me alter my performance. And the director paid no heed at all to Harry. I tried to work out why this had happened—never before, never again—and I decided that Harry didn't want any laughter from the audience to be shared. His approach would have just turned me into a line-giver, with all the bubbling sense of chaotic fun arising uniquely from Harry. Curiously, I was asked to be in a second *Harry Worth* show; perhaps he didn't have the power of veto.

One particular, very talented actor—we'd first worked together at the Mermaid— always blew up on Thursdays. We rehearsed sit-com half days, Monday to Friday; and every Thursday—I was in several shows with this chap—he would find something in the text, or a piece of business or direction, to explode about. We all got used to it and just let it waft by: directors all knew about it, and went quiet, and were very patient and polite. We broke for coffee; came back and eased, slightly awkwardly, back into our smooth groove. At the end of the session the actor apologised, usually with a lame rationalisation, and life went on. Fridays chugged by quite normal and workmanlike, and we recorded on Saturdays. I suppose tension expresses itself in the most balanced of people.

It's an odd beast, sitcom. In a drama, you can swan around, afterwards, convincing each other how wonderful you all were—but you can never really tell. Sitcom, if people aren't laughing, you come off air. This topic, comedy, needs a book in itself.

I've always been interested in actors' craftsmanship, and Leonard Rossiter was a particular delight to work with. The entertaining gas meter/coins scene in *Rising Damp* was a fine tutorial in building to a comic climax. Leonard was supposed to have raided his gas meter, just before I came on as the Inspector to check it. Nobody on the studio team had given a thought as to how the business in the script was to be worked—it all came from Leonard. He asked for a large match box—pre-packed with coins—with an open end, to be fastened on a turn-pin inside one—also open-ended—pocket of his trousers; he explained how he would take as many stolen coins as he could in one hand, and add them to this box in his pocket. The other pocket was to be lightly tacked.

As he backed round the room denying that he'd done anything wrong, and having just convinced me—the gas-man—Leonard burst through the lightly-tacked pocket with one handful of coins, and turned the box full of coins in the other pocket downwards, so that the whole lot cascaded to the floor.

There'd been lots of 'raised eye-brow signalling' among the staff on the studio floor, as if Leonard were being difficult. I also noticed, as we rehearsed the journey round the room, with Leonard (as Rigsby) lying to me through his teeth, that he would

glance at the studio monitor. He stopped, and asked the director 'It's all mid-shots and tight shots you're taking of this sequence. Isn't that going to spoil the gag? The audience has seen me stuff the money into my pockets… wouldn't it build the tension better if they could see me with desperate hands in pockets—at least some of the time?' There was a general sigh from the floor…

A voice from the gallery 'You want me to go looser?' Leonard, very patient, very reasonable: 'I think it'll make the gag work better; I mean, if they can't see…' A long-suffering, 'O.K.' and it was done.

A balance of shots on face and pockets was arranged. Then, when we got to the pay-off, we found that the waterfall of coins onto the BBC studio composition floor made no sound. Leonard again: 'We need a bit of ply, something like that, where we finish, or the audience won't get the sound of clinking coins they'll be expecting.' It was organised.

And, when we came to record it, the whole sequence worked perfectly on one take.

'My word, we seem to have hit the Jackpot, Mr Rigsby.' That was my pay-off line — you can check the episode on YouTube. Incidentally, when I first got this *Rising Damp* script I thought 'Hullo, I didn't know these episodes were an hour long: what a thick script; I must have been mistaken.' No. Leonard Rossiter could speak faster than any actor of his day: so writers had to give him a lot more words than was usual. His only, possible, rival was Richard Briers.

As in Mel Brooks' *The Producers,* it was assumed that only Jews could get away with a sitcom called *Heil Honey I'm Home!* It told of the domestic life of Adolf Hitler and Eva Braun—and their neighbours the Goldensteins. It was the pattern of rehearsal and the atmosphere that still interests me. Commercial TV was, by that time, trying to work with only four days' rehearsal per episode, and if you have a lot to learn, it's murder. On *Heil Honey* we'd start rehearsing, working for an hour or two—then the back room heavies would march into the room and ask the director to show them results, so far. We'd perform seven or eight minutes and they would leave the room, towing the director after them, and we'd get a break.

The director would return, with re-writes, and we'd start again. This happened over and over. Someone from upstairs would come down and check us out, there'd be a consultation, we'd get another re-write; we'd try it. On the recording day, as a sop, we were told we would have the luxury, privilege, of recording the show twice: it would give us polishing time (a substitute for the other, proper, missing day's rehearsal) and if there was anything good from the first show, well, the team could save it and stick it into the final cut; bonus, win-win. At the first run the audience was mostly older school kids, and the performance technically jagged. By the time I was on the show Maria Friedman was playing Rosa Goldenstein: she had an immensely long, distraught, monologue that still kept being changed. Not long before the second recording, Rosa was given yet more changes to her big speech: asked to cut some lines and alter others. She was clearly distressed; but she took it, the new lines. On the second recording the response was patchy, but there was some laughter. Rosa struggled badly. So we were kept back, while the heavies re-took and re-took her stuff, verbally leaning on her, driving her. And I kept thinking… fascist Jews? Hmm. She was brimming with tears, but tried. (Curiously, there was an old but accomplished violinist with a couple of lines in the show: we gathered he was Maria's dad, Leonard Friedman. He stood by and didn't intervene, didn't say a word.) Here was a management ruthlessness—director and creatives—I'd discovered in America; but this was worse than anything I'd, so far, known. Incidentally, only one episode was aired, and it's been flagged as 'perhaps the world's most tasteless situation comedy'.

So, I was in lots of episodes of lots of different shows, and it was during a rehearsal of *Robin's Nest* that the writer Brian Cooke approached me and asked, 'Do you fancy fronting a sitcom of your own?'

'Keep talking,' I said.

'Well, you're a manic-depressive and I've had this idea.'

I'm not a manic-depressive, but I wasn't going to say anything to stop him. He'd been in harness with Johnnie Mortimer for some years and wanted to see if he could write something solo. Up came *Keep It in the Family*.

The basis of the show was a family living on top of each other, dad—Dudley Rush—working at home and coping with three women: his wife, and two daughters still living downstairs. Brian had been a cartoonist, so he made Dudley—me —the illustrator for a strip called 'Barney the Bionic Bulldog'—which I was quite unable to draw unless I was wearing my empowering glove puppet, Leo the Lion. And he created Dudley barely able to make his deadlines, pursued by an angry boss.

*Keep It in the Family; the Rush living room, designer's Sketch*

What I liked about this show was that the husband and wife (Pauline Yates as Muriel) were jokey, not ripping strips off each other, and we had a good sex life: Brian often started the shows with me and the missis in bed. He wrote the first two series himself; the best. The third and fourth series he—purportedly—oversaw. Then the fifth… I'll come to that.

Our boss was a very experienced comedy director, Mark Stuart. Mark was an ex-sergeant, lean, a craggy New Zealander, and you supposed he'd seen everything and was used to the gamut, the works, the full experience of life, anything, everything; you couldn't surprise him… No-o-o: Pauline Yates shocked him. Pauline was quite delightfully frank and indiscreet. A conversation arose (out of the script) about wifeswapping.

Mark growled 'It's supposed to happen, I've read it happens—does it really happen…?'

'It happens, Mark', said Pauline. She was married to Donald Churchill and she described how a group of men in their street (it all happened round Purley, I believe), encouraged by Donald, had regularly brought couples together, chucked their car keys in a heap in the middle of the room, gave them a stir and then each bloke picked out a set; and the rule was, they got to go to bed with the wife of the guy whose keys they'd picked. Pauline's complaint was that there were some absolutely gorgeous women in the group, but the men… And you had no choice, you had to go with whoever picked you. Mark blushed. It was hard to believe he would, but he did. Pauline loved that.

Regularly something came up in an episode that set her off with a story, and I can still hear Mark's voice… 'Pauline, please…! Do we want to hear this, I don't think we do.' Well, it was only the eighties: Liberation still had some way to go.

One of my daughters in the series was delightful Stacy Dorning; a member of a theatre family—Robert Dorning was her dad. An early daughter was Jenny Quayle, whose father, Anthony, I had met once at Broadcasting House.

Anthony Quayle was one of the supreme triumvirate who kick-started the modern RSC; and a brilliant Aaron in Olivier's *Titus Andronicus* (which I saw). Quayle had 'blacked up' for that, and we had a conversation about whether it would ever be possible for a white actor to play Othello again; and what was political correctness and where did it end. I had an opportunity to challenge Quayle with a famous story embedded in theatre lore about a note he gave to an actor at Stratford. This actor had been struggling with a major role in rehearsal and eventually found the courage to approach Quayle and confess that he was at a loss and could Tony, please, help him. Quayle is supposed to have brooded, reflected and then, after a while, lifting a finger, to have said, 'New bread.' Quayle laughed; said it might well have happened, but he couldn't recall it.

From Series Three Sabina Franklyn took over Jenny's part. She, too, was from a theatre family, daughter of the excellent actor William Franklyn. Sabina was a splendid, practical, straight-talking foil to Stacy.

Perhaps the biggest laugh I ever remember getting in *Keep It in the Family* was in the episode in which I was called for jury service. As usual, Dudley (me) was behind with his cartoon drawing and so worked through the night. Though filled up with black coffee, I nevertheless fell asleep during the hearing of the case. The issue being tried centred on a prim lady, played by Pat Coombs, who'd been propositioned by an intruder in her bedroom. She was so inhibited that she couldn't bring herself to say, in open court, what the intruder had asked her to do. She could only manage 'How would you like me to blank-blank you?' So the presiding judge agreed to her writing down the intruder's request, and this was passed from one juror to the next. Next to me in line happened to be an attractive lady. She read the message but, as she turned to hand it on, she noticed I was asleep. So she shook me awake before passing the message to me. The audience, rightly, imagined that the complete message would read, 'How would you like me to f***k you? I got as far as, 'That's a very kind offer, but…' And there came this gale of laughter. The complete line is '…I'm a married man.' But no one heard that. Later, an actress who'd seen this episode told me she'd been watching it in bed and had rolled onto the floor in paroxysms of mirth.

Not an original joke, by the way, but—as they say—the old ones are the best.

Dudley and Muriel were a happy couple; that was very pleasing, and a pointed contrast to *George and Mildred,* which Brian co-wrote. He also risked quite daring, brief, flights of fantasy—Dudley imagining he was Napoleon, or a cowboy; terrific fun to play. Most daring of all, once, Brian took a chance and opened an episode with a scintillating exchange of one-liners between Dudley and Muriel. Here it is:

DUDLEY: COMPLETING MAKING A BOARD GAME) There she is 'Flabby Fanny'. She completes the set. (HOLDING UP CUT-OUT CHARACTERS). Weedy Walter, Chubby Charlie and… Drunken Duncan. D'you want to play?

MURIEL: I'm busy. I can't make lunch and play stupid board games.

DUDLEY: Stupid? That's what they said to the man who invented Monopoly. Now he's a millionaire - Sid Monopoly.

MURIEL: Who's going to buy a game called… what is it?

DUDLEY: 'Heart Attack'.

MURIEL: Who's going to walk into a shop and say 'I'd like a Heart Attack please'?

DUDLEY: Exactly what they said to Arthur Scrabble!

MURIEL: What did he invent?

DUDLEY: (LOOKING ASKANCE) Tiddleywinks.

MURIEL: Oh, I'm quite good at that.

DUDLEY: Only 'cos you cheat. You tiddle when you should wink.

MURIEL: None of your inventions ever work. That stupid pen that wrote under sand…

DUDLEY: The Foreign Legion was very interested.

MURIEL: And your revolving goldfish bowl for fish that couldn't swim… stupid. (EXITS TO KITCHEN)

DUDLEY: (CALLING) I got a nice letter from the RSPCF… anyway, this is different. It's a game. Vegetarians have never had a game they could call their own.

MURIEL RETURNS FROM KITCHEN CARRYING STEAK ON ONE PLATE, ORGANIC SALAD ON THE OTHER.

MURIEL:    What about 'Carrot, Carrot, Who's Got The Carrot?'

MURIEL:    Pardon?

MURIEL:    We played it when I was little. A row of us would stand and one of us would have a carrot behind his back. And whoever was 'it' would have to guess which one.

DUDLEY:    That's 'Who's got the ball?!'

MURIEL:    We played it with a carrot.

DUDLEY:    It doesn't matter. I mean, it could just as easily have been a… a… lamb chop!

MURIEL:    In Nineteen thirty… flum flum? They were rationed. My mother wouldn't give me a lamb chop to play with.

DUDLEY:    Just as well. They're full of cholesterol.

MURIEL:    Rubbish. It hadn't been invented then.

DUDLEY:    Look, cholesterol has always…

MURIEL:    That's your new word, isn't it! cholesterol. You used to think it was a religious holiday.

DUDLEY:    Ah, not any more. Not since I saw the light. (SITS AT TABLE) Vegetarianism… this is the way to eat. Mr. Adams convinced me, and he's got no axe to grind.

MURIEL:    He's our greengrocer.

DUDLEY:    Well, yes, but… what's that? (INDICATES HER PLATE. DISAPPROVING.)

MURIEL:    It's a steak. You can't have forgotten already. It's only been one day.

DUDLEY:    You're not going to eat it in front of me?

MURIEL:    Of course I am. We haven't all gone funny.

DUDLEY:     Oh. (MUNCHING HIS SALAD) What's it like?

MURIEL:     Delicious. You can really taste the cholesterol… yum-yum.
            How are your alfalfa sprouts?

DUDLEY:     Marvellous. And they're good for you. Mr. Adams says so.

MURIEL:     They're good for him. Eighty pence for a tiny little bunch.

DUDLEY:     D'you know, he's seventy-two. And he's got the arteries of a
            thirty year old athlete.

MURIEL:     Which one?

DUDLEY:     He didn't say. (INDICATES SALAD) You know it's all organically
            grown, this stuff. You know what that means?

MURIEL:     Yes, I do. But not while I'm eating, please.

DUDLEY:     FALTERS IN HIS CHEWING. LOOKS DOUBTFULLY AT HIS FORK-FULL
            OF SALAD.

DUDLEY:     Why? What does it mean?

MURIEL:     It means… well, no artificial fertilizers. It's been grown in
            genuine, you know.

DUDLEY:     Has it?

MURIEL:     Yes.

DUDLEY:     (LAYS DOWN FORK) It's very filling, actually.

MURIEL:     You'll never be a real vegetarian. You were eating chocolate
            biscuits this morning.

DUDLEY:     Only the one. I opened the packet… just to look at them… and my
            tooth got caught in it.

MURIEL LOOKS. FRONT DOORBELL RINGS.

…And the only way to make it work was to be very fast, American style.

When playing sitcom, unlike the kinder, live theatre, you only get one chance to see if something works. The Saturday we recorded this episode it so happened that our entire live invited audience came from an old folks' home. Their response was always a beat behind the last gag. Brian never risked this style of comedy writing again. Pity.

Incidentally, Mark never added in canned laughter.

Knowing which bit of the comic machinery you represent in a given story is a never-ending source of fascination to me. We were blessed on *Keep It in the Family* with some wonderful guest appearances from—for example—my mate Roy Kinnear, Pat Coombs, and Robbie Coltrane who, without a word spoken, knew what was their function. But once, a young actor was hired to be one of my daughter's boyfriends. He had just one scene, but wanted to make the most of it. So he charged every line he spoke with extra content, with subtext. Mark Stuart was the boss, so we waited for him to sort it out. The young man didn't understand. The humour depended on giving the same straight, comic feed that Frankie Howerd had worked to get in *Up Pompeii.* Stacy tried to find words to explain. A small, caring but concerned committee of us formed, trying to help this young man see the light. Suddenly Mark turned to me: 'I can't do this. You've directed—you try', and walked away. For some time—you don't have much time to rehearse sitcom—I tried to explain how situation comedy didn't require the same concentrated energy and charged emotion as *The Duchess of Malfi* or even *Dracula.* You just imagined yourself in a pub, or killing time in a dentist's waiting room—and you made your delivery audible, that's all. I told the chap he'd been cast to be just—himself. Sadly, at the recording he couldn't quite let go of the thought that he had this one chance of getting to Hollywood. Somehow, Roy and Pat and Robbie—who fronted shows in their own right—instinctively knew their role was to 'give me the straight' in *Keep It in the Family.* Generosity is best shared. We were all winners.

At the end of each series we'd go our several ways and wait to hear if Philip Jones, Head of Comedy at Thames TV, would give the thumbs up to schedule another series. There was a day when Mark said to me 'there'll come a time when your show's been running for ten years and you'll still all be the same ages; weird medium, isn't it?'

But that's not what happened. John Ammonds, director of *The Morecambe and Wise Show,* died; Mark was offered the show. It would be his swan song in TV comedy and he might as well go out at the very top, he thought. He had a boat in a basin on the Thames, already, near the studios and was thinking legacy, and next phase of his life. He left us.

By then, writer Brian Cooke was so rich he was advised to leave Britain for a year to spend some of his money stashed in foreign banks. We ended up with scripts strenuously crafted by a father and son team—Dave and Greg Freeman—not up to the snuff we were used to—and we had an absolutely useless director. For the first time we were spending the first day of rehearsal collectively re-writing the script. Awful.

Actors combining to 'improve' a comedy script is almost always a disaster. Once, working on an episode of *Beggar My Neighbour* I was surprised that, straight after the read through, the principals in the cast began discussing what they'd *prefer* to say rather than what the writers had written. Peter Jones was one of the leads and, as he was a fine script writer himself, his dissatisfaction with the text could be justi-fied—his re-writes were enhancing. But changes went on being made till a couple of days before recording, and I sent up a silent prayer, thankful that I didn't have a large part. Peter, in fact, wrote me a new line that got a huge laugh. I was sitting behind a desk (as usual) and Peter entered with a coat draped over one shoulder. 'Instead of your first line' he suggested, 'why don't you ask me if I'm trying to sell you a carpet.' I did. Big audience guffaw. But in the case of *Keep It in the Family* we were all comedy *actors,* not comedy writers, so it was a kind of torture to spend a couple of days of precious rehearsal coming up with lame, unfunny lines invented by—an incompetent committee. Writing for sitcom is a rare and special skill and needs a mind attuned to its artificial discipline. Seldom do people in real life speak sitcom.

So, through Series Five we slowly declined, our ratings dropped and we gently died. And then Eric Morecambe died. So the Hand of Fate left Mark bereft of his grand bowing out from the biz—and left us with a show that could have had another five years in it.

Meanwhile, Brian had gone to the States—and piled up even more loot: our series became transformed into a U.S. version titled *Too Close For Comfort* which ran much longer than we did, in which Ted Knight played me. I've never seen a frame of that show. He died too, not so long after.

At its zenith, *Keep It in the Family* hovered around Number Five—at one point we were Number One!—and I wouldn't have missed it for the world. Seeing smiles break out, for years, on strangers' faces, friendly people asking—could I really be the chap on TV who drew bionic bulldogs with a lion puppet on his fist? Many recognised a bit of themselves in Dudley's haphazard life. Way beyond anything else I've done, making people laugh is what they value most, what everyone remembers. Recently, Anna and I turned up to queue at a very booked-up theatre. The doorman spotted us, came up and said 'You're one of our favourite actors. Come on in.'

It's an experience you have to get used to—it was very new to me to begin with—to be approached on the street by strangers everywhere. Always very pleasantly… The only performer who was rude to a fan, that I ever saw, was Charlie Drake. It happened in the BBC canteen: someone spotted him and approached him with a piece of paper and pen. 'No! Can't you see I'm having my lunch.' We are entirely dependent on people liking what we do. How can you risk bawling out your bread and butter?

What is it that makes an utter stranger accost you as if they had known you all their lives and ask to shake your hand, or stand beside you for a photograph, or sign a book or a scrap of paper? I was never a major celebrity, yet at one time it happened so often that I couldn't help reflecting on it. In time I concluded that I represented luck. There were rabbits, rabbits everywhere you looked, but a happy accident had put this particular rabbit on a million screens and here was a rabbit that made you laugh. Me. So you could just about tell me from the other rabbits. What good fortune!

I also noticed a surprising contrast. People who had seen me in a drama or a comedy were courteous, friendly, warm and congratulatory without exception.  But in my five-year phase of a hundred cheap commercials, I'd go into a pub and I'd suddenly hear a voice—loud—'See that bloke that's just come in. He's the one that does that potato ad.' 'No. He's older.' 'I bet you it's him.' 'No, this one's too short.' I bet it's him, I'll ask him. Oi. You're the one in that ad, aren't you?' As I turned to face this, asking 'Are you speaking to me?' There'd be: 'Told you. It's his voice. Told you.' Laughter. Commercials turned me into a commodity. And they provoked rudeness and derision. Very, very odd; very interesting…

Of the many fans who wrote me letters, it was David Taylor who took the pains to create a *Keep It in the Family* fanzine. He's my longest, most loyal fan and we're still in touch.

Sitcom has been the chief carrier of my professional life—fine times. (Much of it is clickable online).

But, once you've fronted a show, the Business is reluctant to offer you anything less than another lead—for some years, at least. So for a while, things went quiet. It's more a sense of status in the management mind, I think, not the actor's. Most actors are not burdened with false pride and will grab any work that's going.

And so it was pleasant to be asked to be in *Bonjour La Classe.* By this time BBC1 had picked up the 4-day rehearsal bug, to save money: that makes life hard. Peter Woodthorpe, who'd had a brilliant career—I'd been on stage with him at the time of his flowering at the Royal Court in 1956—was cast as the English teacher. The shortened rehearsal caused him great difficulty, he struggled to remember his words and as a fellow professional it was distressing to watch. Fortunately I only had a lot to say in one episode. I featured as Gilbert Herring, a music teacher. He was a surprisingly rounded character—you knew what it would be like to be in a room with his egregious self—and his life climaxed with a satisfying cacophonic disaster. I was pleased with that. You can catch it on YouTube.

*Conducting Herring's Magnificat*

**5.15**
Dolly Skilbeck (right) may be guilty of over-reacting to things in today's *Emmerdale Farm* on ITV.

**8.0**
Dudley Rush (Robert Gillespie, left) is in a quandary while attempting to *Keep It in the Family* on ITV.

*The Manhood of Edward Robinson*? What are the chances of him finding the romance he feels life owes him? Nicholas Farrel and Cherie Lunghi (above) in *The Agatha Christie Hour* on ITV. **9.0**

**9.0**
The film on Channel Four tonight portrays the difficulties of an immigrant family trying to build a life in Birmingham, starring Shulka Bhatterchajee (left).

**7.30**
It's Freddie Starr's big chance at charades tonight on ITV.

**8.0**
Will a shock spoil Dudley and Muriel's holiday in ITV's *Keep It in the Family?*

no trouble solving the ...gram before tonight's game of words and numbers. Ted Moult has the dictionary.

**5.15**
**Years Ahead**
ROBERT DOUGALL
FERGUS ANDERSON
First of a new series specially for older people. The programme looks at current issues including leisure activities; and there's a news round-up. This week, there's an interview with Hugh Rossi, Minister of State for Health and Social Security, a look at Remembrance Day in the 1920s, and an introduction to some regular features. For an introductory leaflet, send a large SAE to: *Years Ahead*, PO Box 4000, London W3 6XJ, OR: PO Box 4000, Glasgow G12 9JQ, OR: PO Box 4000, Belfast BT2 7FE. Your comments on the programme are also most welcome.

quick temper," says Sandra. "She's vulnerable herself and has a lovely sense of humour."

And that's just what Liz needs. The moment her comedy ladies as Penelope Keith, Wendy Craig and Liza Goddard.

"If I get just half-way to their standards I will be thrilled," says Sandra.

## Dudley draws on the girls

★ROBERT GILLESPIE is surrounded by lovely young women when he comes back as cartoonist Dudley Rush in a second series of KEEP IT IN THE FAMILY (ITV, 8.0 p.m.).

Says Robert: "I can still hardly believe it, I like them all very much.

"I've been in the profession a long time and tend to get cast with all blokes. This is a lovely change."

The girls in his screen life are Pauline Yates, who plays his wife, Muriel, Jenny Quayle and Stacy Dorning, who play their daughters Jacqui and Susan.

The other important member of the cast is the toy lion, Leo.

Dudley and Leo are to be seen in bed together in the first episode because Dudley has a broken ankle, which doesn't help the family's chronic financial problems.

**STACY DORNING**
*Darling daughter*

advance repaym per m... This is time, b... given t...

● **DAILY MIRROR** Junior Crossword Book 36 ...

# I once acted in the West End

**It was extremely rewarding** to be able to work with Peter Hall—at last. Almost at once it became clear what he was good at: he excelled with sharp, biting, shrewd, worldly writing—often political; he understood how texts held audiences. Later, working at the RSC, I learned that Ian Judge had cut our *Twelfth Night* using Peter's text: brilliant, ruthless. I could never have believed that you can leave out the description of Sir Andrew Aguecheek as having been knighted 'with unhatched rapier, and on carpet consideration'—I knew that description from grammar school. It tells the audience that he's rich enough to have bought his knighthood, and that his sword has never been drawn in battle—so the audience can enter Sir Andrew's terrified mind when he's forced to fight a duel. And it was in our version at RADA: my tutor Muriel Byrne remarked 'ha ha ha it's so amusing, so pointed'. But if the language has become impenetrable to a modern audience, best to cut it… that might make sense.

I was to be Father de Leo in Tennessee Williams' *The Rose Tattoo* at the Playhouse Theatre (Julie Walters played Serafina). To induct us into his singular mysteries, Peter played videos of his version of *Orpheus Descending,* also by Williams: it was cut to shreds, but vibrant, thrilling. I had missed Peter's *Lysistrata* (masterly, so I'm told) but saw his scintillating *Tartuffe* at the Haymarket.

However, I also saw his *Twelfth Night* there—which was awful: why? His first *Godot,* the scandalous one at the Arts, was superb; the one at the Old Vic, very, very boring—and miscast. *Pygmalion,* with Michelle Dockery—brilliant. *Vanya,* Rose Theatre, pudgy. So, a man with a potent talent in a certain sphere: not good on the lyrical stuff, but of limitless energy, and ambition of such scope that he believed it could encompass universes. Through every rehearsal break negotiating, glued to his mobile, yet unafraid to loosen

*Peter Hall, Julie Walters:
it's OK to get laughs*

his stays, open up to us with an intimate tale of his parents' sacrifice: how, straitened as they were, they had denied themselves a second child, to give their only one (himself) every possible advantage in life. Ahhhhhh, so that's why—and it came to me suddenly—that's why he was so generous to Lilian Moubrey! I had wondered… She had played my eighty-year-old wife in *The Good Woman of Setzuan* back in 1956; and then Peter had cast her in a surprisingly prominent part, as Mrs Kovacs, in *Shadow of Heroes* at the Piccadilly in 1958. Why? Part of the magnetism for me, of theatre, was stories like this…:

Lilian played men at the Old Vic during the 1914-18 war in a company led by Sybil Thorndike and Lewis Casson. She'd married a man in Germany who turned out to be a Nazi, and abandoned her. She'd ended up in Ravensbrück concentration camp (just like my aunt Lili), got out, and was rescued by the Cassons. Her troubles had made her almost completely deaf—but she lip-read effortlessly, her voice was undiminished—clarion clear—and she had an unquenchable energy and spirit. 'You're a good driver', the Cassons always said of her—driver of a scene, they meant; impressive. It was good to have tea with Lilian—and hear her refer to one of the theatre 'greats' as 'Sybil'—I got so used to this that I too started calling Dame Sybil Thorndike 'Sybil'; I was ticked off for it—it was supposedly sacrilegious. When I introduced Lilian to my ma, Lilian said 'Your mother? No-o-o… your sister, surely!?' That sort of thing goes down well. Once, stupidly, I booked tickets for me and Lilian at the National Film Theatre. Some of the material was archive death-camp footage. I shall never forget her horrified reaction to clips of unspeakable… unspeakable… She twisted and writhed. At the time, I was too young to grasp that there were some experiences you can never get over. I was interested and curious for historical reasons, but I never could get Lilian to describe any of it. I knew Lilian till she died. Last place we had tea was in a care home near Brighton. 'Robert, I'm never going to leave this place, am I?' she said to me, one day. Ninety-five, or so, when she went.

Peter Hall I think recognised in Lilian a fighter, an indomitable battler, himself. I'd meant to have a conversation about her with him, but it got lost somewhere.

As for *The Rose Tattoo:* it was torpedoed by its designer—as I describe in Part One of this history—and it was curtains for me in the West End as an actor.

'Robert, that was terrific, but if we use you we'll have to up the ages of everybody else in the show!' I began to be second choice for some terrific parts—hair going grey, white, in places. And then…

# They finally found my CV

## The Royal Shakespeare Company (1994–96)

**Maureen Chain rang me one day,** and I listened and thought 'I must be dreaming'. I was with the William Morris Agency by then, and there was a consensus that I'd make my mark in TV and, marginally, in film, and that the stage would forever be unforgiving of my height and looks. After all, I'd burnt boats in a burst of madness all those years ago when I turned down Sir Laurence… I must explain.

There had been a competition, years back, for a place in the first National Theatre company. At that time, theatre managements, agents and established performers all assumed, without a second thought, that the old rules would apply: casting for coveted stage work would be available to a limited pool of actors already in circulation; getting into the National would depend on a comfy, accepted show business stitch up. And then an astonishing thing happened. As awareness grew of this complacent approach there was an enormous public outcry, especially from Equity, which— after a tough fight—persuaded the theatre moguls to climb down and agree that auditions to join the Company would be for the entire profession.

So, I lined up in a queue of three thousand performers for the first audition. I passed. The second audition, held before Laurier Lister, had whittled down the number to seven hundred plus, and I passed that, too. We were now down to fifty; and these final auditions would, naturally, be held before Sir Laurence himself. It seemed to go fine—can't remember whether Sir L spoke to me—I've a feeling he did: I'd met him once before with Rosemary Hill—she'd worked for him during the war—when she and I had gone to seek his support in re-opening an old theatre in Aldershot; very courteous and practical he was. A few days later Olivier's administrator, Pieter Rogers, telephoned me to say that I'd been accepted as a member of the first ever National Theatre company! Great; could he tell me—was there a specific role, of any kind, inscribed in the contract? He said he'd check. I learned that, no, it would be a play-as-cast engagement. I told the person on the telephone that I couldn't, on reflection, accept, and said why. Pieter rang me again. He was sure there would be interesting work for me to do, but he couldn't undertake to write a part into the agreement. I explained my

*A Midsummer Night's Dream; 'Moon'*

experience at both the Old Vic and Royal Court and said I couldn't face a year of half a dozen lines and huge understudies; again. Impasse. End of story…?

To my amazement, Pieter rang one more time. Now Pieter Rogers had become a very big and influential wheel on the management/production side of stage and TV (I'd first met him at the Royal Court), and I was truly surprised that he should take the time to persuade a ten-a-penny actor to join this new company. Even more amazing, we were on the telephone for about forty minutes, and in the end he told me I was making the mistake of my life. Perhaps he was right; I shall never know. It was oddly flattering, and I'll never understand why he took the trouble. Was he just a very nice man; would that explain it?

I saw the National's early shows at the Old Vic, where I'd started. Olivier was a miraculously extreme Captain Brazen in *The Recruiting Officer,* and Maggie Smith, I remember, dared to stick on a silly moustache for her trouser role as Sylvia. I'd had fond hopes, once, of a life in the classical theatre. To be immersed in plots that changed history, or lit up the adventures of the human mind.

But, from that momentous meeting in David Croft's office all the way to *Keep It in the Family,* the telephone rang most consistently to ask me to help tell anecdotes of ordinary life on TV, in a mildly caffeinated form. Once, perhaps twice, I'd auditioned for the Royal Shakespeare Company—tokenly, in front of a senior stage manager. If you nagged enough the RSC felt they had to see you, and no harm trying; it gets you out of the house. No go. It was to be life on the small screen.

So, what was this that Maureen Chain was trying to tell me? 'The RSC wants to see you'! What! For what? It can't be—no—that was in the other life I was going to have, performing in the classics. Too late, that's gone. Well, someone has dropped out last minute and would I like to meet Ian Judge, mainly, but also a couple of other directors. And I was offered Fabian in *Twelfth Night,* Technicus in *The Broken Heart,* and Starveling in *A Midsummer Night's Dream.* Yes O.K., but I won't understudy. That was agreed, and there was two and a half years' work.

My one private, but serious, reservation about signing up arose from my knowledge of what it was like to be in for a long stretch with a company uneasy with itself, doing uneven work. Well, it fell out that the group I joined at the RSC was the most talented, supportive, affectionate lot of players you could possibly imagine working with. It was actor paradise. The only cross word spoken in all that time was between an actor and director: Philip Voss didn't agree with what Michael Boyd was asking him to do in *The Broken Heart*. (Philip was right. Iain Glen, who'd worked with Boyd before, threw light on this: he'd seen the best ever production—and the worst—both directed by Michael, and when it was bad, it was very, very bad).

The crowd-pullers at Stratford-upon-Avon when I was there were *Twelfth Night* and Adrian Noble's show, *A Midsummer Night's Dream*. Adrian was boss. I'd first come across *Twelfth Night* at grammar school, then RADA, and here was I, attached to it again. Ian Judge got it right, though. He toured us round Stratford town to make his point: the play was about English life; country life. Oh I know it's set in Illyria (which is in the Balkans) but that's just Shakespeare's cover so no one can sit out there and say

'Oi, he's having a go at me!' Sir Toby, the bored country gentleman finding things to do; his silly, courtier friend down from the city, looking for a rich marriage; the uppity estate manager, and so on. Emma Fielding was piquante and gorgeous as Viola, and the scene where she and brother Sebastian (Robert Bowman) find each other was as moving as it should be (and often isn't at all). A dash of Ian's genius came from his setting the great scene when Orsino recruits Viola (dressed as a boy) to go and make love on his behalf to the woman he wants to marry—Olivia—on a great big double bed. Each of them reclining very close, lusting after the unattainable, talking lyric love. We had a Feste who could sing and play an instrument—as well as be funny.

My daughter Lucy saw *Twelfth Night* nine times and *The Dream* six (or was it the other way round) and sometimes brought Amber (Lucy's friend, both nine). *The Dream* was good—in my view, not as definitive or completely satisfying as *Twelfth Night*—but it had the best group of mechanicals I have ever seen. Desmond Barrit as Bottom was as near perfect as dammit, and Daniel Evans as Flute killed himself, playing Thisbe, in so many inventive ways that he made the audience helpless. I decided that Starveling—me—who is cast as Thisbe's Mother, unexpectedly *likes* the idea of playing her—and got my one big laugh acting it in this way at Stratford, in London, in America, in the film we made and, at last, in Mendelssohn's incidental music show which Richard Hickox devised for the Barbican and other venues.

Returning to the theme of self-destruction: I got on very well with Ian Judge, but quickly noticed that some people loathed him. He was very clever, very funny, waspish at times, but (rather like Joan Littlewood) if he couldn't find the exposed, vulnerable underbelly to stick the butcher's knife in—if you stood up to him—then he showed you respect. Us lot gave as good as we got. Result: a brilliant show. Kenn Sabberton who played Snug in *The Dream* (a brilliant Lion, by the way) had, once, been reduced to tears by Ian and said he'd rather not be in the company than work with Ian Judge again. It wasn't long before I heard that Judge is known in the profession as The Poisoned Dwarf. Limiting; but a very talented man, on his day.

There was some naughtiness. It's odd about getting naked: a much-loved member of the company used to flash himself in the wings, at times, so as to be glimpsed by the actors on stage; but he was always fully buttoned when he was on set. It was nothing like the destructive, irrelevant joking-around I'd experienced at The Old Vic.

I remember, at the fiftieth performance of *Twelfth Night,* in the wings with Tony Britton, when he said to me, pointing with profound affection down to his feet, to the boards, to the stage 'This is where the theatre lives; this is home—eh?' And then, as the cue to enter approached he'd say 'Come, let's astonish them, let's give them a blinder,' and we'd bowl on stage together. Exhilarating; you knew why you were there.

Tony was startled when I told him that I was fifteen when I first saw him on stage in Machiavelli's play *Mandragola* at the Library Theatre in Manchester, being splendid in Noel Iliff's company.

Tony and I had been in *Robin's Nest* together; there was an unforgettable moment in one episode (I was playing a detective sergeant) when Tony had to go along a line of suspects at an identity parade, and hear each one of them give a meal order to a waiter. Something like 'Veal, courgettes and roast potatoes.' Tony never got through a single rehearsal without collapsing with laughter; same rehearsing in the studio. I thought, he's got it out of his system—once we're recording, he'll keep a straight face.

*With Tony Britton, a wonderful Toby Belch; 'This is where the theatre lives'*

WILLS'S CIGARETTES

THE PRINCE OF WALES AT STRATFORD-ON-AVON

And I could not believe it when he broke up, yet again, in front of our audience, as the cameras rolled. They loved it but, for once, it spoiled the impact; the re-take didn't get the laugh it should.

When Tony began rehearsing Sir Toby Belch he sought to play him with a false belly and a drunkard's roll—the standard, historical approach to the part (the trap Richard Burton fell into at the Old Vic—see Part One). Ian Judge would have none of it. Untiringly, he persuaded Tony that Sir Toby was a bored patrician, living in the country and making his life bearable with bouts of mischief-making; that he was magnificently upper class compared with Malvolio's ambitious vulgarity. Ian was right and Tony was very, very funny—and moving—as Toby.

Tony thought one of the actresses very fanciable; it led to his musing about pubic hair. We had a Turkish production manager (formidable fellow); it had emerged, in a discussion, that the Turk preferred that region shaved. 'No', Tony said 'I like that little dark triangle.' And he drew it in the air. In case you wonder what actors do in the wings, as they prepare to go on stage, you now have some idea.

I stayed in Loxley, where Desmond Barrit had a cottage, too, with his chap. Desmond was very large at the time, and didn't drive, and I'd give him lifts back to London—in my mini—and I used to wonder why it laboured up the long climbs out of Stratford, till I realised it was Desmond!

I couldn't tell if it was an individual's idea or Company policy but, suddenly, it was announced that there would be a two-week Festival open to us all. Was it prompted by sheer restlessness—once all the shows are playing, a year in a small town can feel like a sentence—perhaps it was to startle shy talent out of the undergrowth? Performances were scheduled for every kind of time and venue around our main repertoire. The audiences would just be ourselves and our guests. On offer was new work—a festival of curiosities: extracts from diverse sources, native, poetic and foreign; and the City Waites. A sort of auction was held at which each of us could bid to join an event—and nobody wanted to direct the City Waites, so I jumped at the opportunity.

The City Waites were—are—an early music group, and became queasy if asked to play anything from the 19th Century onward—simply couldn't bear romantic music— and revelled in ballads, catches, folk music and the like. The group was led by Lucie Skeaping and her husband, and they wanted to perform two of the best

'Jigs'. Jigs were an after-show entertainment presented on the Elizabethan stage—not dances but short musical plays—comic, licentious, scurrilous, iconoclastic, fulfilling the same function as the satyr plays of ancient Greece—a corrective to the principal drama. There are very few jigs extant in any European language, and both our chosen stories were inspired by Boccaccio.

There we were with a glorious, vast wooden chest big enough to hide a man in—borrowed from RSC props—and beautiful dresses, ready to perform *Singing Simpkin;* and we waited for Adrian Noble. Seventy people had packed into the performance room, led by Guy Woolfenden, Head of Music, who thought our super-soufflé was so splendid that he'd leant heavily on Adrian to show up. We reserved one empty chair just for Adrian, and were hearing that he was getting closer, closer, was on his way. Then the clock caught us out and we had to start, and the whole jamboree went off like a rocket: absolutely brilliant from everybody—actors, musicians, singers; but the boss failed to pitch up. I'd hoped to persuade him, partly on behalf of Lucie and Co., to give us an experimental stab at the Jigs on a couple of nights after performing a tragedy—*The Broken Heart,* say—and I talked to him a couple of times, but he didn't bite. A shame. Jigs, I hear, have been performed at The Globe in London, since.

Alex Jennings had come off stage from playing Oberon in *The Dream*—and then acted a large part at midnight in a new work at this Festival; just once! What an amazing guy, an acting workhorse, and never below par. Sometimes, having had the luck to see Olivier, Michael Redgrave and their peers in fullest flight, I imagined Alex as Macbeth, or James Tyrone in *Long Day's Journey…* —could he stretch to that? Could be, one day? But he's really good. The stage is Alex's habitat, like a fish in the right water. Our half of the RSC company was led by Alex, playing Theseus-Oberon, and Stella Gonet as Hippolyta-Titania, and I was in awe at the amount of work Alex could get through. Desmond Barrit, who had trained as an accountant and entered show business late, was very funny about Alex—said he always lived beyond his means. 'Alex is to finance as Arthur Mullard is to classical ballet' said Desmond (Arthur was a gor-blimey actor with an ex-boxer's nose and physique). Alex had a wife, two small kids and dined on caviar.

After Stratford, and the Barbican in London, we went all round America with *The Dream;* then ten weeks on Broadway at the Lunt-Fontanne Theatre. In New York an actor who'd been in *Fearless Frank* came to the stage door and said 'hello'. I saw my best RADA friend Linda, and caught up with Mikel Lambert—she'd played The Woman in *Mr. Joyce is Leaving Paris*—now living in the US. Mikel had parted from her husband Jeremy—with whom I'd once worked at the Mermaid Theatre—not long after he came home and announced that he'd suddenly realised he was Jesus Christ.

The RSC got me a lovely flat on West 66th Street and Anna came over with 10-year-old Lucy; her friend Amber joined us for a while. After Broadway we went to Yellowstone and the Grand Tetons, and saw moose, and bears, and elk, and heard the newly introduced wolves howl.

There's a detailed diary of my time in the States with the RSC on my website www.littlejump.co.uk.

I write there about standing ovations, and as it's spreading like a bacillus in London I want to mention it. There is a curious, neurotic response in American audiences that impels them to stand and applaud at the end of a performance. Here, in the UK, this would be stimulated only by a uniquely magnificent show—and very, very rarely. When it happened in New York after—by that time—a very creaky performance of *A Midsummer Night's Dream* I knew it couldn't be a response to quality. So what prompted this behaviour? I'd noticed it when I first came to New York and I evolved a tentative theory. By the end of our American tour I was sure I was right: many people, not used to theatre, are bussed into town in parties for a Broadway treat, and pay enormous sums for a ticket. If, after seeing a show, you feel privately let down and disappointed, then the extortionate cost is painful. But if you can convince yourself that you are not competent to judge what you've just seen, and you notice a handful of punters cheering and raving (as there usually are) then to stand up in solidarity with them and praise the performance means that YOU HAVEN'T WASTED YOUR MONEY, after all.

My agency, William Morris, took itself off and closed in London. I had been surprised at their patience, their tolerance, since I hadn't made them a huge amount of money, and had turned down unappetizing work.

Only for a fleeting second did I think of writing round for employment.

So: what to do with the rest of my life? Devote it to Beauty and Truth, perhaps, to Keats' quest—find some Urn, Grecian or otherwise to contemplate? More about the Urn later—also about Beauty and Truth. Meanwhile I was… directing again.

*Twelfth Night: Clive Wood, Emma Fielding, the perils of cross-dressing*

# Once you taste blood

Directing again

**Out of the ether came a phone call** offering me *London Assurance* for the Irish-centred Juno Theatre Company.

One attraction was the version: re-invented so that one, key leading character would never be cast, but would be played by another member of the company—male or female—when available, by wearing a half mask. Minor characters (there's a whole-company scene at the end) would appear as sculpted heads on broomsticks, their words spoken by available on-stage actors changing voices. The other delight was the set: two, large four-faced boxes on wheels which could be re-positioned to convey changes of location. Brilliant. The play could be done with seven actors. (Was this Beautiful?) The play is a fair version of the 'old-man-who-should-know-better trying to marry an unsuitably-young-girl' story. (Therefore ageless and True, so perhaps Beautiful). I took it on. As a consequence I met an ex-schoolmaster, name of Denis Delahunt, who played Sir Harcourt Courtly, very well. We toured the play round home counties village halls, finishing at the Dublin Theatre Festival—it would be my sixth!

Denis knew of a north Islington pub theatre called The Rosemary Branch run by Cecilia Darker, a striking, energetic ex-dancer. Surely we could pool resources, energy, and put on shows together, there? To be restless and easily bored—yet having no power—is an interesting state. Neither Denis nor I had funds, so he made the case for asking actors to work for nothing—we wouldn't even give them tube fare—but tempting them with showy acting parts: it didn't work.

True, there were partial successes. And after Denis, I went on directing.

Three shows have a particular resonance for me. Once, coming home and turning on the radio, I heard most of a mesmerizing play about a mistress and her ex-slave meeting as gladiators for a fight to the death. There were indeed female gladiators in old Rome. With difficulty I reached the author, Deborah Cook, and she agreed to have the play staged at the Rosemary Branch. The entire play is about the two women—the aristocrat and the slave (they're top of the Fights bill)—steadily arming them-

*Making Dickie Happy, Tristan Bates Theatre*

selves in their dressing room, talking over how life's chances got them into this pickle. I received my most cherished review of all time for this show.

The critic, Howard Loxton, observed that, since the women started the play in street gear and finished fully armed, there must have been some sort of director's hand in it. Yet the actresses seemed to wander about the stage, in their dressing cell, as if entirely motivated by their own whim. 'Just as if the play hadn't been directed at all.' Yet, yet the girls finished facing the open arena door, in a blinding light, bloodthirsty crowd baying, knowing, as they stepped out, that only one of them could survive.

I have always cherished reviews that rated a show a knockout, but didn't look directed. It's not so easy to pull that one today. Directors know that, unless they do backflips to be noticed, it will be said 'Of course, with such a brilliant cast, the thing played itself—not much need for the director to do anything, really.'

The play, *The Main Event* (part of a double bill *Sex, Death and a Baked Swan)* was superbly costumed and set by Kevin Freeman, and there was the most chilling, thrilling, just-audible undulating sound of the mass audience in the arena enjoying the supporting bill of fights. At the beginning of the play there is a stage-manager character showing the women to their quarters, and I got the actor to assume a very heavy limp, and a disturbing, PTSD delivery, to suggest he was an ex-fighter. Curiously not understood by management or author—but grasped by Loxton in his review—it gave the event an unsettling, eerie start: brilliantly played by Rob Pomfret, who will appear again.

Then there were the Jeremy Kingston plays. *Oedipus at the Crossroads* had wowed a lunchtime audience in 1977. For an age I'd wanted to put *Crossroads* together with Sophocles' own *Oedipus Tyrranos.* That would make stark the folly of believing in oracles; by implication, it also rubbished Freud. All good research shows that incest between mother and son is the least common; and is most common (of course) between brother and sister. Freud's hang-ups haven't been helpful. There's a strong biological sexual revulsion between mums and their boy children, and whatever incident messed up Freud's life, it has confused generations. Two shining truths, in Jeremy's witty script.

Even the Oracle at Delphi would have been pushed to predict that paying actors nothing, would get me an ex-BP oil executive to perform the Old Shepherd. Robert

The second play, *The Main Event*, takes us to the dressing room of a couple of *primae matronae* at the London Colosseum (not the Coliseum, note: these divas are gladiatrix not sopranos). Rob Pomfret plays a limping stagehand (is he a survivor from the arena?) forced by some rather nasty flooding to put both stars together, despite contractual stipulations. Thus Claudia, a patrician senator's wife turned fighter, finds herself encountering her former slave whom she named Greeneyes. Fliss Walton makes a very haughty but no less human Claudia and Toni Darlow a spirited Greeneyes. The slave identifies herself as Welsh and in earlier days was an accomplished harpist, but this is a racial identification rather than location, as she was clearly not reared there. She has previously been her mistress's slave in Rome and has an English lower-class accent, equivalent to her slave-girl Latin.

As the two of them prepare to face each other in the arena we learn their back-story: how love made a grand lady into a gladiatrix; how a slave sentenced to the arena for murder won her survival. Deborah Cook offers us intriguing situations and her historical research seems faultless but these are in no way antiquarian pieces. She also has much to say about sisterhood and marriage. Women today may not have such low legal status as under Roman law but you never feel that they are talking from a distant past since men really haven't changed all that much.

I can't pay director Robert Gillespie a bigger compliment than to say you don't notice his direction. It is a different matter with set and costumes: Kevin Freeman has cleverly transformed the space to create an atmospheric setting for both plays, aided by Stephen Ley's lighting, while for the second play sound designer David Peto has provided a track of clanging doors and noisy spectators to remind us how close we are to the blood and sawdust.

These plays might not work so effectively in large venues but are ideal pieces for intimate spaces and make a well-matched pair. They provide three good parts for women of which these actresses make the most.

*Howard Loxton* © Sunday 1st May 2005

Pennant Jones, a singular individual, had taken early retirement; had just launched his new career playing Harold Shipman—and was very, very moving as the Old Shepherd. Robert is, miraculously, an expert on both Shakespeare and Samuel Beckett, has at least three ideas a week—sometimes three a day—some of which are brilliant: he invented a *Comedy of Errors* for seven actors (which I directed) where the twins meet each other in mirrors. We've maintained a professional relationship, on and off, to this day. (Robert was at uni, I was in rep, with Ian McKellen.)

The rest of the cast was an uneven—but oddly powerful—mix of talents; the set, so inadequate and unfinished that I turned it upside down, with good effect.

Fortunately the Fates grinned, sheepishly, and Jeremy's critic colleagues were generous. They gave the play remarkably good reviews, given the messiness of the acting; we got away with it.

The version of the Greek *Oedipus* was not inspired, but honest. Daringly, I tried it with just one chorus member. The Sophocles shook and shimmered with questions about how far man—humans—can take charge of their lives. Oedipus, a fit young chap overtaken by bad luck; without fault except, perhaps, for a hasty temperament. As a helpless infant his life is re-directed by parents holding a sincerely held—but disastrous—belief. It's of interest that Sophocles, as a youth, fought to save Athens from the invading Persians—and Athens won: it had been a time of great hope, of optimism. By the time that Sophocles wrote *Oedipus Tyrranos,* Athens was becoming tyrannical itself, and a regional pain in the butt: you can read the *Oedipus* play as a big STOP sign—a warning: no matter how well-born and seeming-lucky you are, events—and flaws in your character—can trip you, stop you in your propitious tracks, kill you.

Sadly, Sophocles seems to have lived long enough to see Athens smashed—by fellow Greeks, naturally. People won't be told.

In Jeremy's invention (the second half of the evening) young Oedipus is humorous, just out of university and—instead of killing the angry old warrior he meets on the road—contrives to have a chat with him. Natalie Haynes, witty and shrewd champion of the Classics, caught the show and expressed her delight at this alternative way for armed men to sort out their 'issues'.

We humans are offered autonomy, Jeremy suggests, some degree of control over our own lives. The enemy—the existential threat—isn't a mysterious cosmic power, perhaps unknowable, perhaps invincible: it's other humans with agendas. Jeremy puts the Delphic Oracle—its priesthood—in control of a statewide apparatus: instructions are fed through apparatchiks to every city, town and hamlet in Greece. Tiresias, the magic man, is supreme leader—ayatollah and Pope in one wrapper. He is mortal, but canny—has a smart side-kick learning the business, so there will be continuity for the regime. It's an unsettling play, but funny. The threatening monsters are human, not divine; perhaps we can save ourselves from them?

*Making Dickie Happy,* the other Kingston play, is a deft comedy of manners, and completely out of reach to a jobbing, semi-pro actor, and quite impossible for an amateur, except of the scarcest kind. After a number of par-boiled shows I knew I had to

SEX, DEATH AND A BAKED SWAN

Londinium c.200AD and three Roman women are determined to survive....

by Deborah Cook

The Rosemary Branch Theatre,
2 Shepperton Road, London
N1 3DT.

26 April-29 May
Previews from
15 April.

## The Arts

# Oh! Oedipus, you are saucy

Temptations and togas: Alex Hughes as Oedipus and Richard Earthy as Teiresias

### THEATRE

**Oedipus: a double bill**
Rosemary Branch, N1

**Rachel Halliburton**

FATE and farce join hands in this somewhat surreal double bill, which starts in the grip of deterministic doom-mongering, and ends in an innuendo-filled world of togas where the late Frankie Howerd wouldn't seem out of place. While the first play — Sophocles's Oedipus Rex — poses vast questions about the existence of rational man in a world he cannot control, Jeremy Kingston's comedy Oedipus at the Crossroads takes a saucy spin of the wheel of fortune, and reveals a king who is a closet queen, doped up prophets who don't get the munchies and an inconveniently maternal sheep.

Puzzled? You should be — for Times theatre critic Kingston's ribald retort to the ancient Greeks turns the whole Oedipus myth on its head by introducing a tragic hero (a sonorous Alex Hughes) who refuses to believe in fate. But would Apollo have been appalled at the — classically well-informed — variations, which show

Oedipus's supposed father buggering boys in order not to produce the son who will kill him, the Delphic oracle transformed into a sinister intelligence bureau and Oedipus himself as a man who gets touchy when people comment on his fat ankles.

Director Robert Gillespie's production flares into irreverent life for Kingston's play, after a rather solid and declamatory rendition of the Sophocles.

Sophocles, even more than other Greek playwrights, believed in treating audiences as if they were citizens there to debate his plays, yet while the cast members certainly involve the crowd, they seem frustratingly two-dimensional, treating Oedipus's dilemma as if it were a morbid costume drama rather than a visceral confrontation with forces that defy his intelligence and his morality.

By contrast, Kingston's own response could well have contended as a comedy in an Athenian festival. Less concerned with bottom humour than Aristophanes, his secular twists should bring a knowing grin even to those terminally obsessed with iambic trimeters.

● *Until 23 February. Box office: 020 7704 6665.*

pay the cast of *Dickie*. Just wishing, willing, wanting to act isn't enough. What makes the difference? I watched Lucy learn to place her fingers on a violin string in tune: I was in awe of that; that's harder than acting. All humans love, hate, envy, laugh, cry—nevertheless, it's not easy to become a competent *performer*. How's it done…?

Jeremy Kingston, luckily, was willing to back his own show; I signed up too, and Cecilia Darker made three. Of course we couldn't pay Equity rates (the Rosemary Branch has sixty seats) but our offer was good enough to attract surprisingly talented people.

The three salient personalities in *Making Dickie Happy* are Noel Coward, Agatha Christie and Lord Louis Mountbatten—when they were young—so that's tempting. Also, at this time Jeremy consented to publicly 'come out'. Way back he'd said to me 'Don't for one moment think I'm straight…' although he had been married, has two dearly beloved sons. Now in 2004 he decided to fanfare this in spectacular fashion in *The Stage*—which got us a hugely valuable, double-page splash—all for the sake of selling his show. The play flaunts these youthful, high profile people when they are very young and toiling on the baby slopes of love. Could there be a more perfect moment to show your amative hand?

Homosexuality was by now legal, of course, but still plenty of frissons were generated by stories like this, especially around prominent people. In the play there's a gorgeous scene between Noel and Louis about who fancies what and when. But it's the presence of a hunky young waiter that makes the play go round. All the navy lads and Noel have detoured to check out this prodigy: for straight male readers, think pursuing a rumour that a young Marilyn is waiting tables at a hotel in Shanklin, Isle of Wight, and is open to offers. This part was especially difficult to cast. He has few lines, but a deadly effect throughout the story and—right buttons pressed—gets enormous laughs; when indifferently played, the play goes lame. Re-enter Rob Pomfret to be spectacularly good as Cyril. The whole cast was wonderful.

Kevin Freeman designed a fabulous twenties setting for the other especially memorable scene in the play, when Christie and Coward meet by chance in the evening and engage in a close, acerbic literary debate—magically lit by gently glowing tables. Along with the fluid sex, it's another exhilarating strand in the play: Agatha and Noel's nuanced contest about ART. Full of Beauty and a generous dose of Truth.

The Mountbatten girls—2nd Countess Mountbatten and Lady Pamela Hicks—came to the show (with family); they collared me and—non-aggressively—remarked 'Louis wasn't gay, you know!' I simply grinned—because they'd clearly enjoyed the play. Ten thousand pounds, between three, it had cost us. We packed the theatre, Jeremy got raves, we had to put in an extra matinée—and we made our money back; we were a penny short on the divi and Jeremy coughed up the brass coin.

*'Here's looking at you, Cyril'*

# Brothers (& sisters) under the skin

## Cardboard Citizens, & The Arcola (1998-2009)

**And the phone rang again.** In Hackney, in an ex-police gymnasium, I was Luka in a re-imagined version of Maxim Gorki's *Lower Depths*. The gym was the HQ of Cardboard Citizens, a company founded by Adrian Jackson, making theatre and offering training in theatre skills to homeless people; the play is set in a homeless shelter. There were fourteen in the cast and we played a game with the audience of 'spot the pro'. Whenever Adrian produces a blockbuster show, he casts key parts from members of Equity—so half of us were professional, half homeless. Out of those, three or four actors confused the audience: pro or homeless?

I'd have worked for nothing. Adrian routinely presented his dramas to hostels and day centres, so was bound by statute: we all got the same flat rate. Cardboard Citizens was inspired by Augusto Boal's Forum Theatre; Boal empowered the voiceless in Brazil—Adrian was a disciple, and official translator. No two homeless stories are the same. The only thing I found in common, among the people who attended—young or old—was a readiness to learn a skill (and, possibly, ownership of a short fuse).

Memorable, was the Cits production of *Mincemeat*—in two incarnations. First, we devised it. It took flight for 6 performances in a derelict Robertson's jam factory near Tower Bridge. And then we brought it back for an unforgettable four week run in Curtain Road on top of Burbage's The Theatre—well, near enough.

*Mincemeat* is the true tale of a military operation in 1943 when a body, planted with misleading papers, was dropped in the sea off Huelva in Spain to fool the Germans. The Huns were never sure about where the invasion from North Africa was heading. A book and a film are based on this story, *The Man Who Never Was*. But the 'drowned' body's identity had always been a mystery. Steve Hudson played the Body, and I played Charlie (Chaplin), the Body's guide and mentor. Then, as we worked on the show, a historian confirmed that the corpse picked out from all the others in the morgue to be dropped in the Mediterranean was that of a homeless man, a vagrant, originally from Wales; at the end of his life this guy had hung around King's Cross. Just as extraordinary, there was one person still alive who'd handled the body: an undertaker. We filmed him: Steve (the Body) and I had a conversation with the undertaker's image projected, eerily, on a crumbling wall in the jam factory. The high-ups, in war-time, had chosen a homeless man with no family—so there was no one to complain, or to fight for compensation; a smart choice—for a classic, successful piece of deception. The nobs stuffed his corpse into a marine officer's uniform and… dumped him in the sea. At the end, I spoke a version of Chaplin's speech from *The Great Dictator.* It was magnificent coarse theatre: I mean that there was a rough, muscular directness in our performances. We achieved subtlety with large, but well-chosen, strokes. It was the best of community theatre. At one of Robert Pennant Jones' imaginative Christopher Marlowe presentations in the ancient Rose Theatre a gentleman, not of my acquaint-ance, cosied himself up to me on the front row and said 'Saw you in *Mincemeat—* wonderful show. I thought I was going to hate it… all that revolutionary rubbish at the beginning—and then when you stopped and changed direction—magnificent, very moving.' It was Charles Spencer of the Daily Telegraph; he gave us five stars.

Adrian's method fascinates me. He assumes, without contradiction, that anyone can achieve performance excellence—if they spend time. I've seen him work hours on a sequence of perhaps five lines with an untrained, but willing, person and simply not accept that she or he would be anything but excellent by performance day. Each of us had to be strong-minded to put up with that. Most people throve, but every now and then someone would wilt under the strain and explode. But it was wonderful to have a nob—an educated, widely knowledgeable toff, Cambridge educated—show absolute confidence in your ability; simply know you would get there; as if it were a divine ordinance. Some say he's harsh; I have always felt that Adrian has a touch of genius. The end of what he achieves is intensely benign. Not everything he tries works, of course—why would it?—but when it does, it's unique, in a class of its own; fine.

I was directing at the Arcola Theatre when the Twin Towers were smashed. In New York I'd found a play by Adam Rapp, *Ghosts in the Cottonwoods:* scary, dark, ghoulish—but very funny. My young lead actor casually wandered in to say, 'There's something strange happening.' Outside in the Arcola lobby the boss, Mehmet Ergen, had stuck a TV set. We took a break; I strolled out to look. Centre of frame was a structure in the sky pouring flames and black smoke. The channel cued a replay and I watched a plane fly into the guts of a tall building; many times.

Rapp's plays are disturbing; visceral, too bloody for many stomachs. *Ghosts* is about a family buried deep in the Appalachian woods, stuck in the 1970s. There is in it an American icon, a backwoodsman, part film character, part frontier hero—a leathery loner who sews up a gunshot wound on stage, then makes poetical love to his hostess. It's John Wayne parodied to the ultimate. Entirely hilarious. This part, Newt Yardley, was brilliantly played by (experienced amateur) Denis Delahunt. Denis was most successful the more a character was unlike himself. It's a quirk I've noticed from my earliest days in theatre. Many actors flounder when asked just to—be. In our production of *Passion Play* Denis was cast as an adulterous husband, and he got really cross with himself when he just couldn't be believable, genuine. But as Newt Yardley, he deserved an Oscar.

At the end of the play there is a note of hope—a young couple attempting to dash clear, out of the woods, away from the spooky, half-civilised family tribe that sucks on them. But the hope is killed, poisoned by a miscarriage; the oozing, bloody product visible—strictly according to author's instructions, and deliberate.

A writer's metaphor for the state of the nation, perhaps, or for some of the nation? Anyway, it was too much for the reviewers; they found it pitiless. A most spectacularly good set, perhaps the best I've ever had made, was built by Jon Bausor.

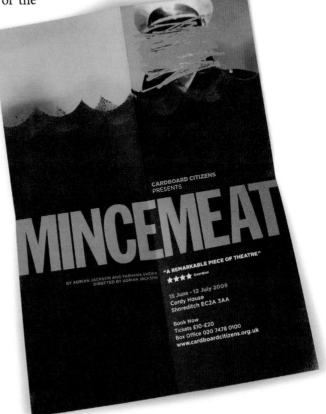

*Mincemeat,
immersive
theatre*

**New Tricks.** Once more the phone rang and I was asked if there was the remotest possibility of my sounding Italian. I had no agent, I was not expecting to work, but the caller was a respected woman casting-director who remembered. I said I did French, I did German but… 'Call in anyway,' she said. I guessed she was in trouble. I dropped in at Mays Court and executed the text in my most extreme version of Brando as Vito Corleone. I took forever to speak a single sentence. Nobody laughed. It was taken seriously. The show was the BBC's *New Tricks* in an episode called 'Roots', and it became quite clear that all the real Italians had, for one reason or another, disappointed. I was asked back, to meet the director, Brian Grant. He began, 'Robert I wonder if you could…' 'Speak it a bit quicker?' I finished his sentence. 'Please.' So I did. And I ended up murdering my best friend on an allotment over wine and a wartime quarrel. It was sheer pleasure to work with Tamzin Outhwaite. That was 2013.

**Joan of Arc:** 'My agent wants to know,' asked an actress working in one of my productions, 'do you still act?' 'I do,' I said, 'if asked.' Which led to my being flown to the pretty medieval town of Loches in France to play a priest for a group of Mormons from Utah making a film of the life of Joan of Arc. I wondered why Mormons would go for Joan. And then I realised that the 'historically proven' miracles in Joan's short life boosted the Mormons' own pitch perfectly. We were treated handsomely. They offered to pay for a 'plus-one' (unprecedented in my show-biz experience), so Anna came out for the jolly, and we enjoyed a scrumptious chateau-and-limestone-cave-laden wander back to London.

**Broken:** Following my skirmish with the Catholic Church as long ago as *A Consumer Guide to Religions* (page 29) I hadn't expected Jimmy McGovern to offer me such a spectacular opportunity to highlight for the public a deeply sad, centuries old, aspect of the Church's very bad behaviour.

Oddly enough, I fancy that just as I was cast as the transvestite Alec in *Mary's Wife* because actors with a reputation to protect turned the part down (Alec was a really fat, juicy part on prime time television) I believe I got the opportunity to play a paedophile priest opposite Sean Bean in *Broken* because no other performer of stature wanted to do it. It's one of the very best-written scenes I've ever had the delight to perform in my entire career as an actor. It wasn't possible, I discovered, to speak any other words but those set down by McGovern—they're perfectly chosen for what they need to do.

I'm not the first actor to notice that many members of the audience have difficulty in distinguishing the traits of the written character from the life of the actor himself. Many actors—through the ages—have for this reason avoided taking on roles which could damage their suitability for other work. Of course, if you make a speciality of playing baddies or eccentrics (as Donald Pleasence did) that's another matter. You'll earn a crust doing that.

Father Matthew was deeply, but entirely realistically, vile.

I was startled at how articulate and open and frank Jimmy McGovern was when he spoke in detail at a BAFTA event about his layered and complex life-long engagement with the Church.

Clean, fresh air. It's what the drama's for—so I think.


***Lost In London:*** Now I had an agent again, and he got me to meet Woody Harrelson at the old Central St. Martin's College of Art. Surrounded by a roomful of people, creating and chatting, Woody started to trade lines of dialogue with me: he wanted a taxi driver who was a hundred years old and not as zippy as he used to be—but that was dreary, so what about making him a slow-liver on principle. So I offered 'It's not the destination that matters, but the journey that counts', and 'we are all in the hands of the goddess Kali who is both a creator and destroyer.' I was hired. The entire story of *Lost in London* is an apology by Woody to his wife for a terrible night, years back, when he featured in the London tabloids and came close to divorce. Woody liked to quote Mark Twain: 'Humor is tragedy plus time.'

Not only was the film rehearsed for months, it was rehearsed between 11p.m. and four in the morning because… because Woody wanted to shoot the whole ninety minutes IN A SINGLE TAKE and SCREEN IT LIVE. Since the action flowed from sets

*Exorcising Joan: RG and Milly Thomas*

built in the old art college to nearby streets and back again, the traffic could only be controlled in the dead of night. Astonishingly, it was the first film he'd ever directed.

Harrelson is one of the most generous people I've ever known. I was posted a framed copy of my page of script (with the alterations), given a hoody (which Lucy wears in New York) and a fat booklet of production stills.

Uniquely heroic, however, in my eyes is John Hembrough: he hand-held the entire ninety-minute movie as it was going out live. As a comedy adventure it stands up pretty darn well. The best scene is a hilarious bust-up between Woody and Owen Wilson—but the show is full of delights.

# Arts

# 'It was the worst night of my life'

Fifteen years ago, Woody Harrelson found himself in London on the run from police. Now he's turning that wild night into a single-take film and beaming it live into cinemas. **Ryan Gilbey** joins the hell-raising director and multiple Jesuses on set for the final run-throughs

I t is almost midnight on Monday and Woody Harrelson is showing me around the set for his directorial debut, Lost in London. An unused building in the centre of the capital has been commandeered to house assorted locations, including a club with burlesque trimmings where gold statues dangle from the ceiling and a police station complete with cells and interview rooms.

There's just one problem: Harrelson doesn't seem to know where he is. "Hold on," he mumbles. "I lost track of what floor we're on. Where's the ...?" His bleariness has always been a considerable part of his charm: that sleepy Texan drawl, that quizzical gaze, half-amazed and half-sceptical. But padding around in tracksuit bottoms and a fleece, his eyes faintly bloodshot, the 55-year-old actor looks positively somnambulant. He smiles as he recognises his cinematographer, Nigel Willoughby. "Nigel, where's the room where I get booked by the cops?" An affectionate chuckle: "Next floor up, Woody."

No wonder Harrelson is dazed. In making Lost in London, he has taken on the biggest challenge of a 32-year career that has stretched from the sitcom Cheers to Natural Born Killers, from True Detective to the Hunger Games series. Shortly before we meet, it is announced that he will play Han Solo's mentor in a new Star Wars spin-off due next year. But tonight he can't think about anything except why he decided to write, direct and star in a movie about the worst night of his life – and then shoot it all in one unbroken 100-minute take in 14 locations across London, complete with chase sequences on foot and by car.

So far, so Victoria. But, while Harrelson was inspired by that German hit, which used the one-take, single-camera approach to tell the tale of a frantic night in Berlin, he needed to go one better. "That film is genius," he says. "It's an inspiring work of art. Ours is a different animal." Willoughby says: "It was me who told Woody we had to do it all with one camera. He said, 'Victoria did that. How can we improve?'" Harrelson then came up with the idea of combining elements of theatre and film by live streaming

**'There's something about the terror of making this film that I love'**

Lost in London to cinemas as it is being shot. "I'm an adrenaline junkie," he grins. "There's something about the terror of it that I love. It's keeping me up at night."

Though the movie can't claim to be the first to be broadcast as it is being shot – that honour goes to My One Demand by the art-film trio Blast Theory, which was transmitted online and to a single cinema in Toronto last year – it is certainly the largest-scale project of its kind; it will hit more than 500 screens in the US on Thursday evening and one in central London in the early hours of Friday morning.

The film has its origins in a disastrous evening that Harrelson spent in London in 2002. It began with a spat with his wife before progressing to a raucous evening at the nightclub Chinawhite. "It was hellish," he says ruefully. "I'm never going to that club again." By the time it was over, he had smashed up a taxi and fled the scene of the crime to hail another cab, hotly pursued by his first driver and the police, who arrested him on suspicion of causing criminal damage. "I was a freaking idiot," he told newspapers at the time.

*Rehearsing: L Woody, R John Hembrough with steadicam*

***Peterloo* and Mike Leigh:** Working with Mike Leigh on the film of *Peterloo* can't be compared with any other theatre or film experience.

On my first day on the film Mike reminded me that we'd first met, way back, in the same episode of *Maigret,* and how the rest of the cast had been niggled that he was the only one of us to get to Belgium (or was it France) to be filmed on a canal boat.

*Peterloo* is Mike's epic about the Manchester massacre of 1819. The most astonishing aspect of the process was how much of his time Mike was prepared to devote to each performer, working one to one; no matter the size of the part. Mike sat with me, and with his own pen, on his own scrap of paper, devised a genealogy for my (invented) Cheshire Magistrate. Over a number of sessions I distilled my final persona from three, beginning with a list of eleven (real) people that Mike had approved (I can even reveal that in 1745, as a little boy, I saw Bonnie Prince Charlie leave Manchester, sent off by cheering and weeping crowds).

One young actor, making up the rear in a line of a couple of dozen mounted hussars, complained that for all he had to portray—he didn't even think he'd be in the final cut—surely he could just have been asked to turn up on the day, mount his steed, and do his couple of shots—instead of spending weeks going to the National Archive at Kew, downloading and reading volumes of historical background mailed to him by our (inspiring) historian Dr Jacqueline Riding: but that's just what I loved about Mike's approach to his project.

I read the research papers, at home, for eight or nine weeks. I worked on the film (on and off) for seven months and gave birth, profoundly midwived by Mike, to a single, short speech in the final movie.

Pushed, I'd say Mike's method is not merely a single discipline but a resilient compound of devising, some improvisation, a pinch of Stanislavski and a salutary dose of Brechtian alienation. The experience was so singular I kept a detailed diary.

Acquaintances have suggested to me how left-wing Mike's work is: they say it's raw, or socially proscribed, even pervading a slight whiff of boiled cabbage. To me it's the work of a defiant outsider; quintessentially. And it's what I like so much about Mike. It isn't obviously in the cards for someone like him to put together such a mighty oeuvre, to be known and discussed everywhere film matters.

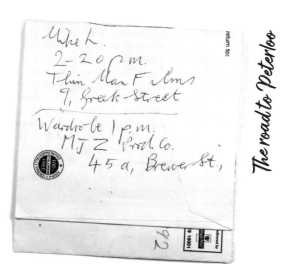

*Mike Leigh in Maigret, 1963*

And I admire the fact that he refuses to dent his own, peculiar, rules of engagement. 'We're going to make a film for seventeen and sixpence' he said to the group of Magistrates on the first day. And he did.

Almost time for the…

# Finale: Beauty and Truth?

**Some of my close friends at RADA** had been to university. Several of them had read quite a few books. Aside from exploratory trips over the two years in my car to Oxford, to Blenheim or to Bath, we not infrequently sat through half the night, examining and explaining everything—as one does. Kerry Jordan from New Zealand was a philosopher, and Margaret Collins, from Perth (Oz), a walking littnut. As aspiring actors, we were in the arts field so I listened-in to the talk about Beauty and Truth. I quickly learned that this association of ideas arose from the musings of highly respected poets and aesthetes. Keats was a name that came up, and Ruskin. I knew of Keats by name; finis. I was very young.

Sixty or so years later I thought I would look for the origin of these stimulating conversations. Yes, the concept of the lively tension existing between Beauty and Truth comes from a poem by John Keats. It's called *Ode on a Grecian Urn*. The imagined urn has on it a scene of 'love about to—possibly—happen'. Here is the final stanza—you may know the last two lines:

*O Attic shape! Fair attitude! with brede*
*Of marble men and maidens overwrought,*
*With forest branches and the trodden weed;*
*Thou, silent form, dost tease us out of thought*
*As doth eternity: Cold Pastoral!*
*When old age shall this generation waste,*
*Thou shalt remain, in midst of other woe*
*Than ours, a friend to man, to whom thou say'st,*
*"Beauty is truth, truth beauty,—that is all*
*Ye know on earth, and all ye need to know."*

This poem, I note, is still studied. The story on the urn freezes an event which might end in many ways. It prompts, in the reader, fertile invention, and perhaps a desire to complete the story—how they do this will depend on their inclination to optimism, romance, dullness or despair. (Anna believes it's a reflection on the transience of love, and life). Beauty and Truth are not equivalent, of course, they are not interchangeable. And mostly, these days, scholars think the last two lines are a load of total bollocks. But more to the point, you will not find two people who will agree on the precise, heady mix of Beauty and Truth in the case of any piece of art.

Tim Turnbull has written a punchy, funny *Ode on a Grayson Perry Urn* which matches the openness and ambiguity of the Keats original.

My clever RADA friends' introspections, all those years ago, on Beauty and Truth distilled into one perplexing thought: how can you tell if a piece of art is good or bad? I found myself at the keyboard again… could I tell some Truth about some key aspects of being alive?

*One good urn deserves another*

# Death

**I had wondered if there was...** but could not think of... a single, modern text which dealt with death, Truthfully.

One June day in the year 2000 I put an actress, a screen and a bag of props in my small car and drove to Reading University to play *My Heart* before a highly intelligent audience of every age. I wrote it because I wanted to address the last taboo. It seemed to me that English society had—just about—accepted the ordinariness, the normality of sex, but all around me people carried on as if death was optional. In America, 150 years was already on offer; immortality, a few years away...

Grants for theatre enterprises are available, but you're likely to croak before you get the money. Your baby, your pet idea has to fit into a narrow slot of 'wanted' projects—of course—a script about death looked still-born.

So I telephoned Vicars and club secretaries and local activists; I offered them a deal: let us have your venue free, and you can keep all the takings for your own pet project—we helped complete a village hall. Every taker was, in practice, generous and let us have a slice of the price of entry. We operated in London, and within driving distance of London.

The adventure began in 1990 in the bay window of a semi-detached house in Neasden owned by the fellow who kicked off the Natural Day of the Dead, and wrote the *Natural Death Handbook.* He was Nicholas Albery—of that distinguished stable of theatre entrepreneurs (there was once an Albery Theatre). I telephoned him and, provided I ordered his book, he let us initiate our show at his house. At the end of his secular Day of the Dead event (modelled after Mexico's) he invited celebrants to stay on and watch a show. Lit by a standard and some table lamps we acted *My Heart* for the first time. Nicholas whipped round and handed us twenty-five quid. A bright woman, a mature divinity student at Reading Uni, watched—and so we went to Reading.

The story is of an old chap (me) waiting by the telephone for news of his heart transplant. The phone keeps ringing, but it's never the right message. Jo Girlestone played nine different parts—blokes as well—changing miraculously on stage behind the screen; she was wonderful (pics page 206, 236). We toured without a stage man-ager by using a foot switch to cue the telephone, whenever we were on stage together.

Eventually, the NHS hired us—for proper union money!—to perform for their palliative care volunteers. Especially memorable… we fascinated one particular nurse with our drama, and she kept coming. Could it be that she felt we were telling the Truth about that aspect of human existence to which she'd given her own life? Is that what brought her to show after show?

We'd probably still be on the road if Jo hadn't gone travelling. I'm not sure the play was Beautiful—it got a lot of laughs and it had a tragi-comic twist at the end—I believe it was the Truth, though.

Lucy directed *My Heart* at Uni and I stayed away, to avoid looming (Anna said it went well). In the end Lucy decided directing wasn't what she wanted to do in the theatre. And I said that what she did want—which is to make happen, produce, organize—means she'll never be out of work.

In America, I asked around—when you guys are immortal, where will you all put yourselves? How feed the kids, where will you house them? Where's the room, the space, the capacity? Have you done the math? Response was a shrug, mostly; sometimes a line or two about conquering space. God came up.

There's been some movement, on death, since. Optional? Mmm… maybe not.

Twelve days before she died, Lucy's Hungarian grandmother (my mother) held her new born grandchild in her arms—glowing with pleasure. No hint in the photo of this enchanting moment that the last seven years of her marriage were a Strind-

*My Heart, Jo Girdlestone, RG*

bergian nightmare. At the age of seventy—it hit her hard—she realised there'd be no second chance; no handsome hussar to scoop her up onto his mettlesome nag and ride her off to re-start a more romantic, a better life—the polar opposite to living all her days with an accountant. She punished my father for denying her that alternative life back home in Hungary, with her young officer. Yet, at her funeral, my father had the effrontery to write on his card 'To Magda, with love, celebrating fifty-two years of happy married life.' Why?

I'm sure this was the jab in the ribs that provoked me to write *Love, Question Mark* which is about

# Love, Sex & Marriage

**When relationships break down**—I was at RADA when I first noticed this—the collapse is widely treated as if it happens because of a—a 'mistake,' because of some error: the couple-forming system is believed to be very sound, but prone to fail. So the advice is—be more careful, take counselling, read self-help books and, next time, you can get it 'right'.

People do not cross the road to see plays about steady, uneventful, undramatic marriage-for-life pursued with unwavering fidelity—the couple having had their first physical contact only with each other. Statistically, that category in the pie-charts of human conduct—I would think—is microscopically small; perhaps invisible—is it non-existent? Then why is it thought to be normal—or something to aim at? Whereas… 'Cheating' partners make prominent copy.

Rosemary Hill sat me down one evening, when I first knew her, in her flat in Lansdowne Crescent. She'd had one son through a marriage, and now had a boy of four and a little girl of two by a very high ranking radio, then TV, producer at the BBC. Rosemary pointed at a fire-side seat and said, 'Donald came home one evening, a little late, and sat right there, on that seat—there. He told me he had something to say to me. He hoped he hadn't seemed a little odd, the last few days, but he'd been struggling with something important. But at last it was resolved. Towards dawn, God had spoken to him and had told him that it was his duty to go to Australia and start television there… taking with him a nineteen year old girl.' Rosie was a very funny woman, and laughed and laughed.

She wore two heart necklaces. I asked what they were. There were twenty or more miniature hearts of different kinds strung on each necklace—they were not folk art, no, she said. Each celebrated a passionate encounter; the hearts were a scorecard—she'd been a pioneer, then, in New York. Rosemary had been a junior stage manager for Olivier at the New Theatre during the war and she'd married her boss, David Kentish, a drinking man. Touring America, she broke with him and came back with two heart necklaces. She wasn't 'morally degenerate'—she was an enthusiast, she liked what she did. After a productive life, she drank herself to death.

*Love, Question Mark* came to be written to shine a light into a fairy story…

In the play, I brought Maria over from Argentina to ask her a few questions. Maria is a prostitute, so I thought she would know a few things, especially about men.

I had better explain. I'd written a stage duologue about a guy of some years who, after a long and largely uneventful marriage, loses his wife. Looking forward to a serene third age, he gets a tremendous shock. He realises that the shapes women make still affect him. Because he has money he avoids the tedium, and degradation, of hanging about bars and places for hours in the hope of lifting someone out of their customary sphere and steering her to between his sheets; or if she's not fussy, spreading her on top of them. Through channels—the doorman of a hotel—this guy Michael acquires a list; it's global. He sticks in a pin and in walks *Maria* from Buenos Aires, to his pleasant apartment.

The first act of the drama shows some of the many shades of love on the market—call it attachment, or however you like to think of it; and a limited tutorial on selling sex. The second act is Michael and Maria trying to get close. He has made a promise to himself that he will stay detached; it doesn't work. He wants Maria to stick around; her intelligence, her personality, her beauty and charm are… Slowly, her power over him grows—she senses that. They bargain, they explore deals. Then an unexpected telephone call reveals that she has two kids. A boy and a girl, and they're on their way over. She'll have to take care of them herself, now. Can Michael —he's never had a child—adjust to this drastic, threatening, alteration to his settled life? This is not the relationship he had in mind…

Chemistry

The fairy tale—wherever you travel—suggests we are a naturally monogamous species of ape. But just think of the art we'd lack if we were. Anna Karenina wouldn't make sense—she'd merely be a patient with a clinical condition, needing treatment; that's all. *Eastenders* would be un-writable.

Most storytellers don't take sides: they delight us with the many shades of infidelity; it's where the money and fame lies. And, globally, quite a few societies simply deliver sex wholesale, in a marketplace dominated by males.

Yet people have persisted in inventing complex rules of conduct around the way we humans should mate. Mary Whitehouse was our last serious public moralist and she seemed, to many, to have a valid picture of how we should be, sexually. I never entirely grasped what she felt we should aim for—or what she thought was possible for us, or best for us, or good for us—for men and women. She struck me as confused, muddled. But she had a go.

Whitehouse's moral guidelines are based on what scientists describe as 'second order' explanations. For example: 'Why does that man keep breaking into houses and stealing things? Because he is a bad person.' Even as a child, I didn't find this convincing, I questioned this.

Take *Anna Karenina*… you could try to account for Anna's conduct because of her father's aloofness, always away on state business with little time for her. Or, perhaps it was that her ambitious mother's preoccupation with running a successful salon, and her constant intriguing, meant that Anna was brought up by nannies? Could be… But infinitely more important is the fact that—for very good reasons —Anna Karenina changes her mating preferences. Is she right to do that? Society's rules (constantly changing) censure her, but her deepest instincts are unfailing. She feels she's breeding from the wrong man. Men and women mate opportunistically, though for women there's the added complication of time out for childbirth and child rearing. That has led to the most spectacular example of a large animal species successfully getting its genes into the next generation. The fleeting moral rules of Karenina's Russia make her tragic. Today, she'd be hardly five minutes' gossip.

So as to get away from second order explanations, the kind that great art seduces us with, I wrote Act One of *Love, Question Mark* shot through with hormones and neurotransmitters, amygdalas, oxytocin and a nucleus recumbens. Suppose you're a heterosexual male, post-pubescent, and are treated to an image of a nubile, unclothed female then, via the light entering your eyes, you'll experience a warm sensation, mediated by receptors in your brain, which you're helpless to hold out against. Your culture may help to avoid an atrocity, but your response is inescapable.

At last—a first order explanation for the effects of what—love?

Today, I'd add a bit about the vagus nerve and the powerful dialogue between your gut and your brain as you size up a mating opportunity.

In *Love, Question Mark,* Maria was played by Clare Cameron. I couldn't pay Equity rates, so the fee limited our scope, and the two of us scratched our heads, puzzled how to find an actor to play opposite her. In a perfect world, he'd be as old as I was then. I was looking for the poetry of desperation: that tenacious wanting that stays with male humans almost till death.

Clare, a most energetic person, set up auditions. The part of Michael is so huge you need health and fitness to attempt it. We finished by casting an ex-Harrovian Lt. Colonel: Stuart Sessions of the Ghurkas; too young—and gay. But diamond keen. Stuart was entirely stage-struck, so was willing to put up with the most exhausting crash course in how not to be embarrassing on stage. Lucy, my daughter, helped give it life at the New Diorama—she produced; that knocked off the roughest early knobs and nodules. We took flight at the Old Sorting Office in Barnes and at The Courtyard Theatre, Hoxton, and then soared for four weeks at The Tabard (now the Chiswick Playhouse).

The reviews were more perceptive than I expected. Is the public narrative changing? Is the whopper about monogamy, like the Cheshire cat's grim grin, losing its potency?

You can try to understand men and women by re-reading Tolstoy or Barbara Cartland—or John Donne or Will Shakespeare or Simone de Beauvoir or *Private Lives* or *A Doll's House*—it may be a help: it's certainly enjoyable. But these, to me, are wonderful, permanent sea-going adventures, with no land in sight. But watch Attenborough's magical explorations of the natural world—or listen to Farming Today on BBC Radio 4—and a light begins to shine.

Ray Cooney's *Run For Your Wife* and Ibsen's *A Doll's House* are both successful stage dramas with women at the centre. They're different, though. I would like to be able to distinguish between them. One is True and hideous, perhaps; the other True

*War, love, death:*
*The Red Baron*

and Beautiful. *Love, Question Mark* seemed to me to be Truthful. Was it Beautiful?

I find $E = mc^2$ very comforting. E is for energy, m for mass and c is the speed of light. It describes how energy and mass are equivalent and can turn into each other. It's True and very Beautiful, and always gets good reviews. I suppose it was my early interest in science that made me wonder if our mating habits could be understood beyond ideas like 'Good and Evil'.

So, is Art just entertainment; pleasing decoration; froth? Not explanatory—at all?

From birth, all our genes tell us to do is 'seek advantage'! Each time I meet a fellow human the three Fs kick in—I have a choice: I am given the chance to Feed, to Fight or F… Fall in love. 'That is all ye know on earth, and all ye need to know.' Question is, which combination will best help get my genes into the next generation? The rest is culture, imagination, inventiveness. There's drama there, I think. And that's what *Love, Question Mark* is about and why I wrote it.

# War

**War was to be next.** There are true accounts of women following their husbands into war by dressing up as men. Not so difficult in the days when soldiers didn't change their gear or freshen up more than two or three times a year. I wrote a text based on such a woman, and we—Clare, Stuart and I—began work on it: 'Lt. Colonel' Stuart was very helpful there.

It's such a daunting canvas, though, war, and the most bewildering question. *La Grande Illusion,* the 1937 Jean Renoir film, is my vintage, and I once saw it and was told that it's about the futility of war; but it isn't. There's nothing futile about war. It's a thing we do; have always done; it's a very important thing we do. It might be worth asking—is it inescapable?

I remember when Lucy was small and we were going through a book of world cats and she was naming them; and when she said a cheetah was a leopard I pulled her up, firmly, and an onlooker told me off for being unfair to her. And I was reminded, suddenly, that our chief design fault—us humans—is that we have to learn everything from scratch as we emerge from the womb—often with a piercing wail! Lucy was

The Red Baron, Royal Air Force Museum

never bombed and she has to take it from me that it's no fun—not really. Anna and I know enough about war (though neither of us was physically damaged by it) to convince Lucy that it's best to avoid it, if possible. But when we think of the wonderful discoveries and inventions war has brought on, the social progress, the good changes: what do we say? 1918: voting—just one dramatic alteration among many. And because our survival has been threatened, the pace, the pace of it, the speed of change in time of war is breathtaking.

Given the fascination with war stories in our trade, I wonder if we could remotely manage to get by without going to war? All those Westerns, those divings at dawns, those dam-bustings, those mounds of rubble and the great triumph of re-building; the media games all based on war.

Perhaps it would be good, nice to stop it, re-direct its energy, but would we cease to be ourselves—and would we get bored?

We never got round to performing the cross-dressing war story, but…

Recently, I'd discovered that Manfred von Richthofen, the WW1 German fighter pilot ace, changed his view of war. I wrote a piece about him and we launched it for a brief flight at the RAF museum, Hendon.

Manfred had become known as the Red Baron, because he painted his Albatros aeroplane red. In the play he is talking urgently about war… he's entirely sold on it at the start of the conflict, like the hero he was. Then, a much-loved pilot colleague was killed; and he himself only just survived a head wound. After that, bit by bit, he changed: he seemed to sicken of the slaughter to the point of wanting out. Then one day this super-skilful pilot was shot down… but in the strangest of circumstances: on that day he broke all his own rules of flying combat conduct; he pursued an enemy over Allied lines. Why Manfred acted the way he did, on the day of his death, is still a mystery.

When it comes to conflict resolution you can learn a certain amount from watching wolves run their lives, but the stars are the Bonobo chimps—they've cracked the business of avoiding trouble: ninety-five per cent of their waking time is spent in smooching each other up. So there's no time for much else.

One of the unexpected delights of being in rep at Ipswich all those years ago was the real-life lesson we all enjoyed on love, power, lust, creativity, variety, invention: a case came up in the local court… The wife of a prominent country gentleman was suing for divorce. Her husband was Mr Cobbold, a leading figure in the local brewing enterprise Tolly Cobbold (chairman or a director or both).

The wife told the court that it was the habit of her husband to harness her, naked, to the shafts of a Roman chariot and drive her round the grounds of their estate. He would playfully flick his whip at her to keep her going. It emerged that he had ordered the replica chariot to be made at a town forge (stimulating the local economy). When asked why it had taken her so long to make a complaint—she had been trotting round the grounds for nine years—his wife told the court that her education, at home, in the ways of men had been minimal and vague. She admitted that she was surprised when her husband, following their nuptials, made this request, but thought it might be a regular part of married life; expected, from a dutiful wife. She assumed her friends were participating in similar practices. None ever dreamt of speaking of such matters—then. Why was she suing for divorce, after all this time? She had grown tired of it; of the whole thing… and she wasn't getting any younger. It would be nice to try… a change.

I maintain this supports my idea that there's nothing to fix—you can't 'fix' relationships. There are variations. If it's bad, scram; don't expect miracles.

Anna and I have had the luckiest time; seventy something years of relative peace in a most quarrelsome part of the world; and we'll be sorry to leave Lucy watching as clouds threaten, blackening the horizon. We, our species, us lot, unfortunately, take after the other kind of chimpanzee.

The damnedest thing is, no matter how many individuals get killed, the sex drive is so magisterial that we've not only replaced the sacred dead, but—it's yet another bummer—we're covering our earth faster and faster with more of ourselves, exactly like a growth on a petri dish—about to run out of nutrients.

It might be that we have the best brains ever evolved in the universe: they are good enough to see that we can't grow—anything—limitlessly on a habitat with limitations. Hardly a sign of more than a handful of brains getting it, though. We still look over the mountain at the tribe in the valley below and wonder if we're strong enough to do them in, and grab everything they've got for ourselves. Those three Fs again. But there's an alternative to 'fight' and it isn't an 'f' word it's a 'c' word: C. C for-Co-operate…? Ah, but it's slow, a slow word, slow—so boring; *War* has much more fizz; it's much more exciting. Is there the slightest chance we could settle for boring…?

Curtain call

**As Lucy and I are both theatre people I shall end with this.**

Actors are not often particularly good company, I've found. I admire them for their courage: that determination to memorise huge swathes of another person's text —which anyone can do—to submit themselves to the drudgery of it. But then to quote, to voice the material as if it was the utterance of themselves—not themselves, but themselves subtly re-emphasised, transformed to evoke the habits of a person not-themselves—since they can shift, convincingly, from speaking words apt for a mediaeval monarch, one day, to those fitting a garrulous dustman the next: that is hard to do. Yet the best of us do it seemingly effortlessly. It's at its most successful when the trick doesn't show.

Most people haven't a clue how difficult it is to act well—not until, by some accident or chance, they try it themselves. Most miraculous of all is when a theatre practitioner of moderate intelligence becomes utterly convincing, on stage, as a nuclear physicist. And in the last, oh, thirty years the standard of acting in the UK has become quite superb.

If I could take you back to my first experience of watching actors on stage, you'd catch your breath at the difference in quality. It happened all the time… a performer would come on stage and I'd be obliged to look down until he or she went off. Nowadays you may disagree with an interpretation, perhaps the casting, but you don't wonder why on earth the person is in the trade at all. Much of it comes from the fading away of the stage super-star. Superb as some of them were, their overwhelming grandeur was a distortion. It's unimaginable, now, to come to rehearsal in a company and find someone 'doing a Wolfit'. The rest is training. Older actors would tell me, 'This drama school nonsense, Robert! I never went to drama school; you can't teach acting, you've either got it or you haven't.' Now, actors turn up before a show to warm up without being formally called.

We are living at a time of utterly wonderful theatre practice in the United Kingdom.

I'm really delighted to have lasted long enough to see it. I hope you are. Let us celebrate it!

*Prince Hal (later Henry V), Stratford-upon-Avon*

## Bottom's Dream

*"God's my life! Stolen hence and left me asleep! I have had a most rare vision. I have had a dream past the wit of man to say what dream it was. Man is but an ass if he go about to expound this dream. Methought I was—there is no man can tell what. Methought I was and methought I had—but man is but a patched fool if he will offer to say what methought I had."*

Was I dreaming…? Some days I wondered… As I was putting this book together, news of a pandemic was reaching me. Plague stalks Shakespeare's scenes, but the scale of our plague is new in my life. I shared Bottom's bewilderment. I was cancelling my theatre tickets.

For a while, perhaps, I thought, we shall return to the spell-binding craft of the single storyteller, making magic on his glowing screen, with his ten gestures and seven timeless props.

And there has been the partial lifting of our heavy tread on our planet, the only home we have—that's an unexpected gift. I thought of that blistering quarrel between Titania and Oberon in The Dream—a glorious piece of writing—in which she ascribes the world's sickness to their jarring relationship; how the discord between herself and Oberon has overthrown nature's good balance:

> *"…Therefore the winds, piping to us in vain,*
> *As in revenge, have suck'd up from the sea*
> *Contagious fogs; which falling in the land*
> *Have every pelting river made so proud*
> *That they have overborne their continents:*
> *The ox hath therefore stretch'd his yoke in vain,*
> *The ploughman lost his sweat, and the green corn*
> *Hath rotted ere his youth attain'd a beard;*
> *The fold stands empty in the drownèd field,*
> *And crows are fatted with the murrion flock;*
> *The nine men's morris is fill'd up with mud,*

*And the quaint mazes in the wanton green*

*For lack of tread are undistinguishable:*

*The human mortals want their winter here;*

*No night is now with hymn or carol blest:*

*Therefore the moon, the governess of floods,*

*Pale in her anger, washes all the air,*

*That rheumatic diseases do abound:*

*And thorough this distemperature we see*

*The seasons alter: hoary-headed frosts*

*Fall in the fresh lap of the crimson rose,*

*And on old Hiems' thin and icy crown*

*An odorous chaplet of sweet summer buds*

*Is, as in mockery, set: the spring, the summer,*

*The childing autumn, angry winter, change*

*Their wonted liveries, and the mazèd world,*

*By their increase, now knows not which is which:*

*And this same progeny of evils comes*

*From our debate, from our dissension;*

*We are their parents and original."*

Even then Shakespeare knew the harm, the damage we can do to each other, and to the planet on which we live. Four centuries ago, he set that down. What an insight from a canny, gifted mind. I was lucky enough to be on stage when two fine performers, Alex Jennings as Oberon and Stella Gonet as Titania, fought their epic battle. After Titania spoke her final line there was that awestruck silence which held… for what seemed… oh… minutes… as everyone—audience and cast— took in the size and implications of her outcry; not only Beautiful but True… The magic of live theatre.

Theatre has never done much harm; and it's done a very great deal of good. It keeps us thinking and feeling, laughing and crying; it challenges us to change our ideas. It will renew itself and it will return. As to which disguise and what costume she—Melpomene or Thalia—will be wearing, who can tell?

In its many forms, theatre will survive.

# Tales from the Green Room

## Playing a Lover (1960s)

When I started in the theatre in the Fifties, people my height could not fall in love. You had to be a minimum five feet nine to go in for that sort of thing. I'd discovered that at RADA: I only ever played one straight juvenile, so I made a pitch to play young character parts—at RADA.

But here I am (below), in 1960 on television in a play called *Limes from Sicily* by Luigi Pirandello. The director was a friend of mine; that made all the difference. And it's a very sad story: a young Sicilian farmer sells his inheritance to put a

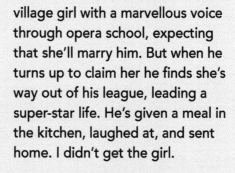

village girl with a marvellous voice through opera school, expecting that she'll marry him. But when he turns up to claim her he finds she's way out of his league, leading a super-star life. He's given a meal in the kitchen, laughed at, and sent home. I didn't get the girl.

I was offered a second chance in 1961, in *Ladies from a Spa*, a half-hour play for BBC TV. It was the story of a timid daughter of thirty, with an ailing mother who exploits her own helplessness to keep her daughter as a companion and carer for life. For the chained-up daughter Celia (played by Avril Elgar), there's just one glimmer of hope—me. I was her almost boy-friend, Harry Jordan. We'd got as far as awkward kissing in a hotel lounge…

Here's the moment (above right) on the top of a high office building when Celia boots her mother's new handbag into the street. It's a proxy for what she—briefly—wants to do to Ma. Self-preservation kicks in and Ma, astonishingly, allows Harry and Celia one more evening on the town together, before the two ladies return home to their spa in the

provinces. The last shot is of Harry (me) hailing a taxi to take me and my gal into London town. Did Harry get his girl, this time? No-one will ever know.

On the face of it (below), this looks more promising... I'd gone to Lincoln in 1963 to direct, but the boss, Kay Gardner, insisted I play a couple of leads first. She had an idealistic rush to the head and decided to try a verse play by Henrik Ibsen (Love's Comedy) on the local audience. She cast me as Falk, a passionate, radical young poet whose aim in life was to change the world... just what young ladies dream of getting swept away by.

And it nearly worked: for a while she was hooked. But then, would you believe, she got hitched to Guldstad (John Savident, the older guy in the picture). A businessman, solid, rolling in cash and assets and status, a long-term prospect, reliable. There was lots of passionate, hot exploration on the way but, in the end, my character was a bit of a nutcase. He was Ibsen's view of the defeated, poetical reformer, way ahead of a society not yet ready for his visionary ideas. I didn't get the girl—my third attempt. And I was never again engaged romantically with a lady on screen or stage, for the following sixty years.

# Unparliamentary Language (1963)

I was in my room in digs with a local vicar at Ipswich Rep when I began work on this sketch. The script unit of *That Was The Week That Was* had asked me if I could think of something performable to do with a list of words and phrases which were—at the time—thought to be inadmissible in Parliament. So I tried to make a single sentence out of them. I seem to recall that Willie Rushton performed it and that it went well.

As to the vicar… he often cornered me to sound off with an emotional polemic against the Mother's Union. He was entirely convinced that they were trying to take over his church and especially dictate how he should run his parish.

He went so far as to describe them as 'the enemy'.

I didn't feel qualified to help him.

---

### COMMMONWEALTH PARLIAMENTARY STYLE

I pity the understanding of the Honourable Member, / when he has his mouth shut he is quite handsome that way. /

Insincere / fool, / maintaining an astonishingly high standard of imbecility, / getting round the ruling, / indulging in favouritism, nepotism and slavery of the capitalists - / lousy, / boozing, / dishonest / pin-head! /

Go back to the gutter! / Lift the commode for somebody, Bengal cobra! You should have been locked up, / dirty / quasi-apartheid / fascist / liar.

Sit down! / Tell the truth for a change, / treacherous, / white-livered / villain. /

You shut up! / Conventions are not being respected in the House!! / Eye-wash! / No confidence in the chair-! / The Minister has a duty to make a truthful statement / dishonourable / rat-bag! /

He possesses the skill of a lady who is adept in setting right a disorderly house, / hypocritical / parrot - / talking through his hat, / slippery, / purring cataclysmic cat. /

Lies!!! / Nothing could be further from the truth; the Minister knows it! /

Why the hell / vomit things from his mouth? / Filtered foolishness! / Egotistical gas! /

Bluffing us, cheating us / the red-faced Members / disgusting / tummy / sounds like a cracked gramophone record. /

It has more curves than Marilyn Monroe! /

Rascal / rank idiot / squib / stooge! / Fraud perpetuated on this country / Dirty / prostitution of this Parliament - / to shamelessly conceal one's foul actions - / Sultan! /

Hero? / Why don't you do it like a man and not a worm? / Lying / rogue - / don't you feel ashamed / pinching / Communist / rats / tummies!? /

Robert Gillespie
4th March 1963.

## *Distant Point,*
## a Soviet play at
## Ipswich rep (1963)

One of the rare entirely satisfying
provincial offerings I was ever in.

Dreaming of a better future...
On the left is our leading lady,
Julia McCarthy, being completely
genuine, tricks-free, and moving,
as Glasha, a peasant woman. I
was Matvei Malko, a Russian Army
general, and on the right is Yvonne
Coulette, who played my wife; in real
life Yvonne was the wife of Denis
Carey who had directed me twice at
the Old Vic Theatre—so there was
lots of backstage gossip and inside
info and politics to chew over in the
four weeks we were together.

Written in 1935, the play resonates
with optimism based on the solid,
practical achievements of the people
of Russia; a wonderful sense of
human betterment drenched the
play. It was as if the painful yearnings
of Chekhov's characters seemed
about to be fulfilled at last. The
author felt free to express the last

vestiges of joy before the horrors of
Stalinism, mass murder and blatant
economic mis-management could
no longer be ignored or avoided or
explained away.

Translator/writer Hubert Griffith on
the playwright Alexei Afinogenev,
and *Distant Point:*

"I remember him as a young man
interested in the widest aspects of art
and literature, and I remember him most
of all as the author of one flawless play
that moved me, with my fifteen years'
experience as a dramatic critic, rather
more than any play has ever moved me on
any European stage. It was the voice of
the future speaking, with the trained and
cultured accent of the past."

## Filming *Mr. Joyce is Leaving Paris* (1972)

Robert Bernal as Joyce is being filmed. Behind the camera is Harry Hart. He was a pioneer of new—at the time barely thinkable—ways of shooting movies, both in terms of sequence length and mobility. Today you hardly think about how it's done when you sit in the cinema and—somehow—travel 360 degrees around a character or a scene.

Like most innovators Harry found that the film industry strongly resisted change. He believed Mr. Joyce... to be perfect for illustrating how a quality feature-length film could be produced at a fraction of the usual cost, and as a way of recording a land-mark stage show for future audiences.

The rig was set up in a room in a Bayswater hotel. All crew were perched between the rig and the ceiling of the room. Only Harry and his assistant had to be on the acting floor. It was his way of avoiding the chronic over-crewing enforced by the unions at the time.

Director Derek Banham wrote:

'I have been asked many times why I became involved in such a ludicrously low-budget production with an eccentric inventor/cameraman, an impossible schedule and terrible working conditions. The answer is that I had been a professional director for three years and all I had directed were TV commercials.

I desperately wanted a longer, more serious piece of work and when I saw the play I thought the cast were absolutely right in wanting to record it. It was a hugely interesting play and they were all making a great job of it, particularly Robert Bernal who seemed like a re-incarnation of Joyce himself. It was an irresistible challenge.

Although it is a very rough piece of work I am extremely glad I did it. I managed to get the film completed early in 1973'.

**Robert Bernal** as James Joyce, from the film of Tom Gallacher's stage play, *Mr. Joyce is Leaving Paris.*

Bernal was an eccentric, but hugely talented, actor who made you believe that the historical James Joyce was living again before your eyes. He died at an absurdly young age, just as his worth as a performer was being recognised.

"MR JOYCE IS LEAVING PARIS"
BY
TOM GALLAGHER

THE STORY OF HOW THE
PLAY WAS FILMED

## *Let's Murder Vivaldi*—a TV play that worked brilliantly on stage
(1972)

Tom Conti took over the part of Ben in *Let's Murder Vivaldi* at the King's Head for the final week—Jack Shepherd had played the part for most of the run, but had to leave due to a prior commitment. That such well-known actors were keen to perform there illustrates the pulling power of the King's Head, and was a huge attraction for our audiences.

This is Tom with Diane Mercer as Julie. Julie's been having an affair with an older man—it's a stormy relationship—Ben is upset.

Both artists had to fake performing on violin and piano, as the lights go down on the play... 'murdering' Vivaldi.

## Freewheeeelers, Series 8, Southern Television (1973)

Director Chris McMaster believed that young viewers would enjoy an adventure with all the elements of international crime and menace and 'bad boy behaviour' so popular with adults. He was right. Hugely successful, it ran for five years.

Photo: young heroes in a pickle: art student Sue Craig (Wendy Padbury)

with boyfriend Dave (Martin Neil), menaced by Crouch (Neil Mcarthy) behind the sofa and Naylor (RG) with the gun, in a heady tale of art forgery, vengeance, canoe chases, spooky chateaux, interpol etc. etc. Exciting.

Wendy Padbury (married to Melvyn Hayes, and pregnant at the time of the series' end) was still able to play teenagers—just.

# *Revival!* by Tom Gallacher, Dublin (1973)

Tony Doyle played three different characters in this play. He became one of the most talented actors I have ever worked with, and a close ally and confidant in planning productions, especially at the King's Head. He died absurdly young, just as he was becoming a major force in television and on stage.

The older man, Julian Somers, was very fine; he played an actor-manager with a fixation about spiritual self-improvement, who came out of retirement to play Solness in Ibsen's *The Master Builder*—and planned to throw himself off his own tall building—like Solness. But unlike Solness, he hoped to emerge on a Buddhist 'higher plane'—having left his lesser self dead on stage… for his family to cope with. In Gallacher's *Revival!* they did—they humoured his delusion for a while; it didn't make much sense, but the audience loved it.

Author Tom Gallacher thought Julian Somers' portrayal was not hopeful and joyful enough, and not certain that his spiritual transition to a higher state would succeed; so he asked for the part to be re-cast. This was at a time when I believed that authors ought to have the last word on how their work should be realised. And it led to the painful and embarrassed political and social contortions that experienced theatre people will recognise only too well. Replacing, on an author's whim, a good actor doing a good job was a huge irritation—Gallacher was obsessed, insistent, adamant. I still wonder, now he's popped his clogs, whether he's in the place he imagined for his character in *Revival!*…?

Photo, next page: Maev Alexander, Tony Doyle, Diana Fairfax—playing daughter and wife of the actor-manager (Julian Somers).

## J.B. Priestley: A Literary Giant (1980)

I first heard this man's voice on the wireless when I was a child, during the war: John Boynton Priestley was asked by the BBC to give regular morale-boosting talks on the Home Service. His Yorkshire intonation provided a sharp, re-assuring, friendly contrast to the standard, clipped and 'posh' delivery of almost all broadcasters of the day that we ordinary folk were meant to model our ideas on and take very seriously.

J.B. Priestley's *Postscript* broadcasts drew millions, and only Churchill was more popular with listeners.

His practical, down to earth view and sympathy with all his listeners led, eventually, to his talks being cancelled—they were thought to be too left wing.

My whole family used to listen to him unfailingly—we loved his voice and his ideas—as we looked up at the map of the war's progress my dad had pinned high on the kitchen wall.

I could hardly believe that, in 1980, at the age of forty-six, I would be directing this celebrated man's play, *Dangerous Corner,* in the West End; that he would find the time to come and see it, and that I would actually meet and talk to him. A rare privilege; because he died four years later. (Centre: Jennifer Daniel, Peter Dennis)

## *Dangerous Corner* at the Cameri Theatre, Tel Aviv, Israel (1982)

It was the strangest thing to walk off a plane to find myself among people of whose language I couldn't understand a single word. Working in Spain, Italy, Germany or France, familiar words floated in my direction at once. But even though I listened hard for repeated phrases or usages, I only ever got as far as working out that 'lo' meant 'no' and 'ken' meant 'yes.' Yet the actors and crew were strikingly European, by and large—given that they were surrounded by Arab lands. They told me how they had, doggedly,

recovered their almost-vanished spoken language; rather in the way that the Welsh have revived theirs, but not the Irish—who haven't succeeded, not really.

I've never discovered what all this says. I know the play, the faces. (that's me, and J.B. Priestley). I also have heaps of reviews from Israel and still not the faintest idea what the writers said about performances, or sets, or direction or quality of play or translation.

I can see that the bent arrow on the danger warning sign in one version, implying a dangerous corner, has been left off the other. Too late to find out why, I think.

## Thames TV Greats
(1980s)

A snapshot of some of the company's fleeting assets, taken to celebrate its phenomenal success in the '80s.

For a couple of seasons I qualified.

Back row Left to Right:
Max Bygraves, Eric Morecambe, Ted Rogers, Glyn Houston and Jeremy Beadle.

Next row Left to Right:
Lionel Blair, Ian Krankie, Me. Above me, Sarah Kennedy and Matthew Kelly. To my Left is Henry Kelly. The 'schoolboy' ('Wee Jimmy Krankie') is Janette Krankie, beside her is Ernie Wise. The cut-out is Des O'Connor.

# A Midsummer Night's Dream at the RSC
## (1994)

Desmond Barrit gave a wonderful performance as Bottom the weaver, leading one of the best groups of 'rude mechanicals' ever assembled. Here's Bottom giving a ride to Titania...

Altogether a superbly talented, devoted, generous and friendly company of players working together in that memorable 1994 RSC season.

Picture: ALASTAIR MUIR

The familiar with the fantastic: Stella Gonet and Desmond Barrit in Adrian Noble's mysterious and funny production

Telegraph 6th August 1994

ADRIAN NOBLE's beautiful, funny and mysterious new staging of the *Dream* (sponsored by Allied-Lyons) begins with a sly homage to Peter Brook's famous adventure-playground production, with Hippolyta first encountered on a swing. Having paid this historical debt, however, the show moves into its own distinctive terrain, creating a haunting and increasingly addictive spell.

Noble and his resourceful designer Anthony Ward never let the audience forget that we are in the midst of a dream. At certain points in the evening, we hear the sound of heavy breathing, as if we were eavesdropping on the sleeping Shakespeare as he conjures up his own play. And again and again the show achieves a disconcerting mixture of the familiar and the fantastic, the homely and the strange. In our dreams, the production suggests, even the most humdrum of us become "the lunatic, the lover and the poet" who, as Theseus reminds us, "are

■ OPERA AND BALLET

ROYAL FESTIVAL HALL 071 928 8800
ENGLISH NATIONAL BALLET
2 - 6 August THE SLEEPING BEAUTY
Mats Wed & Sat

's brother.

## *My Heart*, a duologue about death (1999-2001)

Jo Girdlestone played nine parts: scientist, Buddhist zen master, nurse, parson, stage manager, nun... Here she is as an ex-flame, celebrating past good times with a gift for me to remember her by— her spare false teeth: she wants me to remember her smile. She wore a veil to sneak up on me—surprises could endanger my dodgy heart.

Awaiting my heart transplant, I was offered various spiritual support systems. This is Jo as a barely resistible nun, offering me all the comforts and rewards of the Catholic Church. Below, costume and props from the show.

## *Oedipus Retold* at the Tristan Bates Theatre, The Actors Centre (2013)

Tom Shepherd (Oedipus), Richard Earthy (Tiresias), Luke Hornsby-Smith (Young Priest), Jack Klaff (Laius), David Shaw-Parker (Shepherd).

Young Oedipus refusing to kill his dad: the moment when Jeremy Kingston's comic re-write disrupts the old Greek story. If dad goes along with this idea, then all that unpleasantness about Oedipus marrying his mum would be avoided.

## Shaw's Women
## Tristan Bates Theatre,
## The Actors Centre
(2014)

Bernard Shaw, for a man of his times, wrote sympathetically and fairly about women. Eliza in *Pygmalion*, and *Saint Joan* are notable examples. His short plays also feature entertaining, independent-minded women. I directed a double bill of two of them.

In **Village Wooing**—the main play—Madeleine Hutchins was quite superb as the shop-girl who snares a stuck-up intellectual into becoming a practical —happy—grocer. It's a difficult text to bring to life, but triumphantly possible in the hands of the right performer.

A bonus was the ingenious setting by Matilde Marangoni, which got rave reviews: in the first scene the audience watched transfixed— enthralled—as Madeleine transformed the deck of a cruise ship before their eyes into a village grocer's shop; some nights it got a round.

A: Mark Fleischmann
Z: Madeleine Hutchins

## Shaw's Women
## Tristan Bates Theatre,
## The Actors Centre
(2014)

**How He Lied to her Husband**
also features a clever woman (of a
certain age, this time) coping with
an over-enthusiastic, poetical young
lover. Again, Matilde Marangoni's
setting took the breath away with its
elegance and luxury.

This play has a special resonance
for me because, as a RADA student,
I played the middle-aged husband to
an old folks' audience (twice). It was
an extra-curricular production set up
and directed by a class-mate—and
I still recall the gales of laughter.

Aurora Bompas: Viss Elliot Safavi
Henry Apjohn: Josh Harper
Teddy Bompas: Alan Francis

# Royalty and me

My first brush with royalty happened at the Mermaid Theatre, Puddle Dock in 1964. John Arden had written a play about King John, *Left Handed Liberty*, for the Shakespeare Quatercentenary, and Patrick Wymark was invited to play the lead. However he couldn't play seven performances due to film commitments. I was a fairly lowly member of the company, but Bernard Miles had a sudden brainwave—he asked me to stand in for Wymark... and on a night I played King John, the Queen and Prince Philip attended. The cast stood in a long line, afterwards, and so it was that I was introduced to Her Majesty and HRH. They were utterly delighted, she was glowing,

and they were both completely charming, so I risked a quip about my pretending to be royalty, while she was the real thing.

**My next brush with royalty** was when I met Sofía, Queen Mother of Spain, in 2017. Her charitable Foundation (Fundación Reina Sofía) supports an Alzheimer's project, and I was hired to act an Alzheimer's sufferer in a commercial for her charity, shot in Spain.

It's a tender little story of a grandad (me), stricken with Alzheimer's, trying to help his grandson build a space rocket to go to the stars.

242

That's Queen Sofía, between me and the boy who played my grandson.

She came to the shoot twice, she was so keenly involved and interested in the outcome of what she believes is one of her most important charities. She thanked us all individually, a charming lady.

You can see the film on YouTube. Google: *Robert Gillespie Reina Sofia*

# Acknowledgements

**Lucy Jackson,** my daughter, is the fount, the original inspiration for all the story-telling, reminiscence and capturing of vanishing history within these two volumes.

**Anna Jackson,** my long-time partner and Lucy's mother, one day mused that since Lucy was a late-arrived child, she'd missed a lot of what I'd done in theatre and television. Lucy also knew almost nothing of her Hungarian or Canadian family and the foreign adventures which are related in Part One. I wrote a paragraph and then I stuttered to a halt, but Anna is very persistent and that tentative start has flowered into two volumes, bringing our journey into the present. Anna has, again, done an exceptional job editing and fine-tuning the text.

**Greg Jameson,** critic and drama buff, surprised me by saying that show-biz books have a devoted, if niche, readership. It lit the fire which led, through various transformations, to the present work. Truly, but for Greg, none of this would have gotten done.

**Paul Warrington,** who has created some of the best-ever posters for my stage shows, is responsible for the design of both parts of *Are You Going to do That Little Jump?* Their appeal is immensely enhanced by the superb photographs he's taken of the flotsam and jetsam that has survived my bumpy ride through life, as well as the images he's captured from a bewildering variety of sources. I'm especially grateful to Paul for encouraging me to pursue the enterprise, and for enthusiastically taking on most of the technical and practical aspects of publication.

**Oxford Editors,** although Part Two has proved less unruly than Part One, have continued to address the challenges of a robust, but sometimes uncivilised, text with useful advice. Thank you…

# What I did, when

| | |
|---|---|
| 1933 | Born Lille, France |
| 1940 | Arrived Plymouth, England |
| 1948-50 | School plays: *The Critic*, *The Miser*, *The Haunted House* |
| 1951 | *Figures of Fate*, Library Theatre Manchester |
| 1951-3 | RADA |
| 1952 | *A Comedy of Errors* (dir. Ann Jellicoe) |
| 1953-55 | Old Vic |
| 1954 | *Rosmersholm* (dir. Ann Jellicoe) |
| 1956 | *The Sheep Well*, *The Good Soldier Schweik*, *An Italian Straw Hat*, Theatre Workshop, Theatre Royal Stratford (dir. Joan Littlewood) |
| 1956 | *Jesus of Nazareth*, the disciple Matthew, Series, BBC TV |
| 1956 | *Case Dismissed*, Associated-Rediffusion TV |
| 1956 | *The Black Brigand*, Series, BBC TV |
| 1956&7 | Royal Court Theatre (The English Stage Company), season |
| 1957 | *A Night to Remember* (Film) |
| 1957 | *The Warrant Officer*, BBC TV |
| 1958 | *Hand in Glove*, Worthing |
| 1958 | *Saturday Night at the Crown*, Worthing |
| 1958 | *Order to View*, Worthing |
| 1958 | *Shadow Squad*, Granada TV |
| 1958 | *The Square Peg* (Film) |
| 1958 | *Miss Em*, Associated-Rediffusion TV |
| 1959 | *Major Barbara*, Royal Court Theatre |
| 1960 | *Escape*, BBC TV |
| 1960 | *Limes From Sicily*, BBC TV |
| 1960 | *The Haunted House*, BBC TV |
| 1961 | *The Alan King Show*, BBC TV |
| 1961 | *Ladies From a Spa* (Series *They Came to a City*, dir. Hal Burton), BBC TV |
| 1961 | The Alan Young Show, BBC TV |
| 1961-6 | Mermaid Theatre, various plays inc. *Treasure Island*, *Shoemaker's Holiday*, *Left-Handed Liberty*, *Dandy Dick*, *Fanny's First Play*, *The Beaver Coat* |
| 1962 | *The Caucasian Chalk Circle*, BBC TV |
| 1962 | *Antigone*, BBC TV |
| 1962 | *The Secret of the World*, Theatre Royal, Stratford (after Littlewood) |
| 1962 | *Hotel Paradiso*, BBC TV |
| 1962 | *They Hanged My Saintly Billy*, BBC TV |
| 1963 | *Siege of the Saxons* (Film) |
| 1963 | *I'm Not Stopping*, BBC TV |
| 1963 | *Wormwood*, BBC TV |
| 1963 | *The Queen and the Rebels*, BBC TV |

| | |
|---|---|
| 1963 | *A Consumer Guide to Religions*, *That Was The Week That Was* (Writing), BBC TV |
| 1963 | *Semi-Detached* (Directing), Lincoln |
| 1964 | *Crane*, Associated-Rediffusion TV |
| 1964 | *Maigret*, BBC TV |
| 1964 | *Kipling (The Head of the District)*, BBC TV |
| 1964 | *The Caucasian Chalk Circle*, BBC TV |
| 1965 | *The Shoemaker's Holiday*, Mermaid (Directing) |
| 1965 | *The Drinking Party* (dir. Jonathan Miller), BBC TV |
| 1966 | *Dr Knock*, BBC TV |
| 1966 | *Mr Sludge, the Medium*, BBC TV |
| 1967 | *Beggar My Neighbour*, BBC TV |
| 1967 | *To Kill a Saint* (TV Film) |
| 1967 | *The Caine Mutiny Court Martial*, Glasgow Citizens |
| 1967 | *Comedy Playhouse*, BBC TV |
| 1967 | *Danger Island*, STV |
| 1967 | *Romeo and Juliet*, BBC TV |
| 1967 | *The Glory of Llewellyn Smiley*, Associated-Rediffusion TV |
| 1967 | *Lucky Jim*, BBC TV |
| 1967 | *Vendetta*, BBC TV |
| 1968 | *The Hero Rises Up* (written & directed by John Arden), Roundhouse |
| 1968 | *Otley* (Film) |
| 1968 | *Light Blue*, BBC TV |
| 1968 | *Hugh and I Spy*, BBC TV |
| 1968 | *Captain Fantastic*, Thames TV |
| 1968 | *Harry Worth*, BBC TV |
| 1968 | *Honey Lane*, ATV |
| 1968 | *Avengers (Have Guns Will Haggle)*, ABC TV |
| 1969 | *Mr Digby Darling*, Yorkshire TV |
| 1969 | *Dixon of Dock Green*, BBC TV |
| 1970 | *Vile Bodies*, BBC TV |
| 1970 | *Up Pompeii*, BBC TV |
| 1970 | *Every Home Should Have One* (Film) |
| 1970 | *Doomwatch*, BBC TV |
| 1970-72 | *Mr. Joyce is Leaving Paris* (Directing), Basement Theatre, Dublin Theatre Festival, King's Head |
| 1970 | *Tottering Towers*, series STV |
| 1970 | *A Severed Head* (Film) |
| 1970 | *The Right Prospectus*, BBC TV |
| 1971 | *The Love Songs of Martha Canary* (Directing), King's Head |

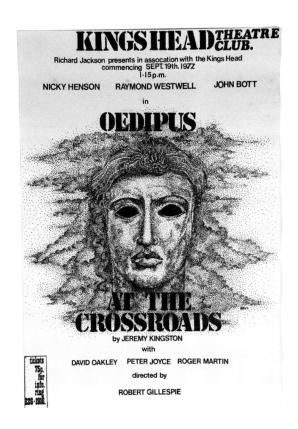

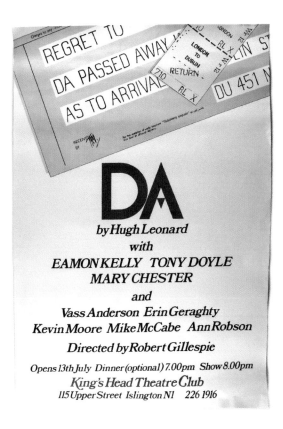

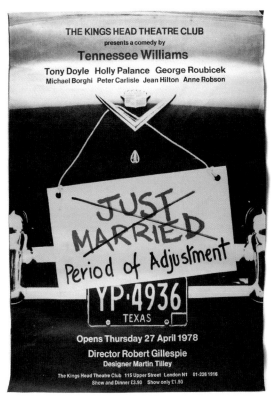

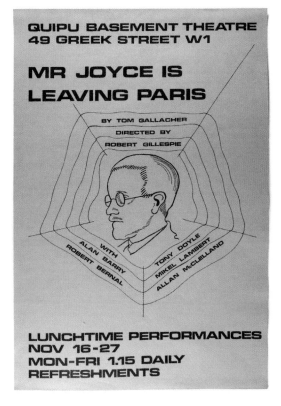

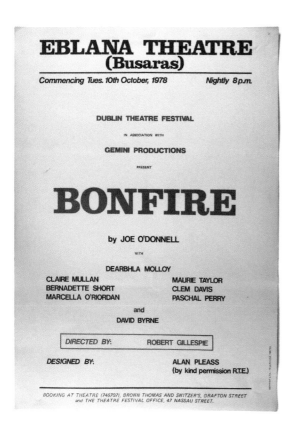

# EBLANA THEATRE
## (Busaras)

Commencing Tues. 10th October, 1978          Nightly 8 p.m.

DUBLIN THEATRE FESTIVAL

IN ASSOCIATION WITH

GEMINI PRODUCTIONS

PRESENT

# BONFIRE

by JOE O'DONNELL

WITH

DEARBHLA MOLLOY

CLAIRE MULLAN                 MAURIE TAYLOR
BERNADETTE SHORT              CLEM DAVIS
MARCELLA O'RIORDAN            PASCHAL PERRY

and

DAVID BYRNE

DIRECTED BY:          ROBERT GILLESPIE

DESIGNED BY:          ALAN PLEASS
                      (by kind permission R.T.E.)

BOOKING AT THEATRE (746707), BROWN THOMAS AND SWITZER'S, GRAFTON STREET
and THE THEATRE FESTIVAL OFFICE, 47 NASSAU STREET.

A Woodspring District Council Entertainment          Director of Leisure Service . . . B. H. Flavell

# PLAYHOUSE          Tel. W·S·M 23521

Week Commencing MONDAY, 12th MARCH
Monday – Friday at 8.0pm          Saturday at 5.45 & 8.30
Seats from £1 (Reduced Prices for Children)  Booking Office open daily (exc. Sun.) 10am to 8pm.  Open throughout the lunch period

MALCOLM KNIGHT
presents

# MELVYN HAYES
(From T.V's "It Ain't Half Hot. Mum")
in

WOODY ALLEN'S COMEDY

# PLAY IT AGAIN, SAM

with
GLORY      RICHARD
ANNEN     BORTHWICK

MOIRA DOWNIE    GLORIA WALKER
LUCINDA MACDONALD   DONNA SCARFF
SUZANNE CHURCH   MIREILLE ALLONVILLE
and
ROGER FOX
as "BOGEY"

Setting Designed by       Directed by        Lighting Designed by
PAUL MILLER        ROBERT GILLESPIE       DAVID LINDSEY

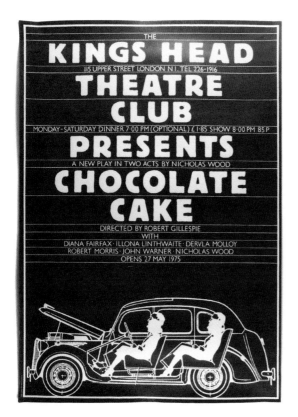

# THE
# KINGS HEAD
## 115 UPPER STREET LONDON N.1. TEL 226-1916
# THEATRE
# CLUB
MONDAY-SATURDAY DINNER 7·00 PM (OPTIONAL) £ 1·85  SHOW 8·00 PM 85 P
# PRESENTS
A NEW PLAY IN TWO ACTS BY NICHOLAS WOOD
# CHOCOLATE
# CAKE
DIRECTED BY ROBERT GILLESPIE
WITH
DIANA FAIRFAX · ILLONA LINTHWAITE · DERVLA MOLLOY
ROBERT MORRIS · JOHN WARNER · NICHOLAS WOOD
OPENS 27 MAY 1975

# KING'S HEAD THEATRE CLUB
115, UPPER STREET, N.1.          Tel.: 226 1916

ALAN WEST ENTERPRISES IN ASSOCIATION WITH THE KING'S HEAD THEATRE CLUB
PRESENTS:

# HEATHER SEARS

IN

# THE LOVE SONGS
# OF MARTHA CANARY
By IAIN BLAIR
WITH
MAEV ALEXANDER     IAIN BLAIR     BOYD MACKENZIE
Directed by ROBERT GILLESPIE

Tuesday, 30th November to Friday 24th Dec.
Tuesday—Sunday inclusive.

DINNER 7.30 (optional) £1.10p          SHOW 8.30 - 60 p.

| | | | |
|---|---|---|---|
| 1971 | *The Kapo* (Directing), Basement Theatre | 1975 | *Hogg's Back*, STV |
| 1971 | *Rasputin*, BBC TV | 1975 | *Whatever Happened to the Likely Lads*, BBC Radio |
| 1971 | *Z Cars*, BBC TV | | |
| 1971 | *The Magnificent Seven Deadly Sins* (Film) | 1975 | *Galbraith and the King of Diamonds*, BBC Radio |
| 1971 | *Catch Me a Spy* (Film) | | |
| 1971 | *The Great Escape Part 2* (Film), BFI Scott Free Enterprises | 1975 | *Couples*, Thames TV |
| | | 1976 | *At the Earth's Core* (Film) |
| 1971 | *Rentadick* (Film) | 1976 | *A Slight Accident* (Directing), Orange Tree |
| 1972 | *Carry On Up the Front* (Film) | 1976 | *The Liver Birds*, BBC TV |
| 1972 | *Dad's Army*, BBC TV | 1976 | *Lord Peter Wimsey*, BBC Radio |
| 1972 | *Salutations*, Young Vic | 1976 | *Witnesses*, BBC TV |
| 1972 | *His and Hers*, Yorkshire TV | 1976 | *Spokesong* (Directing), King's Head |
| 1972 | *New Scotland Yard*, LTV | 1976 | *Softly, Softly*, BBC TV |
| 1972-3 | *Revival!* (Directing), Dublin, King's Head, | 1976 | *A Streetcar Named Desire* (Directing), Theatre Royal Norwich |
| 1972 | *Let's Murder Vivaldi*, *The Problem*, (Directing), King's Head | | |
| | | 1976 | *Rosie*, BBC TV |
| 1972 | *The Adventurers* (TV Film) | 1976 | *Van der Valk*, Thames TV |
| 1972 | *Mr. Joyce is Leaving Paris* (Co-directed, Film) | 1976 | *Happy Ever After*, BBC TV |
| | | 1976 | *The New Avengers*, *The Last of the Cybernauts* (TV Film) |
| 1972 | *The National Health* (Film) | | |
| 1973-4 | *Whatever Happened to the Likely Lads?* BBC TV | 1976-7 | *Robin's Nest*, Thames TV |
| | | 1977 | *Spokesong* (Directing), transfer to Vaudeville Theatre |
| 1973 | *Schellenbrack* (Directing), King's Head | | |
| 1973 | *All Our Saturdays*, Yorkshire TV | 1977 | *Warship*, BBC TV |
| 1973 | *The Kids from 47A*, ATV | 1977 | *A Roof Over My Head*, BBC TV |
| 1973 | *Freewheelers*, series, STV | 1977 | *Galbraith and the Midas Touch*, Series, BBC Radio |
| 1973 | *Napoleon*, *Session 2* (Writing, Directing), Orange Tree | | |
| | | 1977 | *Give Us a Kiss, Christabel* (TV Film) |
| 1973 | *The Only Street* (Directing), Dublin, & King's Head | 1977 | *Da* (Directing), King's Head |
| | | 1977 | *Albert and Me*, BBC Radio |
| 1974 | *Marked Personal*, Thames TV | 1977 | *Midnight is a Place*, Series, STV |
| 1974 | *The Man Who Knew He Was Jesus Christ* (Directing), King's Head | 1977 | *Spokesong* (Directing), touring Holland and Belgium |
| | | 1977 | *George and Mildred*, Thames TV |
| 1974 | *Twigs* (Directing), Dublin | 1977 | *Naught for Thy Comfort*, Yorkshire TV |
| 1974 | *Churchill's People*, BBC TV | 1977 | *Angels*, BBC TV |
| 1974 | *Porridge*, BBC TV | 1977 | *It Ain't 'Alf 'Ot Mum*, BBC TV |
| 1974 | *The Life of Riley*, Granada TV | 1977 | *Oedipus at the Crossroads* (Directing), King's Head |
| 1974 | *The Sweeney* (TV Film) | | |
| 1974 | *Barry McKenzie Holds His Own* (Film) | 1977 | *Return of the Saint* (TV Film) |
| 1974 | *No Strings*, BBC TV | 1977 | *The Professionals*, LWT |
| 1974 | *The Public Eye*, Thames TV | 1977 | *Our Day Out*, BBC TV |
| 1975 | *Paradise*, Royal Court | 1978 | *The Thirty-Nine Steps* (Film) |
| 1975 | *Rising Damp*, Yorkshire TV | 1978 | *Dreamboats*, Thames TV |
| 1975 | *Sadie It's Cold Outside*, Thames TV | 1978 | *Crime on the Knock*, BBC Radio |
| 1975 | *Volunteers!* (Directing), Abbey Theatre, Dublin | 1978 | *Period of Adjustment* (Directing), King's Head |
| 1975 | *Chocolate Cake* (Directing), King's Head | 1978 | *Born and Bred*, BBC TV |
| 1975 | *Gone Away*, Thames TV | 1978 | *The Prisoner of Zenda* (Film) |
| 1975 | *The Sea-Horse* (Directing), Dublin | 1978 | *Spokesong* (Directing), UK tour & return to King's Head |
| 1975 | *The Good Life*, BBC TV | | |
| 1975 | *Private Lives* (Directing), Dublin | | |
| 1975 | *Survivors*, BBC TV | 1978 | *Selwyn*, Yorkshire TV |
| 1975-9 | *The Dick Emery Show*, BBC TV | | |

| | | | |
|---|---|---|---|
| 1978 | *The Sadrina Project* (TV Film) | 1988 | *Blind Justice*, BBC TV |
| 1978 | *Whodunnit*, Thames TV | 1989 | *Latin*, by Stephen Fry, *Creditors*, by |
| 1978 | *Bonfire* (Directing), Dublin | | Strindberg (Directing), New End Theatre |
| 1978 | *A Soft Touch*, ATV | 1989-9 | *Bishop*, BBC Radio |
| 1978 | *The Fall and Rise of Reginald Perrin*, | 1990 | *Heil Honey, I'm Home*, Galaxy TV |
| | BBC TV | 1990 | *Tales From Macedonia*, RV Films-Europe TV |
| 1978 | *Butterflies*, BBC TV | 1990 | *Inmates*, BBC TV |
| 1978 | *The Glums*, LWT | 1991 | *A Jovial Crew*, National Theatre Studio |
| 1978 | *Bristow*, LWT | 1991 | *The Rose Tattoo*, Playhouse Theatre, |
| 1978 | *Leave it to Charlie*, Granada TV | | West End |
| 1978 | *Room Service*, Thames TV | 1991 | *So You Think You've Got Troubles*, |
| 1978 | *How's Your Father?* Yorkshire TV | | Alomo Productions, BBC TV |
| 1978 | *Force 10 From Navarone* (Film) | 1993 | *Bonjour La Classe*, BBC TV |
| 1979 | *Da* (Directing), Greenwich Theatre | 1994 | *Zorn* (Film) |
| 1979 | *Away From the Light*, BBC Radio | 1994-6 | *Twelfth Night, A Midsummer Night's Dream,* |
| 1979 | *Play it Again, Sam* (Directing), UK tour | | *The Broken Heart, Zenobia,* |
| 1979 | *Give or Take*, BBC Radio | | Royal Shakespeare Company |
| 1979 | *Agony*, LWT | 1997 | *The Prince of Denmark Hill* (Film) |
| 1979 | *Secret Army*, BBC TV | 1999 | *Bozo* (Film) |
| 1979 | *Fearless Frank* (Directing), King's Head | 1999 | *The Lower Depths*, Cardboard Citizens |
| 1979 | *Only When I Laugh*, Yorkshire TV | 1999-01 | *My Heart* (Writing, Directing, Performing), |
| 1979 | *Sherlock Holmes* (TV Film) | | London & around |
| 1980-1 | *Dangerous Corner* (Directing), Ambassadors | 2001 | *Mincemeat* (first production), |
| | Theatre, Peter Bridge Productions | | Cardboard Citizens |
| 1980 | *Catchpenny Twist* (Directing), King's Head | 2004 | *Making Dickie Happy* (directing), |
| 1980-3 | *Keep It in the Family*, five Series, written for | | Rosemary Branch |
| | RG by Brian Cooke, Thames TV | 2005 | *Making Dickie Happy* (directing), revival, |
| 1980 | *Mary's Wife*, BBC TV | | Warehouse Theatre, Croydon |
| 1980 | *Beyond the Book*, BBC Radio | 2009 | *Mincemeat* (second production), Cardboard |
| 1980 | *Fearless Frank* (Directing), Princess Theatre, | | Citizens, also BBC Radio |
| | New York | 2009 | *No Signal* (TV Film) |
| 1980 | *Tony's*, BBC Radio | 2010-11 | *Love, Question Mark* (Writing, Directing), |
| 1982 | *Dangerous Corner* (Directing), | | New Diorama, Courtyard Theatre, |
| | Cameri Theatre, Israel | | Old Sorting Office Barnes, Tabard Theatre |
| 1982 | *Singles Weekend*, LWT | 2013 | *Making Dickie Happy* (directing), revival, |
| 1983 | *Outlaw* (Directing), UK Tour | | Tristan Bates Theatre, The Actors Centre |
| 1983 | *Noises Off* (Directing), Cameri Theatre, Israel | 2013 | *Portia* (Writing, Directing), Women's Theatre |
| 1984 | *'Night, Mother* (Directing), | | Festival, Tristan Bates Theatre, The Actors |
| | Cameri Theatre, Israel | | Centre |
| 1984-5 | *I Woke Up One Morning*, Series, BBC TV | 2013 | *New Tricks*, BBC TV |
| 1985 | *Swimming Pools at War* (Directing), | 2014 | *Oedipus Retold* (directing), revival, |
| | Offstage Downstairs | | Tristan Bates Theatre, The Actors Centre |
| 1985 | *Beside the Sea*, Theatre Royal, Windsor | 2014 | *Shaw's Women* (directing), Tristan Bates |
| 1985 | *An Englishman's Humour* (Directing), | | Theatre, The Actors Centre |
| | Peter Jones, one-man show | 2015 | *Joan of Arc* (Film) |
| 1986 | *Marlowe* (Directing), King's Head | 2016 | *The Red Baron* (Writing, Directing), RAF |
| 1988 | *Starting Out*, Central TV | | Museum, Hendon |
| 1986 | *I Ought to be in Pictures* (Directing), | 2017 | *Broken*, BBC TV |
| | Offstage Downstairs | 2017 | *Lost in London* (film), Woody Harrelson |
| | | 2018 | *Peterloo* (Film), Mike Leigh |

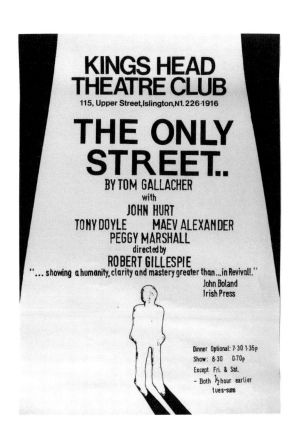

# KINGS HEAD THEATRE CLUB

115, Upper Street, Islington, N1. 226·1916

# THE ONLY STREET...

BY TOM GALLACHER

with

JOHN HURT

TONY DOYLE    MAEV ALEXANDER

PEGGY MARSHALL

directed by

ROBERT GILLESPIE

"... showing a humanity, clarity and mastery greater than...in Revival!"

John Boland
Irish Press

Dinner Optional: 7·30 1·35p
Show: 8·30    0·70p
Except Fri. & Sat.
– Both ½ hour earlier
tues-suns

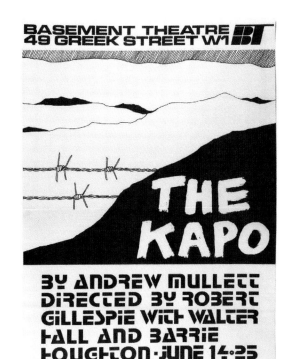

# BASEMENT THEATRE 49 GREEK STREET W1 BT

# THE KAPO

BY ANDREW MULLETT DIRECTED BY ROBERT GILLESPIE WITH WALTER HALL AND BARRIE HOUGHTON · JUNE 14·25 MON·FRI AT 1·15 · NOT FOR THE SQUEAMISH !

5 - 18 JUN

LONDON FRINGE THEATRE

### KINGS HEAD THEATRE

Tennessee Williams'
PERIOD OF ADJUSTMENT

Directed by Robert Gillespie

Show & Dinner: £3.00    Show Only: £1.50

### ICA THEATRE

tues–sat 10 June
Waste of Time

tues 13–sat 17 June
Hesitate and Demonstrate

tues 20 June–sat 1 July
The People Show

all performances at 8pm.    tickets £1.60

### HAMPSTEAD THEATRE

THE TRIBADES

by PER OLOF ENQUIST

directed by MICHAEL RUDMAN

Mon–Fri at 8.00 pm (Sats at 6.00 & 8.00)

### ROUND HOUSE DOWNSTAIRS

CHILDREN'S ACTIVITIES EVERY SAT

### THE WAREHOUSE

From 30 May
Two new plays
David Edgar's
The Jail Diary of Abie Sachs

Peter Flannery's
Savage Amusement

with David Rudkin's
The Sons of Light

### OPEN SPACE THEATRE

A NEW AMERICAN COMEDY
THE BALL GAME

by TOM THOMAS

directed by John Fortune

until 2 July

Tues–Suns at 8.00 pm (Sats: 6.00 & 8.00)

### COCKPIT THEATRE

Gemini Theatre Co presents

FRIENDLY STREET

by ANDY MORTON & GEORGE DOUGLAS

Tickets: 80p

### COMPANY OF 3

BYRON'S CAIN

UNTIL 11 JUNE

TUBE Stamford Brook    (except Mondays)

### HALF MOON THEATRE

WE CAN'T PAY!
WE WON'T PAY!!

a political farce by DARIO FO

Sunday 12 June ONLY
BELT AND BRACES BAND in concert

### ALBANY EMPIRE

### UPSTREAM THEATRE CLUB

for details ring
633 0852

### THEATRE QUARTERLY

TQ Publications

### RIVERSIDE STUDIOS

13 June–2 July

TREETOPS

by Nicholas Wright

Printed & Published by THEATRE DESPATCH LTD

### KESKIDEE CENTRE

for details ring
409 4263

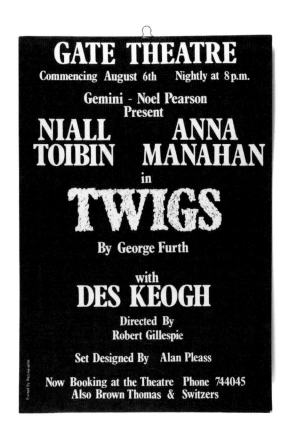

# GATE THEATRE

Commencing August 6th    Nightly at 8 p.m.

Gemini - Noel Pearson
Present

NIALL          ANNA
TOIBIN      MANAHAN

in

# TWIGS

By George Furth

with

DES KEOGH

Directed By
Robert Gillespie

Set Designed By    Alan Pleass

Now Booking at the Theatre    Phone 744045
Also Brown Thomas & Switzers

KINGS HEAD THEATRE
CLUB 115 UPPER STREET ISLINGTON N1.226·1916

"an evening of fiercly good writing delivered with panache & intelligence"
THE TIMES

TOM GALLACHER'S
SCHELLENBRACK
directed by
ROBERT GILLESPIE
with
WOLFE MORRIS
SHELAGH FRASER ALAN BARRY PAULINE CUNNINGHAM
dinner 7·30 £1·35 opt.        show 8·30 70p
except fri&sat – half hour earlier

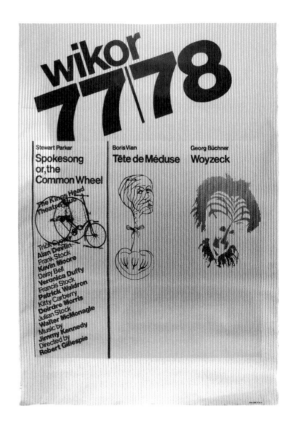

wikor 77\78

Stewart Parker
Spokesong or,the Common Wheel

Boris Vian
Tête de Méduse

Georg Büchner
Woyzeck

The Kings Head Theatre Club

Trish Gonella
Alan Devlin
Frank Stock
Kevin Moore
Daisy Bell
Veronica Duffy
Francis Stock
Patrick Waldron
Kitty Carberry
Deirdre Morris
Julian Stock
Walter McMonagle
Music by
Jimmy Kennedy
Directed by
Robert Gillespie

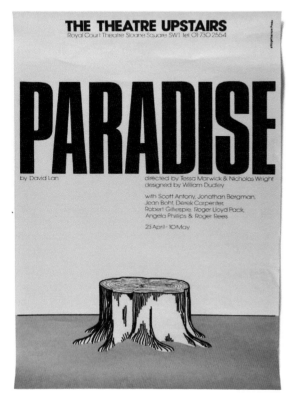

THE THEATRE UPSTAIRS
Royal Court Theatre Sloane Square SW1 tel 01-730 2554

PARADISE

by David Lan

directed by Tessa Marwick & Nicholas Wright
designed by William Dudley

with Scott Antony, Jonathan Bergman,
Jean Boht, Derek Carpenter,
Robert Gillespie, Roger Lloyd Pack,
Angela Phillips & Roger Rees

23 April - 10 May

Capricorn Stage Directions in association with Richard Jackson
present
STRINDBERG AND FRY

CREDITORS
by August STRINDBERG
translation by Michael Meyer

LATIN
OR
tobacco & boys
by Stephen FRY

NEW END
THEATRE
27 New End, Hampstead
London NW3

with
Karen Cooper
Michael Malnick
Howard Samuels
directed by
Robert Gillespie

May 16 to June 11
Tuesday to Sunday at 8pm
May 18 at 7pm

Box Office 01 794 0022

# Illustrations

**P. 90-91**

Designer's sketch for set of *Bonfire* by Joe O'Donnell, directed by RG, Eblana Theatre, Dublin Festival, 1978

**P. 94**

*Dangerous Corner* by J.B Priestley, directed by RG, Ambassadors Theatre 1980. Top: designer's sketch of set. Below: press cutting of Anthony Daniels (Gordon Whitehouse), Stacy Dorning (Betty Whitehouse)

**P. 97**

*Dangerous Corner* by J.B Priestley, directed by RG, Cameri Theatre, Tel Aviv, Israel, 1982. Top: prompt copy, Hebrew text and English text. Below: cast members.

**P. 100**

Top: theatre programme, *Noises Off* by Michael Frayn, directed by RG, Cameri Theatre Tel Aviv, and touring, Israel, 1983. Below: designer's sketch of set for '*Night Mother* by Marsha Norman, directed by RG, Cameri Theatre, Tel Aviv, Israel, 1984

**P. 105**

Israel, Jerusalem, various postcards

**P. 111**

Susan Hampshire (publicity photograph, signed)

**P. 112**

Rehearsal photo and poster for *Fearless Frank* by Andrew Davies, directed by RG, Princess Theatre, Broadway, New York 1980

**P. 117**

US theatre stamps, New York ticket stubs (RG was accosted, visiting the Empire State Building, with a request for an autograph)

**P. 118**

L: Steve Harley (played Marlowe). R: Ernest Hemingway (Leo Rost look-alike…)

**P. 122**

Photo-sheet of the *Marlowe* cast used as a 'good luck' card, King's Head Theatre 1986

**P. 126**

Ernest Hemingway Look-Alike Contest, including prize medallion and bust, Key West, Florida, USA

**P. 130**

Peter Cushing, fan photo, signed; found in my mother's memorabilia collection

**P. 132-3**

Still frame from *The Magnificent Seven Deadly Sins*, illustrating the sin of Pride, by Alan Simpson and Ray Galton, directed by Graham Stark. L-R: RG (AA Patrol Man), Alfie Bass (Mr. Spencer), Ian Carmichael (Mr. Ferris), Keith Smith (RAC Patrol Man). Shot on location in the UK, Tigon Pictures 1971

**P. 134**

Right: Evidence of summons to film for *Picasso Summer* on the Côte d'Azur, 1969

**P. 136**

Still frame from *Barry McKenzie Holds His Own*, script by Bruce Beresford and Barry Humphries, directed by Bruce Beresford; L-R Chantal Contouri (Zizi), R.G. (Dorothy, Count Plasma's catamite), Donald Pleasence (Count Plasma); Reg. Grundy Productions, 1974

**P. 138**

*Survivors*, RG; *Last of the Cybernauts*, RG; *The Professionals*, Lewis Collins, RG, Martin Shaw; *The Avengers*, Patrick Macnee, RG; *Maigret*, Rupert Davies, RG; *The Professionals*, RG; *The Avengers*

**P. 142-3**

*The Professionals* (episode entitled *Rogue*), RG (Steve Ballard), Lewis Collins (Bodie), London Weekend Television 1977

**P. 144**

*Survivors*, RG as Sam Mead; RG was in four episodes, one as John Milner, three as Sam Mead. BBC Television 1975-77

**P. 145**

Top: Maigret, Rupert Davies (Chief Inspector Maigret), RG (Gerard), BBC Television 1963. Centre: *The Professionals* (episode entitled *Long Shot*), RG (Sammy), London Weekend Television 1978. Bottom: *The Avengers* (episode entitled *Have Guns - Will Haggle*), Patrick Macnee (John Steed), RG (Lift Attendant), ABC Weekend Television 1968

GREENWICH THEATRE
Crooms Hill, SE10
Box Office
01-858 7755

The award winning play by
HUGH LEONARD

From January 10th
with Mary Chester
Tony Doyle
Eamon Kelly
Mike McCabe
Kevin Moore
Anne Robson
P.G. Stephens
Bernadette Shortt

Directed by
Robert Gillespie
Designed by
Bernard Culshaw
Lighting by
Nick Chelton

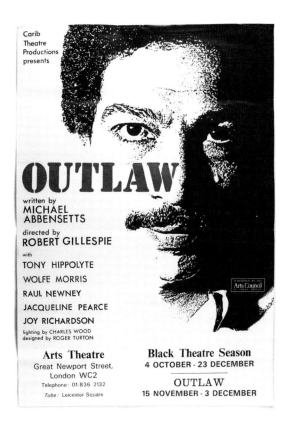

Carib Theatre Productions presents

# OUTLAW

written by
MICHAEL ABBENSETTS

directed by
ROBERT GILLESPIE

with
TONY HIPPOLYTE
WOLFE MORRIS
RAUL NEWNEY
JACQUELINE PEARCE
JOY RICHARDSON

lighting by CHARLES WOOD
designed by ROGER TURTON

Arts Theatre
Great Newport Street,
London WC2
Telephone: 01-836 2132
Tube: Leicester Square

Black Theatre Season
4 OCTOBER - 23 DECEMBER

OUTLAW
15 NOVEMBER - 3 DECEMBER

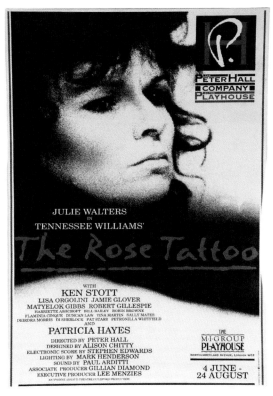

PETER HALL COMPANY at the PLAYHOUSE

JULIE WALTERS
IN
TENNESSEE WILLIAMS'

The Rose Tattoo

WITH
KEN STOTT
LISA ORGOLINI   JAMIE GLOVER
MATYELOK GIBBS   ROBERT GILLESPIE
HARRIETTE ASHCROFT   BILL BAILEY   ROBIN BROWNE
FLAMINIA CINQUE   DUNCAN LAW   TINA MARTIN   SALLY MATES
DEIRDRA MORRIS   DI SHERLOCK   PAT STARR   PETRONILLA WHITFIELD
AND
PATRICIA HAYES

DIRECTED BY PETER HALL
DESIGNED BY ALISON CHITTY
ELECTRONIC SCORE BY STEPHEN EDWARDS
LIGHTING BY MARK HENDERSON
SOUND BY PAUL ARDITTI
ASSOCIATE PRODUCER GILLIAN DIAMOND
EXECUTIVE PRODUCER LEE MENZIES

THE M-I-GROUP PLAYHOUSE
NORTHUMBERLAND AVENUE, LONDON WC2

4 JUNE - 24 AUGUST

OFFSTAGE DOWNSTAIRS

Buddy Dalton & Richard Jackson Present

PRUNELLA GEE and MARY TAMM
with Kevin Arndt & Mick Gough

Directed by: Robert Gillespie
Designed by: Nick Ormerod

in

SWIMMING POOLS AT WAR

by Yves Navarre
translated by Donald Watson

from Wednesday June 19 at 8.00 pm (Not Mondays)
Press Night June 20 at 7.00 pm

37 Chalk Farm Rd NW1
Camden Town or Chalk Farm

OFFSTAGE DOWNSTAIRS
485 4996

Jane Nightwork Productions presents

# MAKING
## Dickie
# HAPPY

by Jeremy Kingston

**5 – 30 March 2013, Tristan Bates Theatre**

Book now: 020 7240 6283 or tristanbatestheatre.co.uk

The Actors Centre, 1a Tower St, London WC2H 9NP
Covent Garden / Leicester Square / Tottenham Court Road

the actors centre

TRISTAN BATES THEATRE

cardboard citizens

"one of the most moving pieces of theatre that many of us had ever seen"
THE BIG ISSUE

A VERSION OF MAXIM GORKY'S CLASSIC PLAY

# The Lower Depths

same as it ever was

**12-30 MAY
THE SECTION** 146 Mare Street, Hackney, E8
**BOX OFFICE: 0171 237 1663**
ADVANCE BOOKING ADVISED

Jane Nightwork Productions presents

# OEDIPUS
## RETOLD

Two plays by
Jeremy Kingston

a bristling, intelligent and funny play The Guardian

**14 Jan – 8 Feb 2014, Tristan Bates Theatre**

Book now: 020 7240 6283 or tristanbatestheatre.co.uk

The Actors Centre, 1a Tower St, London WC2H 9NP
Covent Garden / Leicester Square / Tottenham Court Road

the actors centre

TRISTAN BATES THEATRE

Jane Nightwork Productions presents

# SHAW'S WOMEN

**Village Wooing**

**How He Lied To Her Husband**

Two plays by
George Bernard Shaw
Directed by
Robert Gillespie

**6 – 31 January 2015, Tristan Bates Theatre**

Book now: 020 7240 6283 or tristanbatestheatre.co.uk

The Actors Centre, 1a Tower St, London WC2H 9NP
Covent Garden / Leicester Square / Tottenham Court Road

the actors centre

TRISTAN BATES THEATRE

**P. 191**

*Mincemeat* by Adrian Jackson and Farhana Sheikh, flyer and book cover design, 2009

**P. 192-3**

*Mincemeat* by Adrian Jackson and Farhana Sheikh, Cardboard Citizens, scenes from the 2nd production of a promenade theatre event directed by Adrian Jackson in an unused warehouse, Cordy House, Curtain Street, Shoreditch, London 2009

**P. 197**

RG as a priest in *Joan of Arc*, with Milly Thomas as Joan, BYUtv USA 2015

**P. 198-9**

*Lost in London*, feature film shot in a single take and transmitted live. Produced by Ken Kao and Woody Harrelson, directed by Woody Harrelson, camera John Hembrough, 2017. Press cutting from The Guardian, and production photos

**P. 201**

Top: appointment with Mike Leigh, and wardrobe call, *Peterloo*, 2017.
Below, *Maigret*, L-R: Ewen Solon (Lucas), possibly Neville Jason (Lapointe), Mike Leigh (Paul), Rupert Davies (Chief Inspector Maigret), BBC Television 1963.

**P. 202**

L-R: Brett Dawes (Manfred von Richthofen in *The Red Baron*), Clare Cameron (Maria in *Love, Question Mark*)

**P. 204**

Urn, by Grayson Perry

**P. 206**

*My Heart*, written and directed by RG. Jo Girdlestone (played nine characters), RG (Michael), a touring production 1999-2001

**P. 209**

*Love, Question Mark*, written and directed by RG; Clare Cameron (Maria), Stuart Sessions (Michael). First performed at the New Diorama Theatre 2010 (producer Lucy Jackson), then at the Courtyard Theatre Hoxton, The Old Sorting Office Barnes, and four weeks at the Tabard Theatre Chiswick 2011

**P. 212**

*The Red Baron*, written and directed by RG.
Top: Neusha Milanian (Coco). Centre: Richard Earthy (Papa). Bottom: Neusha Milanian (Coco), Richard Earthy (Papa), Brett Dawes (Richthofen), Royal Air Force Museum, Hendon 2016

**P. 214-15**

*The Red Baron*, written and directed by RG.
L-R: Brett Dawes (Richthofen), Richard Earthy (Papa), Neusha Milanian (Coco), Royal Air Force Museum Hendon 2016

**P. 218**

Bronze statue of Prince Hal (later Henry V) in *Henry IV* by William Shakespeare, outside the RSC Theatre, Bancroft Gardens, Stratford-upon-Avon,

THE KINGS HEAD THEATRE CLUB
presents
AIRS & DISGRACES

The many faces & voices of Des Keogh

directed by Robert Gillespie   musical director David Wykes

20th February ———— 4th March

1.15pm

115 Upper Street, Islington, N1.
226 1916

75p

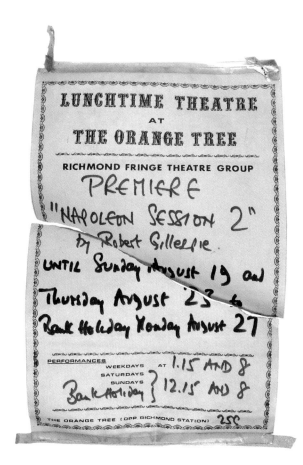

LUNCHTIME THEATRE
AT
THE ORANGE TREE

RICHMOND FRINGE THEATRE GROUP

PREMIERE
"NAPOLEON SESSION 2"
by Robert Gillespie.
UNTIL Sunday August 19 and
Thursday August 23 to
Bank Holiday Monday August 27

PERFORMANCES
WEEKDAYS    at 1.15 AND 8
SATURDAYS
SUNDAYS     } 12.15 AND 8
Bank Holiday

THE ORANGE TREE (OPP. RICHMOND STATION)   25C

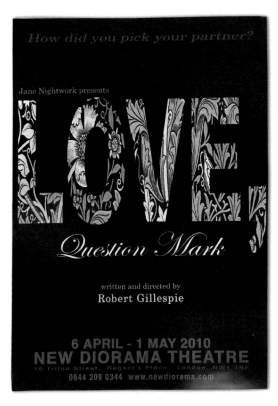

How did you pick your partner?

Jane Nightwork presents

LOVE

Question Mark

written and directed by
Robert Gillespie

6 APRIL - 1 MAY 2010
NEW DIORAMA THEATRE
15 Triton Street, Regent's Place, London, NW1 3BF
0844 209 0344   www.newdiorama.com

KINGS HEAD
THEATRE CLUB
LONDON'S PUB-THEATRE
115, UPPER ST. ISLINGTON N.1.
226·1916

MR. JOYCE
IS LEAVING
PARIS
James Joyce returns from the Dublin Festival

with
ROBERT BERNAL
JIM NORTON    ALAN BARRY
TONY DOYLE    MIKEL LAMBERT

directed by
ROBERT GILLESPIE

OPENS MAY 9TH
TUES WED THURS SUN   DINNER 7·30 opt. £1·10p
                      SHOW 8·30      ·60p
FRI & SAT            "   7.pm    "
                      "   8.pm    "

**Book design**
Paul Warrington
www.tcecreative.co.uk

**Archive photography, and picture research**
Paul Warrington

© 2021 Robert Gillespie

Printed in the UK by
Harrier Print
ISBN 978-1-9997993-1-1

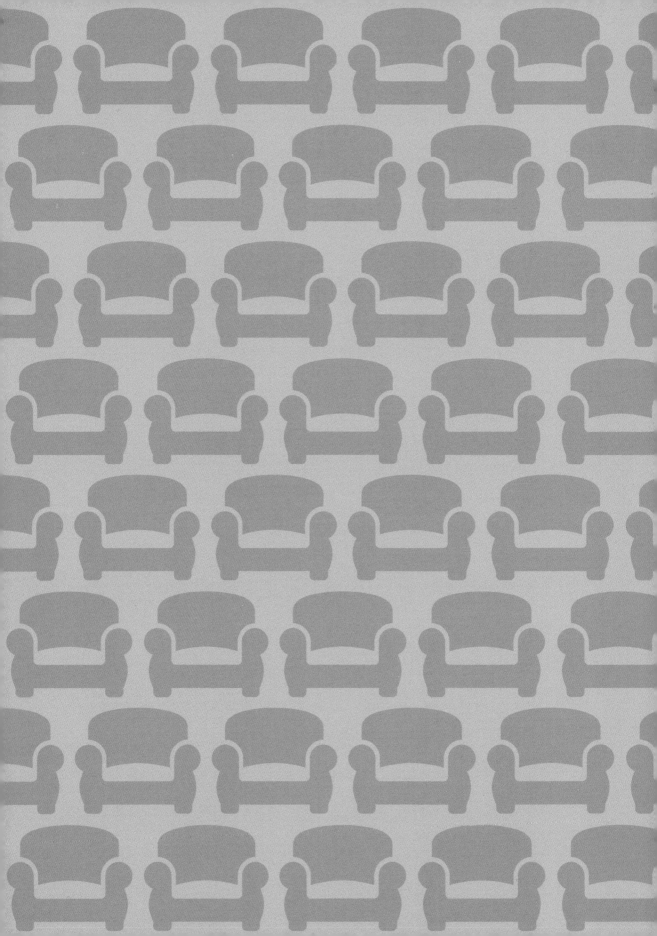